CANADIENS vs LEAFS

THE RIVALRY

STAN FISCHLER

McGraw-Hill Ryerson
Toronto   Montreal

THE RIVALRY
Canadiens vs Leafs

Copyright © 1991 Stanley I. Fischler

ISBN 0-07-551302-1

First published in 1991 by
McGraw-Hill Ryerson Limited
300 Water Street
Whitby, Ontario L1N 9B6

ACQUISITIONS AND EDITORIAL: GLEN ELLIS
PRODUCTION EDITOR: MARGARET HENDERSON
RESEARCH EDITOR: JUAN MARTINEZ
BOOK AND JACKET DESIGN: CAROLE GIGUERE/
  MATTHEWS COMMUNICATIONS DESIGN

Canadian Cataloguing in Publication Data

Fischler, Stan, date
  The rivalry

ISBN 0-07-551302-1

1. Montreal Canadiens (Hockey team) — History.
2. Toronto Maple Leafs (Hockey team) — History.
3. Hockey — Canada — History.   I. Title.

GV848.M6F5 1991   796.962'64'0971   C91-095362-7

Printed and bound in the United States of America

1 2 3 4 5 6 7 8 9 10 RRDH 0 9 8 7 6 5 4 3 2 1

CONTENTS

ACKNOWLEDGEMENTS

The Montreal Canadiens and the Toronto Maple Leafs are two clubs steeped in history and tradition. With thirty-five Stanley Cups between them, they are obvious examples of teamwork and dedication. Just as it would be impossible for a single player to win the Stanley Cup, this book could not have been put together alone.

Keeping that in mind, we would like to thank the following people for their invaluable research assistance:

Juan Martinez, Tracy Pattison, Eli Polatoff, Matt Davis, Todd Diamond, Teresa Faella, David Frattini, Rita Gelman, Charlie Higgins, David Kamsler, Dave Katz, Nick Lanteri, Linda Lundgren, Jeff Resnick, Damian Salvati, Stuart Klitternick, Dave Starman, Matt Messina, Ashley Scharge, Adrienne Nardo, Bernard De Sena, and Andy Schneider.

ACKNOWLEDGMENTS

INTRODUCTION

My connection with the Toronto Maple Leafs and Montreal Canadiens dates back to my tenth birthday, celebrated in March, 1942.

My parents, who could ill afford a substantial gift, nevertheless gave me a very small but handsome Philco Transitone radio which fit snugly on a shelf in my room on the third floor of an old Brooklyn brownstone. I had been a hockey fan ever since my father had taken me to an Eastern League game between the New York Rovers and Washington Eagles at Madison Square Garden in 1937.

But with the arrival of the Philco, I learned of new hockey horizons. One evening in April, 1942, I happened to be turning the dial on my Transitone to obtain news of World War II. As I moved the dial past WOR and toward WJZ, the Philco picked up a strange, yet arresting, voice.

Immediately I knew it was a hockey game taking place and it didn't take me very long to figure out that the teams involved were the Detroit Red Wings and Toronto Maple Leafs engaged in the finals for the Stanley Cup. More than anything I was totally intrigued and captivated by the penetrating voice of broadcaster Foster Hewitt. Hewitt's description of even the most prosaic play carried the ring of a climactic event. A scramble around the net achieved titanic proportions in Hewitt's description and when a goal was scored, he was — and is to this day — unmatched with his inimitable *He shoots!, He scores!!* recounting of a goal.

So, it was Hewitt first who lured me to the radio for the Maple Leaf broadcasts. Then there was the team itself. The Maple Leafs had delightful nicknames, the likes of which I had never heard before nor have heard since.

For starters, there were two defensemen nicknamed Bingo (Rudolph Kampman) and Bucko (Wilfrid McDonald), a goalie named Turk (Walter Broda), a sniper called Sweeney (Dave Schriner), and a coach labeled Happy (Clarence Day). Even the players without nicknames sounded more appealing than your average athlete. While I can't tell you precisely why, high-scoring Gordie Drillon and Lorne Carr had a ring to their names as did the captain, Syl Apps. Even the subs such as Pete Langelle and Johnny

McCreedy sounded delightful, as did Murph Chamberlain and Billy ("the Kid") Taylor.

Perhaps the clincher in terms of my attachment to the Leafs came during the finals. Toronto fell behind three-games-to-none and seemed destined for a hasty exit. But they rallied as no team has ever done in the Stanley Cup finals and won the next four in a row to annex the championship. From that point on, I became a passionate Maple Leafs fan and would remain so until the untimely death of Bill Barilko in the summer of 1951.

My affection for the Canadiens was considerably less intense and developed later. But, again, it was the radio that provided the catalyst. Later in the 1940's, I was able to pick up broadcasts over CBM Montreal, which carried the Canadiens' games. Although play-by-play man Doug Smith lacked Foster Hewitt's intensity, he nevertheless had a style all his own. Even more intriguing was the reaction of Montreal Forum fans when the inimitable Maurice Richard scored a goal. It was thunderous, to say the least.

I never did become passionate about the Habs but I later grew to admire them more as a critic than a fan.

As for favorite players, they numbered in the dozens, but I'll only name a few. For pure skill nobody could touch Max Bentley, whose combination of stickhandling, jackrabbit skating and wrist-shooting couldn't be equalled by Wayne Gretzky on the best day the Great One ever had. Apps and Ted Kennedy were personal heroes. Syl was as straight an arrow as any character in a Horatio Alger book. He was the ultimate role model both on and off the ice. And a remarkably skilled player to boot.

Kennedy, known as Teeder, was a plodding skater who compensated with a work ethic topped by no one. If anybody ever demonstrated that much could be achieved by simply putting your nose to the grindstone, Kennedy was it. Naturally, a robust team like the Leafs had some marvelously tough characters. One was Wild Bill Ezinicki, arguably the best bodychecking forward in history, and Bashin' Bill Barilko, notorious for his snake-hips bodycheck.

The 1947–48 Cup winners were loaded with characters. Garth Boesch was the only mustachioed player in the NHL and penalty-killer extraordinary Joe Klukay owned my favorite nickname, the Duke of Paducah. And, of course, there was the top defense combo of Gus Mortson and Jim Thomson, also known as "The Gold Dust Twins."

Since both the Leafs and Canadiens were top teams when I

began following them, I found the competition between Montreal and Toronto intriguing especially because of the English (Toronto) vs French (Montreal) rivalry, the likes of which was unknown in American sporting life.

When I became a professional journalist, following graduation from Brooklyn College in 1954, my interest in hockey remained at a high level and I vowed that I would someday write a history of the two clubs that had impacted so powerfully on the Canadian sports scene. As for the book itself, its purpose is to compare the evolution of the two distinctly different organizations.

Because of space limitations, less attention has been paid to less successful — or less meaningful — periods. Thus, the abject failure of the Maple Leafs in the Harold Ballard era inspired considerably less attention than the Conn Smythe epoch. The Leafs' decline from 1979 to the present has been well-chronicled elsewhere (especially so in William Houston's *Inside Maple Leaf Gardens: The Rise and Fall of the Toronto Maple Leafs*). Similarly, the less successful Canadiens period of 1980–85 has been well-documented in Goyens' and Turowetz's *Lions in Winter*.

An attempt has been made to compare the success levels of the clubs in terms of individual awards as well as by their season-by-season final standings and other bases of comparison. For me, there can be no question that the greatest Maple Leaf period extended from 1942 through 1951 during which six Stanley Cups were delivered to Toronto. As for the Canadiens, nothing can top the unforgettable fifties, climaxed by five-straight Stanley Cup wins.

My hope here is that the reader gets as much fun out of this volume as I did covering the clubs.

Stan Fischler

ANALYSIS

In the beginning there were Canadiens but not Leafs. Toronto was represented in the NHL by the Arenas, who later became the St. Patricks. The Toronto Maple Leafs were born February 14, 1927, when Conn Smythe, who had purchased the St. Pats, replaced the "wearin' o' the green" with the blue and white.

Toronto won its first Stanley Cup within the context of the newly formed (1917) National Hockey League by defeating the powerful Pacific Coast Hockey League's representative, Vancouver, in the 1917–18 final.

Montreal represented the NHL a year later, challenging the PCHL's Seattle sextet in a series that was called off after five games (2–2–1) because of the dreaded post-war influenza epidemic that cost the life of Montreal star Bad Joe Hall.

Both Toronto and Montreal shared a mantle of excellence in major professional hockey's early years. Toronto won another Cup in 1921–22, defeating Vancouver three-games-to-two; two years later the Canadiens defeated Vancouver two-games-to-none in the semi-finals and Calgary two-games-to-none in the finals.

Both cities produced stars. Toronto had hard-shooting Babe Dye, Cy Denneny, and an excellent goaltender in John Ross Roach. Among the Canadiens' stars were hard-nosed Sprague Cleghorn, Newsy Lalonde, and arguably the most exciting player of the NHL's first decade, Howie Morenz.

With Morenz orchestrating the attack, the Habs won the Stanley Cup in 1923–24 (defeating Victoria). That year the league had two franchises in Montreal (Canadiens and Maroons), and individual teams in Hamilton, Toronto, Ottawa and Boston.

A major blow to the Canadiens and the Montreal fans was the death in 1926 of crack Habs netminder Georges Vezina. His successor, the "anglo" George Hainsworth had some initial difficulty winning over the fans, who preferred a Quebecois puckstopper.

MONTREAL:
CANADIENS
DOMINATE

World War I was reaching its climax when the player-stripped National Hockey Association convened for its annual meeting on November 10, 1917. Some of the foremost Canadiens players as well as stars from other NHA teams had departed for the Canadian Armed Forces, and there was considerable talk about dropping pro hockey for the duration of the war. Petty feuding among the various team officials merely exacerbated the already deteriorating situation, and on November 17 officials of the Quebec franchise announced it was dropping out of the NHA.

The bombshell from Quebec shook the foundations of the NHA, and two more "crash" meetings were held within a week of the Quebec announcement. Apparently the remaining NHA moguls believed a facelifting was needed to restore hockey's stability, although the same teams — Ottawa, Canadiens, Toronto, and Wanderers — were still involved in the organization. The facelifting took the form of a new name, the National Hockey League, which was officially created at a meeting on November 26, 1917, at the Windsor Hotel in downtown Montreal. As a result of the alteration, the only noticeable change in ownership involved the Toronto franchise. Otherwise it was the NHA with a new sobriquet.

Once Quebec announced its abandonment of pro hockey, the entire roster of the dissolved team was put up for sale in a modified form of a draft system. This produced the second shock of the still-unplayed 1917–18 season when the Canadiens obtained from Quebec both Joe Malone and Joe Hall, two of the most formidable skaters on the continent.

Many respected observers regard Malone as the greatest all-around scorer who ever laced on a pair of skates. "He might have been the most prolific scorer of all time if they had played more games in those days," said Frank J. Selke, the former Canadiens managing director who remembered Malone as a young professional. "It was amazing the way Joe used to get himself in position to score. In that respect his style was similar to Gordie Howe's. Joe was no Howie Morenz as far as speed was concerned. But he was a clean player like Dave Keon and Frank Boucher. On the other hand, though, Joe never took a backward step from anybody."

The handsome native of Quebec City played his early hockey for teams in Ontario before being signed by the Quebec Bulldogs. His acquisition by the Canadiens for the 1917–18 season was considered a coup of major proportions. A centerman, Malone could be regarded as the Jean Beliveau of his day.

"Quite often," Malone remembered, "I played fifty or fifty-five minutes a game. They didn't bother too much about changing lines, only individuals. There were only about nine or ten players on each team. I used to stickhandle in close and beat the goalie with a wrist shot. There was no forward passing allowed in the offensive zone and not as much scrambling as there is today. We wore shoulder and elbow pads, but the equipment wasn't too heavy and this was a good thing considering the number of minutes we had to play each game.

"The goalkeepers stood up a lot more. Vezina was a wonderful standup goalie who used to stop more shots with his stick. George Hainsworth and Patty Moran were other good ones. There were no slapshots, but much more passing and stickhandling than today."

Malone's most notable achievement, which came later, was his record-breaking seven goals in a game scored on the night of January 31, 1920, in Quebec City. Three of the goals were scored within two minutes in the third period. Unfortunately, the game was played on a night when the temperature hovered around twenty-five below zero and only a handful of spectators turned up at the rink.

"There was no great fuss made about the seven goals at the time," said Malone. "It was only a night's work as far as I was concerned. The only thing I remember about it is that it was very cold outside."

As a member of *Les Canadiens*, Malone was no less spectacular than he was at Quebec. He missed two games of the twenty-two-game schedule in 1917–18 yet managed to score a total of forty-four goals and scored in each of fourteen consecutive games and three times scored five goals in one game. "The funny thing is," said Malone, "there was more publicity about my record when Maurice Richard broke it than there was when I set it and all the years afterward."

Although Malone's record was shattered in 1944–45, when the Rocket scored fifty goals in fifty games, nobody has been able to match his percentage of more than two goals per game. His compensation hardly matched his production. "My salary," Joe recalled, "was about one thousand dollars a year with the Cana-

---

diens and then went up to two thousand dollars when I joined Hamilton in the early twenties. We could make another three hundred or four hundred by playing with a Stanley Cup-winner and maybe a few dollars more by endorsing hockey equipment. But there were no trophies or additional money for being leading scorer, and things like that."

If the acquisition of Malone was a surprise for the Canadiens, the signing of "Bad" Joe Hall was the height of irony, in view of the fact that his archfoe, Newsy Lalonde, had been named Canadiens' player-manager.

"Joe wasn't mean," said Malone, "despite what a lot of people said about him. He certainly liked to deal out a heavy check and he was always ready to take it as well as dish it out. That in itself was remarkable when you consider that he weighed in at only a hundred fifty pounds. As far as I'm concerned he should have been known as 'Plain' Joe Hall and not 'Bad' Joe Hall. That always was a bum rap."

Whatever the case, Hall and Malone ignited the Canadiens to a successful first half of the 1917–18 season and by midpoint the Flying Frenchmen — by now dotted with English-speaking players — were in first place. Then the roof literally fell in on them. On January 2, 1918, a huge conflagration gutted the Montreal Arena, reducing it to rubble. Both the Canadiens and the Wanderers lost all their equipment — an estimated loss of $1,000 each — and the arena damage was put at $150,000.

Sam Lichtenhein, owner of the Wanderers, had been bemoaning his team's dearth of players since the beginning of the season. After surveying the fire damage he requested player help from the other teams. When they refused, he announced that the Wanderers would drop out of the NHL, leaving the Montreal hockey scene solely to the Canadiens.

In the 1919 Stanley Cup finals against Seattle the Canadiens' "Bad" Joe Hall, who in earlier games had battled vehemently with Seattle's Cully Wilson, appeared to lose his zest and finally left the ice and made his way to the dressing room. Unknown to all the onlookers, it was to be the last time Joe would ever appear on a hockey rink.

Hall was rushed to the hospital, stricken with the flu bug that was causing an epidemic throughout North America. Immediately after the game several other Canadiens, including Lalonde and manager George Kennedy, were bedded with influenza but none as bad as Joe Hall.

With the series tied at two apiece an attempt was made to finish the playoff for the Stanley Cup. Kennedy requested permission to "borrow" players from Victoria to finish the series, but the hosts declined the bid and the playoff was cancelled without a winner.

Six days after he had stumbled off the ice, Joe Hall died of influenza in a Seattle hospital. His friend and admirer, Joe Malone, was the most seriously affected by the news because he believed that Hall never had the opportunity to erase the bad name he had acquired. "There were plenty of huge, rough characters on the ice in Joe's time," said Malone, "and he was able to stay in there with them for more than eighteen years."

The Canadiens entered a period of decline for the next two seasons, which forced owner/manager Leo Dandurand to rebuild. "Leo was quick to see that the team was disintegrating," said Elmer Ferguson who was covering the Canadiens at the time, "and he quickly set about rebuilding. The accent in hockey in those days was largely on weight and power, though a few of the lighter-weight players had risen to stardom." Ferguson reflected:

> Dandurand was thoroughly convinced that speed and skill were the real essentials. He had a keen eye for hockey-playing talent, having played the game himself. Out of the Mount Royal League he picked Pit Lepine, a fine scorer and one of the great defensive forwards of his era. He similarly secured the two Mantha boys, fast-skating Armand Mondou, Wildor Larochelle, Billy Boucher, Albert "Battleship" Leduc, all from amateur ranks. Later he traded Newsy Lalonde for Aurel Joliat and beat the Toronto Maple Leafs to Howie Morenz by a few minutes.

The 1921–22 season began dismally for Montreal. They were walloped 5–2 in the opening game and followed that with a 10–0 debacle at the hands of Ottawa. When they lost their third-straight — 2–1 to Ottawa — Dandurand began worrying. He probed the roster carefully and decided, with many misgivings, that Newsy Lalonde was doing the Canadiens more harm than good.

Dandurand conferred with Montreal's perennial star, but the conference appeared to set them further apart. Disgusted with his treatment, Lalonde abruptly announced his "retirement" on January 10, 1922, asserting that he was insulted by management, which charged him with not playing his best. Lalonde bolting the Canadiens was tantamount to Babe Ruth walking out on the Yankees. It was a national catastrophe and compelled NHL president Frank Calder to intervene and mediate the dispute. Calder didn't achieve a settlement overnight, but Newsy, after missing four games, was finally persuaded to return.

Newsy was never the same player for Montreal after that. Later in the season the Montreal fans began razzing him and soon he was handed the supreme insult: he was demoted to a substitute's role and eventually traded to Saskatoon for young Aurel Joliat.

The moment Newsy started slumping he was replaced on the front line by Sprague Cleghorn, who was a Montreal native and a big, capable leader. He had every bit of the fight in him that Lalonde possessed. "He was a product of a rough neighborhood," said the late Bobby Hewetson, curator of hockey's Hall of Fame, "where everything you got you had to fight for. He played hockey the same way." After using his stick to perform major surgery on several Ottawa Senators he was described by referee Lou Marsh as "a disgrace to the game."

If Cleghorn tended to blemish the Canadiens' reputation for "good sportsmanship," it was consistently restored and upheld by Georges Vezina. "The Chicoutimi Cucumber," apart from being a superb athlete, was the acme of gentility.

Although Vezina never attended college, he was nevertheless a gifted human who once took pen in hand and wrote a short essay called "Sport, Creator of Unity," which his boss, Dandurand, translated from French to English. It read in part: "If fair play is the rule in the NHL, there will be no cause for worry. Speaking of fair play reminds me of the words of the noted English novelist John Galsworthy, who, despairing of what he termed 'the present precious European mess,' declared that he found only one flag that was flying high and true, and that was the flag of sport."

On the ice Vezina proved his mettle repeatedly. In a game at Hamilton during the 1922–23 season, his former teammate Bert Corbeau smashed into Vezina with such force that the goaltender's head was cut open and his nose was broken. Vezina continued playing despite his wounds. A few games later he led the Canadiens to a win over Ottawa, allowing the Senators only one goal, although seventy-nine shots were hurled at him.

"After the game," observed Vezina biographer Ron McAllister, "he left the rink a solemn, plodding figure, in sharp contrast to the wild hilarity of his teammates, who were already celebrating the victory that Vezina had won for them."

Another reporter observed, "Georges has a calmness not of this world."

The commentary was more prophetic than the writer had realized for Vezina's body was being tortured by the early symptoms of tuberculosis. "Beads of perspiration formed on his forehead for no apparent reason," said McAllister. "An expression of pain flitted momentarily across his face, but the great Vezina invariably settled down to the business at hand, turning in his usual matchless performance."

Whether or not Vezina himself was aware of the gravity of his condition is debatable. One thing is certain, and that was his determination to continue in the nets for the Canadiens. There was no outward suggestion that he was faltering.

Although the Habs finished second to Ottawa in the 1923–24 season, Vezina allowed only forty-eight goals in twenty-four games, including three shutouts, for a goals-against average of 2.00. He then blanked Ottawa, 1–0, in the NHL playoff opener and sparkled as the Canadiens swept the series, 4–2, in the second game, thus qualifying to meet a representative from one of the two western professional leagues.

A squabble between officials of the Western Canada Hockey League and the Pacific Coast Hockey Association resulted in a bizarre turn of events. Instead of one team coming east to challenge Montreal for the Stanley Cup, both Calgary and Vancouver showed up. The Canadiens really weren't overly extended. They first dispatched Vancouver by scores of 3–2 and 2–1 and routed Calgary, 6–1 and 3–0. The final game was switched to Ottawa because of poor ice conditions in Montreal, but Vezina was never better. His Stanley Cup record was six goals-against in six games for a perfect 1.00 average.

Proof that Vezina was outfighting his ailment was provided by his uncanny performance in the 1924–25 season. The Canadiens finished in third place behind Hamilton and Toronto, but Georges's 1.9 goals-against average was easily the best in the league. His teammates rallied behind him in the first round of the playoffs to oust Toronto, 3–2 and 2–0, but Vezina enjoyed only one good game — a 4–2 win — at Victoria as the western champs dispatched the Canadiens by scores of 5–2, 3–1, and 6–1 to win the Stanley Cup.

Whether Vezina was debilitated or not in the 1925 Cup series is uncertain, but when he showed up at the Canadiens' training camp in the autumn of 1925, he betrayed the signs of fatigue. "As this gigantic frame, in the grip of dread tuberculosis, gradually weakened, even his public sensed that their beloved goaltender was fading," wrote Ron McAllister. "If his color was a little higher than usual, no one remarked on it."

The 1925–26 season was truly momentous for the National Hockey League. It had expanded into the United States, first accepting Boston the previous year, and now embracing New York and Pittsburgh as well. A second team, the Maroons, had been added to Montreal to provide an English-speaking club as the natural rivals for the Canadiens. Needless to say, the outstanding attraction in the American cities among Montreal players was the redoutable Vezina.

Pittsburgh, one of the new entries, provided the opposition for the Canadiens in the season opener on November 28, 1925, at Mount Royal Arena. There were six thousand spectators in the stands on that rainy night who had come to see the great Vezina, ignorant of the fact that the lean goalie was suffering enormous discomfort as he took the ice for the opening faceoff.

"No one knew," wrote McAllister, "that the great goaltender had struggled to the arena in spite of a temperature of 105 degrees. A deathlike chill settled over him; but with Pittsburgh forcing the play from the faceoff, Vezina functioned throughout the entire first period with his usual dexterous ease, deflecting shot after shot. In the dressing room he suffered a severe arterial hemorrhage, but the opening of the second period found him at his accustomed place in goal."

Fighting desperately against the fatigue and fever that completely throttled his body, Vezina could no longer see the puck as it was skimmed from one side of the rink to the other. Suddenly, a collective gasp engulfed the arena. Vezina had collapsed in his goal crease! "In the stricken arena," said one observer, "all was silent as the limp form of the greatest of goalies was carried slowly from the ice."

It was the end of the line for Georges and he knew it. At his request he was taken home to his native Chicoutimi where doctors diagnosed his case as advanced tuberculosis. On March 24, 1926, a week after the Canadiens had been eliminated from a playoff berth, Georges Vezina passed away.

An enormous funeral, held in the old cathedral at Chicoutimi, saw players and fans from all parts of the country deliver their final tribute to the gallant goaltender. A year later, the Canadiens' owners, Cattarinich, Dandurand, and Letourneau donated a trophy in his honor — the Vezina — awarded annually to the NHL goaltender with the best goals-against average.

Had Vezina been healthy enough to play his normal game in the 1925–26 season, the Canadiens would surely have climbed to the top of the league instead of finishing an embarrassing last, because the Three Musketeers (as the Canadiens' owners were called) had carefully collected some of the best young players in Canada. One of them was Aurel Joliat, a wisp who wore a black baseball cap and defied opponents to knock it off his head. The other was Howie Morenz.

The son of a railroad man, Howie was born in Mitchell, Ontario, a hamlet about thirteen miles from Stratford, in 1903. A little fellow, the young Morenz was often severely beaten by the older boys with whom he played hockey in neighborhood games. From time to time he'd return home so badly cut and bruised he'd often consider quitting the game; but his love for hockey was so passionate he'd inevitably return to the rink. Soon he was the star of the Stratford team which journeyed to Montreal for a playoff game.

Dandurand happened to be in the stands on the night that Morenz dipsy-doodled around the hometown defensemen from the start to the finish of the game. Leo conferred with his aide, Cecil Hart, and both agreed it would be prudent to sign Morenz before the Maroons, Hamilton, Ottawa, or Toronto beat them to it.

Raw speed was Howie's forte as he gained a varsity center ice berth on the Canadiens. Within weeks he was dubbed "the Stratford Streak," "the Mitchell Meteor," and assorted other appellations that almost but never quite described his presence on the ice. "The kid's too fast," said one observer. "He'll burn himself out."

Morenz scored his first goal for the *bleu, blanc, et rouge* against Ottawa on December 26, 1923 before 8,300 spectators at the spanking new Ottawa Auditorium, a curious-looking egg-shaped rink. Ottawa's Senators dominated the NHL that season, thanks in part to a miniscule defenseman by the name of Francis "King" Clancy who would go on to become one of hockey's most delightful personalities as a referee, coach, and vice-president of the Toronto Maple Leafs.

Morenz scored thirteen goals in his rookie season to finish in a tie with Jack Adams for seventh place in the scoring. He was well on his way to becoming the glamor boy of hockey, admired as much by his opponents as by his teammates and fans. He played the game as cleanly as was possible in those rambunctious days of chronic stick fights and butt-ends.

In a game at Madison Square Garden he knocked out four of Bun Cook's front teeth with the end of his stick as the pair battled for the puck. Howie immediately dropped his stick and helped Bun off the ice. Later Cook explained, "It was just an accident. Howie wouldn't pull anything like that intentionally."

Morenz was a superstar in his second year of big-league play. He finished second in scoring to Cecil "Babe" Dye of Toronto and was doing things with the puck that astonished even such skeptics as Conn Smythe, founder of the Maple Leaf empire and the venerable dean of hockey in Toronto.

"The trouble is," said Smythe, "that writers are always talking about what a great scorer Morenz is. Which is true enough. But they overlook the fact that he's a great two-way player."

According to Smythe, Morenz executed "the most amazingly impossible play" he had ever seen in hockey up until that time. It was accomplished against the Boston Bruins who had a big, rugged team.

Eddie Shore and Lionel Hitchman of the Boston defense had prepared to sandwich Morenz between their powerful bodies as he tried to split the defense. Suddenly Howie leaped forward and crashed through like an auto speeding past two railroad gates at a crossing.

Just then a Bruin forward swerved in behind his defense to intercept Morenz. Seeing that he couldn't elude the checking wing, Howie released his shot from twenty-five feet in front of the net. The shot missed the goalpost by a few inches and caromed off the end boards right back to the blue line and onto Shore's waiting stick.

The Bruin defenseman, one of the speediest rushers hockey has ever known, orbited into a breakaway with all the Montreal players caught in Bruin territory along with Morenz. "I was watching Howie all the time," said Smythe, "and I saw him follow up his shot with a long leap in preparation to circling the net. To this day I can't figure out how he managed to stay on his skates as he rounded the cage."

Meanwhile, Shore was away at top speed for the Canadiens' goal. Nobody in the rink, let alone Smythe, doubted that the Bruins would have plenty of time for an easy play on goal and a likely score. That is, all but Morenz. He had put his head down and dashed in pursuit of Shore. "He flashed from the net to the blue line," said Smythe, "faster than I can say 'blue line.' "

Shore was about to enter the final stages of his maneuvering when Morenz suddenly cut directly in front of him, released the puck from the Boston player's blade, and immediately changed direction for another play on the Bruin goal. "Shore," said Smythe, "was absolutely dumbfounded. As for me, I actually was unable to move my mouth, I was so awed by the play. Morenz had done what he was to do for years to come — he took my breath away!"

Many respected hockey observers claim that Morenz and Vezina were responsible for the successful expansion of the NHL into the United States in the 1920s. It was no secret that New York promoter Tex Rickard became a hockey fan the moment he saw Morenz in action. Not long afterward Rickard introduced the Rangers to New York.

"There isn't a team in the league that has not in some way been affected by some aspect of Montreal hockey," wrote Peter Gzowski, "even if the link is as tenuous as the Detroit Red Wings' crest, which is based on the old Montreal Athletic Association's winged wheel."

But Gzowski was quick to point out that Morenz was the leader of "the most exciting team in hockey from the mid-1920's to the mid-1930's." He adds: "While most fans remember Morenz mainly for his blistering speed and his headlong rushes on goal, he also provided one of the most remarkable examples of the passionate dedication to the game — to winning — that has been another characteristic of Canadiens teams. Many people say, of course, that Morenz's fierce involvement in hockey, and in the Canadiens, led to his untimely death, although Morenz's dedication is not unique in the annals of the Montreal team."

Few opponents ever got the better of Morenz when Howie was in his prime, although Joe Primeau, the crack Toronto center, did just that one night when the Canadiens and the Maple Leafs were locked in a Christmas Eve match. The teams were tied, 1–1, after regulation time and nobody scored in the overtime. When the siren sounded to end the game, both clubs headed for the dressing room until they were halted by the referee. Apparently the timekeeper had erred by ten seconds and the referee ordered the players back to the ice to play out the remaining unused time.

This act of recall nettled Morenz who was anxious to get home to his family. Before the referee dropped the puck, Howie urged Primeau not to touch it after it hit the ice; that way the ten seconds would be squandered and everybody could quit for the night. Primeau understood Howie's point but had no intention of complying. Once the puck hit the ice the Leaf center slapped it to the left side where his winger, Busher Jackson, gathered it in and roared toward the Montreal goal. His shot fooled goalie George Hainsworth and Toronto won the game, 2–1.

The competitive spirit of Morenz was matched by perhaps only one other member of *Les Canadiens* — Maurice Richard. But in the twenties, the fires of competition burned fiercest in the heart of Morenz, and only those who were with him at the time can honestly portray the quality of his emotion. One of them was Elmer Ferguson, a veteran Montreal sportswriter who had traveled to Boston one weekend with the Canadiens.

"It was a dark, muggy sort of morning," Ferguson recalled, "the way Boston gets when fog rolls in from the sea on March days and nights. But it didn't seem possible it could be time to get up, and still be this dark, when the knock sounded on my hotel room."

Ferguson rubbed his eyes and wearily strode to the door. When he opened it, there was Morenz fully dressed as if ready to take an early-morning stroll along the Charles River. "Howie," asked Ferguson, "don't you think it's a little early to be getting up? It's still dark. Where are you going?"

"I'm not getting up," said Morenz. "I haven't been to bed yet. I've been out walking around the streets, thinking about that play I missed. I lost the game for the team, and there's no use going to bed, because I won't sleep."

The play that so disturbed Howie was a faceoff he had lost to Cooney Weiland of the Bruins. A split-second after the referee had dropped the puck it flew into the air. Weiland batted it down with his hand and promptly shot it into the net in the same motion. The goal won the game for the Bruins. Eight hours later a sobbing Morenz was still blaming himself for the goal as he slumped into the chair in Ferguson's hotel room. "He buried his face in his hands," said Ferguson. "His shoulders shook because he was crying like a little boy. He was heartbroken."

A Morenz ritual was to arrive at the dressing room at least an hour before game time. "He'd restlessly pace around the long promenade," said Ferguson, "as high-strung as a thoroughbred that is being readied for a race."

It was easy enough for Montreal players and writers to wax ecstatic about Morenz and it was not uncommon for opponents to do likewise. But when the opponent happened to be Eddie Shore, the fiercest defenseman in the game, then Morenz knew he had arrived!

"He's the hardest player in the league to stop," Shore admitted. "Howie comes at you with such speed that it's almost impossible to block him with a bodycheck. When he hits you he usually comes off a lot better than the defenseman. Another thing that bothers us is his shift. He has a knack of swerving at the last minute that can completely fool you. Everybody likes Howie; he's one player who doesn't deserve any rough treatment."

Howie's ascendancy came at a fortuitous time for the Canadiens because they were about to be challenged for patronage by the newly-formed Maroons. In 1924 Dandurand sold half of the Canadiens' territorial rights in Montreal to the owners of the Canadian Arena Company who owned the new Montreal Forum. Dandurand's asking price was fifteen thousand dollars. When Chicago and Detroit applied for franchises, the NHL formally announced that the league was to receive fifty thousand dollars in return for entrance into the league. Dandurand later admitted that his generosity in permitting the Maroons to become NHL members wasn't as altruistic as it appeared on paper. "I figured that having an English team to compete with the French Canadiens would make for a great rivalry," he said later, "and I was proven right."

Dandurand's shrewd wheeling and dealing brought the Stanley Cup to Montreal in 1924 following victories over Ottawa, Vancouver, and Calgary. The feat was hailed in Montreal with appropriate enthusiasm but with a dignity and hilarity that has never been matched in the team's long history.

Instead of the traditional ticker-tape parade that greets the contemporary Stanley Cup champions, the 1924 Canadiens were honored by no less august an institution than the University of Montreal. A public reception was held at the city's national monument, during which each player received what amounted to an honorary degree from the university. The highlight of the civic affair, of course, was the presentation of the Stanley Cup.

That formality dispensed with, Dandurand herded his players to his home for a private party. Members of the team made the trip in private cars, including Vezina, Sprague Cleghorn, and Sylvio Mantha, along with Dandurand, in Leo's Model T. Ford. En route to Chez Dandurand, Leo's automobile broke down and required a rather hefty push. One by one the Canadiens emerged from the car, including Cleghorn who had been nursing the Cup on his lap. When Sprague got out of the car, he placed the Stanley Cup on the sidewalk and joined in the pushing brigade. It took several minutes to get the car up and over the hill, and when this was accomplished the quartet jumped into the car and jubilantly drove off to Leo's house.

Madame Dandurand was delighted to see her husband and the players when they arrived, but she was anxious to pour some of her newly concocted punch into the Stanley Cup. She asked Leo where it was and he, in turn, asked Cleghorn where he had put it. Sprague nearly collapsed with anguish when he remembered that he had left it at curbside. An hour had passed but Leo and Sprague returned to the site and found the Cup sitting there undisturbed.

Theoretically, Morenz, whose ancestry was Swiss, should have been playing for the Maroons. However, the Canadiens had their share of French-Canadian stars to complement Howie, and the one who did it best was the smallest of all, Aurel Joliat. Morenz and Joliat worked together through the years, and when they retired, they had identical scoring totals of 270 goals.

Like Morenz, Joliat was a native of Ontario, having grown up in the New Edinburgh district of Ottawa. He learned his hockey on the frozen Rideau River along with Bill and Frank Boucher who also were to achieve enormous fame in the NHL.

Aurel weighed 135 pounds, at his heaviest, but his size never bothered him. It apparently motivated him to compensate with a vast repertoire of stickhandling maneuvers and pirouettes. "He transported the world of ballet to the hockey arena," said one admirer.

Joliat teamed up with Morenz in the 1923–24 season. The pair jelled perfectly right from the start, although Aurel was to prove that season that he could excel with or without Morenz at his side. The Canadiens had gone up against Calgary in the playoffs and Morenz's shoulder was broken after he was hit successively by Red Dutton and Herb Gardiner. That's when Aurel took over. In the third period he intercepted an enemy pass and circled his own net to gain momentum.

"I traveled through the entire Calgary team," said Joliat, "and faked a shot to the far corner of the net. But even as I let it go I sensed I was covered on the play. So I kept going, rounded the net, and backhanded a shot into the open corner. I tumbled head over heels after that one. We went on to win the Cup and I consider it the best goal I ever scored."

Well stocked on offense and defense, Dandurand realized that his major project would be finding a replacement for the legendary Vezina. Immediately after Vezina collapsed at the start of the 1925–26 season, the Canadiens replaced him with Alphonse "Frenchy" Lacroix who obviously couldn't handle the job. After five games Lacroix was removed, and Herb Rheaume played twenty-nine games for the Habs but also left much to be desired.

Once again luck played a hand in the Canadiens' favor. When Newsy Lalonde was traded to Saskatoon for Aurel Joliat, Lalonde went searching for a goaltender and found an exceptionally courageous young man playing in Kitchener. The son of a plumber, George Hainsworth soon persuaded Lalonde that he was major-league caliber and Newsy signed George to play for the Saskatoon Sheiks of the Western Canada League.

But Newsy, like so many of the Canadiens before and since, had strong ties to his alma mater in Montreal. One day he wrote a letter to Dandurand, advising him that it would be worthwhile keeping Hainsworth in mind. "This kid," wrote Lalonde, "could be the one to take Vezina's place if Georges ever retires."

This was not exactly startling news to Dandurand because he and Vezina had watched Hainsworth play for Kitchener a few years earlier when Georges had actually entertained thoughts of retiring. Vezina was greatly impressed with Hainsworth and Dandurand knew it. "That night," Leo once told author Bill Roche, "Vezina really chose his own successor in the Canadiens' net."

Dandurand launched his pursuit of Hainsworth in earnest as soon as Vezina entered the hospital. But since Hainsworth was under contract to Saskatoon through the 1925–26 season, Leo's hands were tied. As soon as the Western League dissolved, Dandurand was free to negotiate with the little goalie and Leo was right there with a bid.

Dandurand didn't sign Hainsworth without some grave reservations. After all, there was the delicate matter of finding a suitable replacement for the venerated Vezina. Unlike his predecessor, Hainsworth was an English-Canadian who measured only 5', 6", compared to the tall, distinguished Vezina. And furthermore, at thirty-three years old, Hainsworth seemed to be approaching the end, rather than the beginning, of his major-league career.

Hainsworth's debut was something less than impressive. He was beaten, 4–1, in the season's opener at Boston and returned to Montreal where Ottawa outscored the Canadiens 2–1. This was followed by a 2–1 loss to the Maroons, thus confirming the suspicions of Montreal fans that Hainsworth was an unworthy successor to Vezina.

"From their point of view," observed Ron McAllister, "everything George did was wrong. Their loyalty to Vezina was a living thing."

The criticism notwithstanding (one sportswriter referred to him as "a lowly substitute"), Hainsworth played every one of the forty-four games on the Canadiens' schedule and finished the season with a goals-against average of 1.52, topped only by Clint Benedict of the Maroons who registered a 1.51 mark. But George led the league in shutouts with fourteen and outgoaled Benedict in the first round of the Stanley Cup playoffs.

Little by little the Canadiens fans began warming to Hainsworth. He won the Vezina Trophy in the 1927–28 season with a remarkable 1.09 goals-against average and managed to improve on that in 1928–29, this time allowing only forty-three goals in forty-four games for a 0.98 mark. It would be presumptuous to suggest that Hainsworth ever commanded the same total adulation of Montreal fans that Vezina enjoyed, but by January, 1929, Hainsworth had certainly become a hero to many French-Canadians. It was a single performance, however, that captured their imagination.

On the night of January 24, 1929, the Toronto Maple Leafs were visiting the Forum. As the Canadiens were peppering Hainsworth in the pre-game warm-up, a practice shot caught the goaltender unaware and smashed into his nose, knocking him unconscious. A bloody mess, Hainsworth was carried to the dressing room and a call went over the Forum loudspeaker for the Canadiens' spare goalie. He couldn't be located.

Meanwhile the team physician worked over Hainsworth's broken nose, attempting to reduce the swelling around his eye and cheeks. But the blow was so severe there was little the doctor could do, and within a matter of minutes the swelling had completely shut one eye. "Bandage me up," Hainsworth insisted, "I want to get out there."

Neither the doctor nor the Canadiens had much choice. Ten minutes later George skated out to his position for the opening faceoff. The Forum crowd reacted with a distillation of jubilation and fear. The goal-hungry Maple Leafs immediately swarmed to the attack and bombarded Hainsworth with every variety of shot at their command.

"George appeared to be enjoying himself," said one viewer. "He seemed to laugh with mad glee after stopping each shot."

Veteran reporters could hardly remember the fans sitting down throughout the game as Hainsworth portrayed a hockey version of Horatio at the bridge, and soon George himself was yelling and screaming along with the fans. "His face," wrote McAllister, "one-sided and bulging, feverish and red from excitement and injury, loomed livid and macabre above the forest of sticks and whirling forms crowding close about him. This was his night of nights!"

The Maple Leafs managed to jam one shot behind him, but the inspired Canadiens scored a goal, too, and the game ended in a 1–1 tie. From that point on Hainsworth was a Forum hero and played seven full seasons until he was forty years old.

Hainsworth seemed to improve with age. In 1928–29 he recorded twenty-two shutouts in forty-four games and continued to excel for the Canadiens until the 1932–33 campaign. The entire Montreal team from Morenz to Hainsworth was in the trough of a slump that year. It bottomed out on February 21, 1933, when the Canadiens visited Boston and were demolished, 10–0, by the Bruins. Dandurand was furious with Hainsworth, who had given up several "easy" goals and made up his mind to trade him at the earliest opportunity. The result was one of the quickest deals in hockey history.

It happened after the season in which the Canadiens were quickly dispatched from the playoffs by New York. Dandurand had been brooding over Hainsworth's play for a long time when one afternoon, in a Toronto hotel room, he picked up the telephone and called Conn Smythe, manager of the Maple Leafs, whose goalie was tall Lorne Chabot.

"Would you be interested in trading Chabot for Hainsworth?" Dandurand asked.

"Certainly," replied Smythe, who promptly hung up.

Dandurand could be forgiven if he thought the whole brief sequence had been a bizarre dream. He phoned Smythe again to be sure the whole idea wasn't a gag in the mind of the Toronto boss. Thus assured, the two agreed to announce the trade the next day and the deal was completed.

Chabot played only one season for the Habs and registered a 2.15 goals-against average, whereas Hainsworth's mark was a less impressive 2.48. But Hainsworth lasted three full seasons in Toronto, during which the Leafs twice led the league, before returning briefly to Montreal in 1937, where he played a few games before retiring.

"George was one of the greatest goaltenders," said a Montreal observer, "but he had the misfortune of battling the ghost of Vezina as long as he played for the Canadiens."

TORONTO: BIRTH
OF THE MAPLE LEAFS

Despite the high quality of professional hockey in the days following the end of World War I, the play-for-pay game was less than a
financial bonanza, principally because many outstanding players
who had served in the war chose to play amateur hockey rather
than the pro game. Toronto's Mutual Street Arena, with its artificial ice, attracted larger crowds to its amateur games than to its
NHL matches.

At the end of the 1918–19 season Toronto's pro crowds were
depressingly small, and the owners of the Arenas decided to sell
the club to the first buyer. However, purchasers made themselves
so scarce that when a group of Toronto sportsmen collected a
grand total of $2,000, the Arenas' directors leaped at the bid. They
gave the new owners rights to the club name and good will, and
tossed in sticks, sweaters, ice privileges, and a dozen athletic
supporters. They then obtained an NHL franchise for $5,000 — to
be paid off in time — and a new era was ushered in for Toronto
hockey.

The name Arenas was replaced by St. Patricks. Toronto opened
the season on December 23, 1919, at Ottawa and lost the match
3–0. However, the St. Pats returned home four days later to defeat
Quebec 7–4, thereby setting a pattern for the first season. When the
campaign was over, the Toronto sextet had won twelve and lost
twelve, finishing out of the playoffs.

By 1920–21 a feud was developing between the St. Pats and
Ottawa, nurtured in part by the natural superiority of the Capital
City skaters. They beat Toronto 6–3 in the season's opener and
routed the St. Pats when the clubs faced off in the opening round of
the playoffs. The first game of the total-goals series was held in
Ottawa, where the Senators manhandled the Pats 5–0. Toronto
played a better game at home, but Ottawa could hardly be con-
tained and skated off with a 2–0 victory and a 7–0 triumph in the
series. It surprised nobody that the Senators eventually traveled to
Vancouver, where they successfully defended the Stanley Cup.

As humiliating as the defeat by Ottawa had been, Toronto coach
and general manager Charlie Querrie was not overly perturbed.
He had been patiently building the foundations of a championship
team, and when the 1921–22 season began, Charlie earnestly
believed that his Stanley Cup time was soon to come. It was no idle

dream. His hopes were pinned on Cecil "Babe" Dye, a Toronto native whom he had personally scouted and signed. He had briefly lost him in a deal with Hamilton in the middle of the 1920–21 season, but he reobtained him the following year.

A right wing with limitless potential, Dye was unique among young athletes who learned their trade in the renowned Jesse Ketchum School playground of Toronto. When Babe was a year old his father died. Esther Dye raised her son at their Boswell Avenue home and vowed that he would not lack athletic instruction. "Essie" Dye was an exceptional woman, and nobody appreciated her more than Babe. "Mom knew more about hockey than I ever did," he once remarked, "and she could throw a baseball right out of the park." Dye was eventually invited to sign with the Baltimore Orioles but opted for hockey instead.

In his rookie season the Babe played magnificently, scoring thirty goals in twenty-four games, to tie for the league lead with Harry Broadbent of Ottawa. Toronto finished second behind the Senators in regular-season play. On March 11, 1922, before a full house of 8,000 roaring fans in Mutual Street Arena, the teams met for the opening playoff game.

Complementing the offensive artistry of Babe Dye was another rookie, goaltender John Ross Roach, a nervous, restless player who managed to limit the Senators to four goals while Toronto scored five to take a surprising one-game lead in the series.

The two-game total-goals series moved to Ottawa on March 13, and all the home squad required was a two-goal lead to capture the series from Querrie's upstart St. Pats. Superficially, at least, Ottawa had the superior team right down to such accomplished substitutes as Frank Boucher and Frank "King" Clancy, both of whom eventually gained entrance to the Hall of Fame.

Yet try as they might, the defending champions could not penetrate goalie Roach, although Roach's defenses seemed to be collapsing around him. "During the final period," wrote Charles L. Coleman in *The Trail of the Stanley Cup*, "Toronto players were shooting the length of the ice in order to relieve the pressure from Ottawa, who ganged continually in their end. At that time this was good strategy as the rules did not require a faceoff for icing the puck although Toronto was at full strength."

With Roach holding fast, the clock ticked away the remaining seconds, and Toronto held the formidable Senators to a 0–0 tie, good for a 5–4 total-goals advantage and the right to meet Vancouver for the Stanley Cup. The City of Toronto was euphoric over the triumph, and the St. Pats' players were overwhelmed with well-wishers when their train arrived in Union Station.

Babe Dye didn't assert himself to the utmost until the Stanley Cup finals reached the second game. Vancouver, with Lester Patrick behind the bench, edged the St. Pats 4–3 in the first contest, but a goal by the Babe at 4:40 of sudden-death overtime gave Toronto a 2–1 win in the second game. Vancouver went ahead for the last time in the series with a 3–0 triumph in the third match.

Staggering on the brink of elimination, the St. Pats proved their mettle in the fourth game, dispatching Vancouver 6–0. Dye led the rout with a pair of goals and served notice that he would be the decisive factor in the fifth and final game at Mutual Street Arena on March 28, 1922.

Most critics agree that for two periods the final game between Vancouver and Toronto was a Stanley Cup classic. The St. Pats nursed a 2–1 lead in the third period when a faceoff was held at the Vancouver blue line. It was then that the fabulous Babe scored what henceforth was known as the "mystery goal" of Stanley Cup hockey.

Corbett Denneny took the puck from the faceoff and skimmed a quick short pass to Babe, who orchestrated a shot with such consummate ease and speed that nobody in the arena, let alone Vancouver's excellent goalie Hugh Lehman, saw the puck make the flight from stick to goal cage. "Fooled by its blinding speed," said Ron McAllister, "Lehman still waited, crouched in goal.

"A hurried search for the puck began, while Dye, the only man who knew where it lay, skated back to his own defense. The crowd finally roared and pointed to the Vancouver net. There was the puck! Then the light was flashed on and the goal was registered."

The Vancouver skaters were stunned to the core by Lehman's sphinx-like behavior on the shot, as much as by the velocity of the blast itself. Disorganized and disoriented, the Millionaires proceeded to give up two more goals, and the St. Pats emerged with a 5–1 conquest and the Stanley Cup.

Despite Dye's stellar performances — he led the league in 1922–23 with eighteen goals in twenty-three games — the St. Pats were no match this time for Ottawa or the Canadiens, and they finished in third place, just out of reach of the playoffs. A year later Querrie's boys were back in the same place — third, out of the playoffs — except that they had lost more games than they had won and, barring a drastic turn of events, it appeared that they were on a treadmill to oblivion.

THE RIVALRY: CANADIENS VS LEAFS

Two events occurred prior to the 1924–25 season that abruptly halted the St. Pats' slide to the cellar. First the NHL approved new franchises for the Montreal Maroons and the Boston Bruins. This new expansion meant that Toronto almost automatically would ice a better team than the newcomers and, therefore, would finish higher. Second, the St. Pats signed Eddie Powers as manager and Clarence "Hap" Day and Bert McCaffrey as defensemen.

As expected, the Bruins and Maroons were trampled by the established clubs. Boston finished an abysmal last, winning only six games. But it wasn't merely the new clubs that gave impetus to Toronto's rise. With Eddie Powers running the club the St. Pats were once again respectable, and Babe Dye continued pumping home big goals.

Thanks to the Babe's thirty-eight goals in twenty-nine games, Toronto finished a close second to Hamilton in the 1924–25 race. The league arrangements called for the second-place St. Pats to meet the third-place Canadiens for the right to play Hamilton in the NHL finals, but a startling development disrupted the plans. Hamilton players, led by Red Green, organized one of the rare labor strikes in hockey and refused to play unless they were paid $200 apiece extra for competing in the finals. League president Frank Calder angrily rejected their demands and ordered that the winner of the Canadiens-Toronto series be declared league champions and the NHL representative to the Stanley Cup finals.

This time the Babe was overshadowed by a new star on the NHL horizon. Howie Morenz, an unbelievably speedy center from Mitchell, Ontario — a lot closer to Toronto than to Montreal — overwhelmed every skater on the St. Pats. He led Montreal to a 3–2 victory in the opening game in Montreal and a 2–0 win in the return match at Toronto. The Babe, meanwhile, was held score-less, and the St. Pats lost a shot at the Cup. In the finals, the Habs lost to the Victoria Cougars.

Like the tides, the status of Toronto's St. Patricks fluctuated from high to low. In 1925–26 they slipped again, falling to sixth place in a seven-team league. Expansion was no longer a catalyst for the St. Pats. A year later the NHL welcomed a second New York team — the Americans entered the league in 1925–26 — as well as Pittsburgh, Chicago and Detroit. A Canadian division and an American division were formed, and Toronto finished dead-last in the Canadian section.

But in one of those inexplicable turns of fate the fortune of the Toronto hockey club took a permanent turn for the better because of the arrival of the New York Rangers and the firing of Conn

Smythe by the New York club as a result of his refusal to buy Babe Dye from the St. Pats.

A much-decorated veteran of World War I, Conn Smythe had gained acclaim in college hockey circles for his superb steward-ship of the University of Toronto hockey clubs. Each year Smythe would shepherd his varsity sextet to Boston, where the Toronto skaters wowed Beantown fans on the ice while young Smythe impressed newspaper editors with his flamboyant prose and knack for headline-grabbing, a talent he refined with age. Charles F. Adams, owner of the Bruins, was fascinated by Smythe's deportment and remembered him when Colonel John Hammond, president of the Rangers, asked for a recommendation for a man to organize a group of players to be Hammond's NHL entry. "Conn Smythe is your man," said Adams. "You won't find any better."

With customary vigor Smythe spent the summer of 1926 signing players for the rookie Rangers franchise. His selections were impeccably sharp, and before the season had begun, Smythe had signed such stickhandlers as Frank Boucher, Bill and Bun Cook, Ching Johnson, Murray Murdoch, and Bill Boyd.

When the players gathered at a Toronto hotel for pre-season training, Smythe felt content. His team, he believed, with good reason, would be indomitable. One night after convening at the training hotel Smythe chose to take the night off to go to a movie with his wife. It was a reasonable plan, so Smythe was flab-bergasted when Colonel Hammond accosted him in the lobby upon his return.

"Where have you been?" Colonel Hammond demanded.

When Smythe revealed that he and his wife enjoyed a leisurely dinner and a good movie, Colonel Hammond bristled with anger: "Well, that night out has just cost us one of the greatest players in the game. St. Pats just sold Babe Dye to Chicago. We could have had him for $14,000!"

Smythe was unimpressed, and he told Colonel Hammond so. "I wouldn't want Babe Dye on my team no matter the price," snapped Smythe with a brand of finality that either convinces an employer or causes a man to lose his job. "He's not the type of player we need."

Smythe was not about to be fired on the spot; the Colonel wanted more evidence, and for a one-dollar phone call, he got it. Hammond phoned Barney Stanley, coach of the Black Hawks, and pointedly mentioned Smythe's opinion of Dye. Stanley's guffaws could be heard across the continent. When he stopped laughing, the Black Hawks coach sputtered: "Smythe wouldn't want Dye on his team? Why that man must be crazy. It only proves how little he knows about hockey players. I can't understand, Colonel, why you keep a man like that when there's an outstanding man like Lester Patrick loose and ready to be signed."

The Colonel couldn't understand it either. Smythe was promptly summoned to the Colonel's office and given his discharge papers before the season ever began.

"Unwittingly," wrote former Toronto hockey publicist Ed Fitkin, "Babe Dye was mainly responsible for the formation of the Toronto Maple Leafs, because Conn Smythe, angered by the Rangers rebuff, decided he'd get back into pro hockey or bust. Within a year he was back in the NHL, this time to stay."

What manner of man was Smythe, whose genius at selecting players enabled the Rangers to win the Stanley Cup in their very first year of operation?

His fertile mind had enabled him to gain entrance to the University of Toronto, where he majored in engineering. His agile body won him the captaincy of the varsity hockey club, for whom he played center during the months following the start of World War I. Overseas, Smythe served with distinction.

The overseas stint never assuaged Smythe's thirst for education. Upon his return from the war, he headed straight for the university, where he obtained his degree in applied science and continued to stay in close touch with the varsity hockey team. In 1926 he mustered the graduated collegians who had played so successfully for the university and called them the Varsity Grads, a powerful club that won the 1927 Canadian championship and proceeded to capture the Winter Olympics gold medal in 1928. The Olympics set the stage for his first professional venture, creating the nucleus of the Rangers team. Smythe was a hockey genius without peer. Unfortunately, after Colonel Hammond got through with him, he also was without a job.

"Smythe was flat on his back," said Foster Hewitt, "and few would have blamed him if he had stayed down. But that wasn't his way of fighting. He was determined to convince himself, as well as others, that Hammond had made a big mistake. He told friends that he would go out and organize another team that would beat the pants off the one he had organized for New York."

Acutely aware of Smythe's heroic war background — he had been awarded the Military Cross — his friends were quick to support his campaign to return to the NHL. "I always firmly believed," said Frank Selke, Sr., who was to become Smythe's *aide-de-camp* and later the managing director of the Montreal Canadiens, "that the success just ahead of Conn Smythe owed far more to hard work and sacrifice than to any streak of luck. I remember seeing Conn and his wife out scouting young players on outdoor rinks when the temperature ran as low as twenty degrees below zero."

Like Smythe, Selke was accustomed to long, hard work and was devoted to the game of hockey. Selke reorganized the Toronto Marlboro hockey club in 1924, a task that included some extensive fundraising. Aware of Smythe's ability in amateur hockey, Selke approached Conn and convinced him to purchase an interest in the Junior team.

Selke prudently scouted talent throughout Toronto and the vicinity, traveling in a second-hand seven-passenger Reo touring car. Within a couple of years he had stocked the Marlboros with some extraordinarily gifted young players, who later were to be of inestimable help to Smythe. These included Harvey "Busher" Jackson, Alex Levinsky, Red Horner, and Charlie Conacher. In later years Selke rated Conacher as "the greatest all-round athlete I have ever managed," carefully noting that Conacher also was adept at baseball, football and lacrosse. He considered Busher Jackson the "classiest" player he had ever seen.

"Jackson," Selke observed in *Behind the Cheering*, "could pivot on a dime, stickhandle through an entire team without giving up the puck, and shoot like a bullet from either forehand or backhand. In fact, his backhand was the best I ever saw."

But Jackson, Conacher, and company were still a couple of years away from Smythe. Conn went about the business of trying to purchase the St. Patricks so that he could proudly re-enter the NHL. It required one year from the time the Rangers had fired him for Smythe to come through the front door of the major league again.

In that time the fortune of the St. Pats went from bad to worse. Toronto's futility reached a low point on December 21, 1926, when Hap Day put the puck into his own net during a game against Boston.

With each day it became increasingly obvious that the St. Pats were going nowhere. By January, 1927, Toronto hockey fans showed their interest in the team by staying away from Mutual Street Arena by the thousands.

Directors of the St. Pats decided that they were finished and put the team on the selling block. For $160,000 the franchise could be had, and for a brief time it appeared that William Wrigley, of Chicago, would purchase the club. But the purchase of the St. Pats was too great an opportunity for Smythe to ignore, especially since the NHL club was available in his home city. He scoured the metropolis for financial support and put together a company including J.P. Bickell, a part owner of the St. Pats, Hugh Arid, and himself.

The momentous day in Toronto hockey history was February 14, 1927, when an NHL governors' meeting was held in Toronto. Querrie resigned as governor, and Smythe was elected to be his replacement. The name St. Patricks was officially dropped. From then on the team would be known as the Toronto Maple Leafs.

During that same week the Toronto club, now the Maple Leafs, won their first game, 4–1 against the New York Americans. At the same time Babe Dye, the skater who made it all possible for Smythe, was sidelined for the Chicago Black Hawks with a bad back. The Babe soon was to break a leg and miss the entire 1927–28 season. He would play only one more NHL game before being permanently shipped to the minors.

It was too late to salvage the 1926–27 season, and Smythe realized that only a five-year plan to build a new hockey empire would be realistic. To do so he would have to wheel and deal as never before in league history. He decided to build his team around a couple of young aces with rare promise. One of them was Hap Day, a forward who was converted to defense on the night the newly-christened Maple Leafs won their first game, and Joe Primeau. Selke had discovered Primeau when "Gentleman Joe" first tried out for — and was rejected by — the St. Cecilia's Bantam squad, which Selke then was managing. But Primeau worked at his game and improved enough to gain a berth on Selke's St. Mary's squad, which later became the Marlboros.

Primeau and Day would not be enough for a winning team, and Smythe knew it. After the club finished last in the Canadian Division in 1926–27, Smythe suffered what Selke described as one of Conn's most severe depressions about the Maple Leafs' outlook. It was then that Selke saved the day, if not the franchise by recommending to Smythe that he phase out his aging stars in favor of youth.

Smythe realized that gifted but green youngsters needed time to mature, and, as a result, he would be compelled to use a mixed bag until the young Marlboros were ready. Toronto finished the 1927–28 season with a record of eighteen wins, eighteen losses, and eight ties, an improvement over the previous year but not good enough for a playoff berth.

More trading was necessary and more youth. In the meantime, Clarence "Hap" Day was called upon to knit the team together. He was to be so successful that Smythe would eventually call upon him as coach and later manager of the Maple Leafs during their second golden era.

Like so many stars of the twenties and thirties, Day learned his hockey under extremely severe conditions, in a small Ontario village near Owen Sound. At times he would plod miles through the snow to find a place to play hockey, and he eventually became a leader with the Midland Juniors.

Day's courage and ability enabled him to climb the long, hard hockey ladder in Ontario. He moved from the Midland Juniors to the Intermediate sextet and then to Hamilton's Tigers. Hockey was not the only subject on his mind; Day wanted very much to be a pharmacist, and he enrolled at the University of Toronto, from which he eventually obtained a degree. While attending the university he played for the varsity club. It was then that Charlie Querrie spotted Day and persuaded him — not without a considerable battle — to turn pro instead of applying for a job in the nearest drugstore. A left wing converted to defense, Day emerged as a superb, hard-checking blueliner who specialized in skating opponents out of the play.

Day was followed by George Reginald "Red" Horner, who was signed by Smythe in the fall of 1928. Unlike Hap, Red took his basic training in hockey on the Toronto playgrounds, although he was born on a farm, near Lynden, Ontario. By the time Red was ten years old, the Horner family had moved to a house on Spadina Road in Toronto.

In his spare time Horner got a job as a delivery boy for a grocery store on Spadina Avenue, and one day he discovered that one of his deliveries was to be made to Frank Selke, Sr., then coach of the famed St. Mary's hockey club. Horner made a point thereafter of making all deliveries to the Selke residence and learned to synchronize his deliveries so that he arrived when Selke was at home. Each time the youngster delivered groceries, he would strike up a conversation about hockey with the St. Mary's manager.

When he was sixteen Horner tried out successfully for St. Mary's. Selke's perspicacity paid off handsome dividends but not overnight. Horner was used sparingly at first while he honed his skating style in his spare time at outdoor rinks.

When St. Mary's became the Marlboros, it had become apparent that Horner was ready for regular work. In time, Red was named captain of the team. By the beginning of the 1928–29 season, Smythe toyed with the idea of signing Horner and placing him on the Maple Leafs, but he nurtured second thoughts and decided that Red needed more seasoning. He got just that, playing regularly with the Marlboros and a second team that belonged to the Brokers' League.

Just before Christmas, 1928, Smythe called Horner up to the big team. In his debut, against the Pittsburgh Pirates, he drew his first penalty when he decked the Icelandic-Canadian ace Frank Frederickson. In his career he would eventually serve 1,254 minutes worth of penalties, a record that went unbroken for many years. Of course, the kid wasn't too sure that Smythe approved, but it didn't take long to find out for sure.

"Penalties?" said Smythe. "What do they matter? We just write them off as mistakes. No man ever became a millionaire who didn't make mistakes. Besides, penalties show that we have a fighting team."

Horner made a different kind of mistake in his second NHL game, on Christmas night against the Montreal Maroons. He moved the puck out of his zone and detected what he believed was an opening between Nels Stewart and Jimmy Ward, of Montreal. Red skated for daylight. But the old veterans closed the vise on Horner, and in doing so one of the Maroons rapped Red smartly on the hand with his stick. Red skated to the sidelines with a broken hand and was through for the rest of the season. Nevertheless, he already had persuaded Smythe that he was in the NHL to stay.

Horner and Day bolted down the Toronto defense while Smythe tried to construct a formidable attacking unit. Once again the ubiquitous Selke came through, this time with a youngster named Irvin Wallace "Ace" Bailey, from Bracebridge, Ontario, who played lacrosse as well as he played hockey. In 1921 Bailey left home to play lacrosse in Mimico, Ontario, near Toronto, where he also worked in a planing mill.

Bailey couldn't find an opening on any Junior team in his first round of tryouts. The Parkdale Canoe Club sextet left him sitting morosely on the bench until Ace was filled with despair. One day, however, a friend tipped him off that a St. Mary's defenseman soon would be overage and ineligible for Junior hockey. "Get over and see a man named Frank Selke," his friend advised.

Always hospitable to an eager youth, manager Selke gave Bailey a trial on defense. But Mike Rodden, the St. Mary's coach, instantly realized that defense was a mistake. "Young man," said Rodden, "you have no business playing that position. Get on right wing and stay there!"

It was not an easy adjustment, but Bailey realized that he had no choice. As the weeks drifted by, Ace learned that playing forward was not all that bad. He developed into an accomplished scorer and soon moved up to Peterborough, in the Ontario Hockey Association Senior League, which won the championship in 1924.

By 1924 Rodden had become coach of the Toronto St. Pats, who desperately needed a right wing. "Irvin Bailey," said Mike, "the boy I had at St. Mary's is as good as any we'll find." Bailey and Hap Day were, in fact, the only St. Pats who survived Conn Smythe's youth movement of the late 1920's.

If the Maple Leafs were to be molded into a championship team, it would have to be done with Conn Smythe's hands. Consequently, when the 1928–29 season began, Conn was not only managing but also coaching the Toronto club.

Week by week the Maple Leafs' roster changed form. Smythe bought left wing Harold "Baldy" Cotton from Pittsburgh, and he concluded a major trade with New York, sending John Ross Roach and Butch Keeling to the Rangers for goalie Lorne Chabot and right wing Alex Gray. It was by no means Smythe's best deal. Roach played capably for New York, and Keeling became a Rangers star. Gray disappeared from the Toronto scene after skating in a handful of games, leaving only Chabot to help Smythe.

Because of his experience at the University of Toronto, Smythe kept his scouting radar trained on Canadian universities. In 1928 some interesting blips showed around the play of Andy Blair, a beanpole center who played for St. John's College in Winnipeg. Blair signed with Toronto in 1928–29 and found himself right at home with Hap Day, another university player. "Andy," Day recalled, "even wore a Joe College mustache and, believe it or not, played the game with a handkerchief stuck up the sleeve of his uniform." Blair lasted eight full seasons with the Leafs and proved to be a capable if not spectacular performer.

Week by week it became evident that Smythe had transformed his club into a respectable contender if not a championship team. On February 2, 1929, Toronto visited the Bruins' lair at Boston Garden. At that time the home club had played thirteen consecutive games without a loss, but Smythe's troops skated off with a convincing 3–0 victory. As if to prove it was no accident, the Leafs played host to the Canadiens on February 23. The Montreal club had been cruising along with a seventeen-game unbeaten streak, but the final score was Toronto, 2, Canadiens, 1.

The Maple leafs finished the first year of rebuilding with a record of twenty-one wins, eighteen losses, and five ties, good for forty-seven points and third place in the Canadian division. Ace Bailey led all scorers, with twenty-two goals and ten assists, for thirty-two points in forty-four games, three better than Nels Stewart of the Maroons. Rookie Andy Blair finished in a tie for third with Carson Cooper of Detroit and Howie Morenz of the Canadiens.

For the first time Smythe led his Maple Leafs into the Stanley Cup playoffs and wiped out Detroit, 3–1 at Olympia Stadium and 4–1 at Toronto. Those victories catapulted the Maple Leafs into the second round against the Rangers, a team Smythe dearly wanted to beat. The opening game was played at Madison Square Garden on March 24, 1929, and Toronto's best moment occurred before the opening faceoff when orchestra leader Paul Whiteman presented a trophy to Ace Bailey for leading the league in scoring. The Rangers won the game, 1–0, on a goal by ex-Leaf Butch Keeling. In the return match, before 8000 fans at Mutual Street Arena, the Leafs battled nobly but in vain. Holding New York to a 1–1 tie after regulation time, Toronto finally capitulated when Frank Boucher beat Chabot after two minutes of sudden-death overtime.

Conspicuous by his absence from the Maple Leafs roster that season was Joe Primeau, the gifted center who had once disdained a Rangers offer in order to remain loyal to Smythe. Twice Primeau was shipped to the minors, first to the Toronto Ravinas and then to the London Tecumsehs, of the International League.

"All the self-confidence he had built up over the years began to slip away," wrote Ron McAllister. "Mentally Primeau analyzed his game, trying to discover what it was that made him appear such a poor risk to the professionals. And he couldn't find the answer."

But Smythe had never quit on the young center. Conn was waiting for Primeau to develop his skills in the minors, and he also wanted his linemates to complement Joe's unique passing style. All this was to happen in a perfect marriage of passing, skating, and shooting during the 1929–30 season when Smythe's pal, Frank Selke, sent him two of the brightest young players Toronto ever produced: Harvey "Busher" Jackson and Charlie Conacher.

Conacher's shot was the hardest of its day, when slapshots were unheard of and a player beat a goaltender with a quick crack of the wrists.

Scouting Conacher was easy. Charlie learned his hockey on Toronto's venerated Jesse Ketchum Public School rink, and he learned all other sports from his older brother, Lionel, who was to be voted Canada's athlete of the half-century. Charlie broke in as a hockey player guarding the goal, but soon moved to the front line. His career nearly ended at the age of eleven when he developed a passion for mountain-climbing, a somewhat illogical choice in Toronto, where the elevation rarely climbs much above sea level.

To overcome this problem Charlie would find bridges on which to practice his mountaineering techniques. One day in 1920 he challenged the Huntley Street span in Toronto, which crossed a ravine. Young Conacher was proceeding smartly through the iron supports on the underside of the bridge when he missed a steel stepping area, lost his balance, and plummeted some thirty-five feet to the ground below.

At this point fate intervened, and Charlie was intercepted by a pine tree, which cushioned his blow so perfectly that he escaped with only minor scratches, or so it seemed. Unknown to him at the time, his kidney was damaged, but that injury was not to affect him until much later in his life.

When autumn came, Conacher was able to play hockey, and he continued to improve each winter. He eventually became captain of Selke's Marlboros in 1926, a club that won the Memorial Cup for Canada's Junior championship. Conacher's booming shot was his forte, but his skating still left something to be desired. Thus, when Smythe announced that Charlie had made the team for 1929–30, straight out of Junior, there was considerable surprise.

Charlie made his NHL debut on November 14, 1929, at Mutual Street Arena. Chicago's Black Hawks, with the redoubtable Charlie Gardiner in goal, were the opponents, and the fans filling the old Toronto ice palace were frankly skeptical of Conacher's ability to skate and shoot with the pros, especially since he had never had basic hockey training in the minor leagues.

The game was close, but Charlie was never out of place. At one point the puck came to him as he skated over the blue line. Conacher caught it on the blade of his stick and in the same motion flung the rubber in Gardiner's direction. Before the Chicago goalie could move, the red light had flashed, and Charlie Conacher was a Leaf to stay.

At first Smythe used Conacher on a line with Primeau at center and Harold Cotton on left wing; but despite Conacher's instant success, Primeau still failed to click. Just before Christmas, 1929, Smythe made a move that would alter hockey history. He pulled Cotton off the line and inserted Busher Jackson in his place on right wing. Hockey's first and most renowned "Kid Line" was born. Success was as dramatic as a volcanic eruption. Toronto defeated the Black Hawks, the Canadiens, and the Maroons right after Christmas and went undefeated until January 23 of the new year.

"Almost overnight," said Ron McAllister, "Primeau's confidence returned, and a continual flow of original playmaking ideas crowded into his head. On the ice between the powerful Conacher and the rugged Jackson, Joe set a pattern of unselfishness in organizing plays for his fine wingmen to finish off."

Yet the Leafs still were missing something. They slumped in the last part of the season and missed a playoff berth by a full ten points behind Ottawa. Analyzing his roster, Smythe realized that the weak underbelly was defense. He vowed to repair the backline before the 1930–31 season got underway, even if it required a negotiation of major proportions.

ᴛʜᴇ 30's

ANALYSIS

If there was any decade during which the Canadiens and Maple Leafs were more equal than dissimilar, it was during the 1930's. Each club won a Stanley Cup and did so in the early part of the Great Depression era.

Likewise, each team had the elements of a dynasty but they never came to fruition in the manner that people had anticipated.

Another similarity involved the truly superior forward line that Montreal iced, a magnificent trio centered by one of the speediest players ever to grace an ice rink, the Stratford Streak, Howie Morenz, also known as the Mitchell Meteor. His linemates Aurel Joliat and Johnny "Black Cat" Gagnon were not quite on Morenz' level but complemented the center as well as any two wings could.

Toronto's top line went one better. It had a nickname — The Kid Line — composed of Gentleman Joe Primeau at center, flanked by Charlie Conacher — he of the dynamite shot — on the right and Harvey "Busher" Jackson, a splendid sniper who was just as active in nightlife as he was in the NHL.

Another aspect of the leafs that gave them added luster was their innate marquee quality. This was a team of superstars and super characters who not only could lead the league in scoring but also in off-ice capers. This was only natural since Toronto's hockey leader Conn Smythe had established himself as the most flamboyant impresario this side of P.T. Barnum and crowned his early reign by completing Canada's palace of hockey, Maple Leaf Gardens in 1932.

By contrast, the Canadiens were quite content with their smaller Forum which was just as well since the Habs had begun what would become a decade-long descent while the Leafs reaped the benefits of their star-studded cast a lot longer.

One of the saddest sagas centered around the decline and fall of Morenz who was — quite shockingly — traded to Chicago and then New York before returning briefly to the Canadiens in 1936–37 before being tragically sidelined by a broken leg that led to his hospitalization and, tangentially, to his death.

The primary difference between Toronto's productivity and the Canadiens' lack of same was Smythe's ability to replace aging aces with scintillating new stars. As Jackson, Conacher, Primeau, and King Clancy took their leave, in skated the likes of Syl Apps, Gordie Drillon, and Bob Davidson. It was symbolic, perhaps, that in the season during which Morenz died, Apps won the Calder trophy as rookie of the year.

Another distinction between the two clubs was coaching. The Leafs succeeded in large part because of astute operators behind the bench such as Dick Irvin who later would move to Montreal and turn the Canadiens' operation upwards. The Habs groped for the right coaching combination but never found it as the 1930's ended and the Canadiens suffered through one of the most depressing eras of their history.

MONTREAL: THE RISE AND FALL OF HOWIE MORENZ — AND THE HABS

While Conn Smythe assiduously built his Maple Leaf organization, the Canadiens made good use of their head start as an NHL franchise. Leo Dandurand's diligence during the roaring twenties — not to mention his patience — would eventually move the Habs ahead of the Leafs in terms of hockey prestige although it would only be a momentary phenomenon.

The seeds of a world championship team that Dandurand had planted in the mid-1920's finally bore fruit in the playoffs of 1930. The Canadiens went up against the Black Hawks in the first round of a two-game total-goals series and emerged with a 1–0 win at Chicago before 17,476 at Chicago Stadium, the largest crowd to see a game in the Windy City until then, and returned to Montreal where the teams played a 2–2 tie. Thus, the Canadiens came off with a 3–2 edge in goals and moved on to the semifinals against the Rangers.

Paced by Gus Rivers, who scored at 6:52 of sudden-death overtime, Montreal won the opening game, 2–1, and Hainsworth shut out New York, 2–0, in the second and final match, giving Montreal the right to meet the Boston Bruins in the Stanley Cup final. Boston was heavily favored to rout the Canadiens, but Hainsworth was too much for the Bruins in the opener and stopped Boston, 3–0. The Bruins hadn't lost two consecutive games that season and were expected to rebound in the second game of the best-of-three series, but the Canadiens prevailed, 4–3, and captured the Cup.

Dandurand wasn't one to stand pat. He embellished his lineup with a small slick French-Canadian forward named Johnny Gagnon. Swarthy and black-haired with quick darting moves, Gagnon was placed on the line with Morenz and Joliat and immediately dubbed "the Black Cat." He was to become one of the foremost Canadiens forwards in the years ahead.

With the Gagnon-Morenz-Joliat line leading the way, the Habs finished first in the Canadian Division of the NHL and faced Boston, champions of the American Division, in the first round of the best-of-five series. As expected it was a superb series that went down to the fifth game with the clubs tied at two apiece.

Montreal grabbed a 2–0 lead in the finale at the Forum, but the Bruins counter-attacked and tied the score, forcing the game into sudden death. It was finally resolved after nineteen minutes of furious skating when Marty Burke passed the puck to Wildor Larochelle who beat Tiny Thompson in the Bruins' goal.

In the meantime, the Chicago Black Hawks, coached by Dick Irvin, who was to play a major part in the Canadiens saga, reached the finals against Montreal. Cleverly directed by Irvin, the Black Hawks stunned the Canadiens by taking a 2–1 lead in games and a 2–0 lead in what could have been the fourth and Cup-winning game for them. But "Black Cat" Gagnon rallied Montreal with two goals and Pit Lepine followed with two more as the Canadiens triumphed, 4–2.

The finale was the type of match that has since been referred to as "typical playoff hockey." Both teams accented a close-checking defense game, also known as "kitty-bar-the-door," waiting for the one break that would lead to a score. The Canadiens finally got it and the Black Cat once again was the scoring hero, with Morenz supplying the second goal, giving the Habs their second-straight Stanley Cup.

A year later Montreal led the Canadian Division again, but this time they were wiped out in the opening playoff round by the American Division champion Rangers, three games to one. Like the more contemporary Montreal teams, the Canadiens of that era accented style rather than strength. They were an artistic bunch with one collective flaw: size was always against them. The Morenz Line, for example, was nothing more than a collection of half-pints compared with the behemoths on the other teams. Consequently, whenever an opposing coach planned strategy against Montreal, he would give serious consideration to mauling the smallest of Flying Frenchmen. In Toronto, husky Busher Jackson often got that assignment.

Dandurand's dynasty began crumbling in the 1932–33 season, and for no apparent reason. The Morenz line was intact, the goaltending and defense appeared to be sound, and the rest of the roster could hardly be considered inferior. Some of the players, including Gagnon, later charged that they couldn't get along with Newsy Lalonde, who was coaching the team at the time. The behavior of some stars confirms this thinking. Overlooking Lalonde's part in the slump, Dandurand threatened to shake up the team and even went so far as to put Morenz on the trading block. At one point late in the season it was rumored that Leo had fined Gagnon two hundred dollars for indifferent play. Leo clearly established himself in support of the coach and immediately began probing the minor leagues for potential replacements. Oddly enough, he took Morenz with him on a trip to Hamilton, Ontario, and it was Howie's advice that led to a vital acquisition for the Canadiens several years later.

Dandurand had heard some good things about a forward line with the Hamilton Tigers, of the Ontario Hockey Association's Senior League, and after watching the Tigers in action, he asked Morenz whom he liked best. "Toe Blake and Herbie Cain," Morenz replied.

"I agree," said Dandurand.

During the 1933–34 season Howie Morenz's goal-scoring abilities declined dramatically. He was thirty-three years old at the time and had obviously slowed down to a point where he could be more easily stopped by the opposition. Just prior to the 1934–35 season Dandurand dropped his bombshell — Howie Morenz had been traded to Chicago!

After eleven years with *Les Glorieux*, the most popular Montreal hockey player since Vezina was being cast adrift. In addition, Dandurand dispatched Lorne Chabot and Marty Burke to the Hawks in exchange for Lionel "Big Train" Conacher, Roger Jenkins and Leroy Goldsworthy.

In honor of his friend, Dandurand tossed a fairwell dinner for Morenz and solemnly told the audience, "As long as I'm associated with the Canadiens, no other player will wear Howie's number seven." Dandurand's promise was kept by his successors, and to this day the Montreal management has honored that vow.

The shakeup was beneficial to both the Canadiens and Morenz. Although he was admittedly unhappy in Chicago, Morenz played a scintillating game for the Black Hawks and finally scored against his old teammates in the final game of the season at the Forum, a 4–2 Chicago triumph. He received a standing ovation from the Montreal crowd. A season later Morenz was dealt to the Rangers, but he was a shadow of his former self and New York's Lester Patrick was happy to return him to the Canadiens for the 1936–37 season.

Wearing the *bleu, blanc, et rouge* once more proved to be a tonic for Morenz. True, he had lost his old get-away power, but he was reunited with his old buddies, Gagnon and Joliat, and every so often he'd bring the Forum crowd to its feet with one of the exquisite Morenz rushes.

He was doing just that on the night of January 28, 1937, at the Forum when a Chicago defenseman caught him with a body check, sending him hurtling feet-first into the end boards on the Atwater Street side of the north-end net. It wasn't a normal spill and Howie had lost all control as he skidded toward the boards. When his skate rammed into the wood, a snap could be heard around the rink and Morenz crumpled in excruciating pain.

He was rushed to the hospital with a badly broken leg, and there was some doubt that he would recover in time to return for another season of play. Once in the hospital, the thirty-six year-old Morenz began brooding about his fate. Instead of recuperating, he suffered a nervous breakdown. Then he developed heart trouble.

Nobody is quite sure what transpired in the hospital to bring about the utter deterioration of Howie's condition. One theory has it that he was overwhelmed by well-intentioned friends who filled his room with flowers, books, and candy. "The hospital," said one visitor, "looked like Times Square on a Saturday night. The continual stream of visitors tired him."

Perhaps too late, hospital officials forbade all but Howie's immediate family from visiting him. Then, early on March 8, 1937, Morenz was given a complete physical checkup. It appeared he was rallying. It was deceptive analysis. A few hours later, Howie Morenz was dead.

In his book *Hockey Heroes*, Ron McAllister theorized:

> Probably Morenz realized that even if he did recover, he would never be able to make a second comeback. And when

he could no longer see visitors — his one link with the game that had become a whole life to him — the future must have looked terribly black. The terrific strain under which he played that last season, against younger and fresher men, had brought him to a complete breakdown; only genius, drive and know-how had kept him abreast of the game at all.

The funeral service for Morenz was held at center ice of the Forum where thousands filed silently past his bier. Andy O'Brien, of *Weekend Magazine*, was there at the time and recalls the scene as thousands of hockey fans lined up outside the rink that Morenz had made famous.

"Outside," said O'Brien, "the crowd was so great, we of the press had to enter through the boiler room on Closse Street. As I walked below the north end, profound silence left an impression of emptiness, but at the promenade I stopped in breathless awe. The rink was jammed to the rafters with fans standing motionless with heads bared."

The NHL paid an official league tribute to Morenz on November 7, 1937, by sanctioning an All-Star game at the Forum. In it the Canadiens and Maroons combined forces to challenge a select squad of NHL stars including Frank Boucher, Charlie Conacher, and Eddie Shore. The All-Stars won, 6–5, before some 8,653 fans who contributed $11,447 to a fund for the Morenz family. Howie's uniform was presented to his son, Howie Morenz, Jr.

The death of Morenz signaled the end of a significant era in Montreal hockey history and was also the prelude to the downfall of the Habs in the NHL. They reached their nadir in the 1939–40 season, finishing dead-last in the seven-team league. Leo Dandurand had sold his interest in the club and new management realized it was time for a major housecleaning. The first and most important move of the 1940–41 season was the signing of Dick Irvin as coach.

TORONTO: THE LEAFS WIN THEIR FIRST CUP AND CAPTURE THE FANS

If Morenz was the single most exciting character on the Canadiens in the 1930's, his Toronto counterpart was a flamboyant little defenseman named Frank "King" Clancy. A native of Ottawa, King moved up the hockey ladder until he gained a spot on Tommy Gorman's NHL club the Ottawa Senators. As a member of the Ottawa club Clancy played on four Stanley Cup-winners and appeared to be a fixture in the capital city. Then the Depression began, and the Senators' attendance dropped off at an alarming rate. By the time the 1930–31 season approached, the Ottawa management needed money fast. There was only one thing to do: peddle a star to a wealthier club. And the most attractive star on the club was none other than King Clancy.

Thus the Senators played right into Conn Smythe's hands. Smythe had been looking for a colorful superstar, and the moment he heard about Clancy's availability, he decided to get him. There was only one problem — Smythe didn't have the money. He knew that he would lose Clancy to the Rangers or Black Hawks if he didn't find the cash somehow. Always a gambler, Smythe pulled off yet another daring move.

Smythe had become a horse-racing buff, and he owned a colt named Rare Jewel, who just happened to be running at Woodbine Race track in Toronto at that time. The odds were 100–1 against Rare Jewel (optimistic odds at that), yet Smythe put his bankroll on his horse and then cheered him on to an astonishing victory. With the winnings he had enough money to afford Clancy.

Smythe bought Clancy from Ottawa for $35,000 and threw in two extra players, Art Smith and Eric Pettinger, who were worth a total of $15,000 on the NHL market. Clancy cost Smythe $50,000, but he proved to be worth every penny of it.

There are those who believe that Clancy would have accepted a nickle from Smythe if he had suggested that as a bonus. "Clancy liked hockey so much," said Milt Dunnell, sports columnist for the Toronto *Daily Star*, "that he probably would have played for nothing."

"His main forte," said Ted Reeve of the Toronto *Telegram*, "was his ability to break fast, to come leaping off that blue line as though it were a springboard, with the loose puck tossed out in front." He could pass on the dead tear, though not a graceful skater (he was almost running on his blades at times), and he had a wicked shot.

"It was that indefinable something — the competitive spirit — that made Clancy so valuable to the Leafs. And the God-given gift of fun in him that would bring them out of the doldrums with a whoop and a holler. That high-pitched sort of husky voice, his piping exclamations and infectious grin."

While Smythe appreciated Clancy's humor, he was most interested in his ability to help him mold a championship club. Smythe made Clancy's job easier by signing Alex "Kingfish" Levinsky, a Syracuse, New York, native, and Bob Gracie, a forward from North Bay, Ontario. With Levinsky on hand, Smythe was able to retire veteran defenseman Art Duncan and put him in charge of coaching the club.

The defensive results couldn't have been better. Lorne Chabot registered five consecutive shutouts in the first five games of the season. In the sixth game it was assumed that Chabot would retain his flair for frugality since Toronto was playing the Philadelphia Quakers, perhaps the worst team ever to skate in the NHL and one that had yet to score a victory that season. A meager crowd, of 3,500, turned out in Philadelphia on November 25, 1930, and the Maple Leafs obliged by losing 2–1. The Leafs briefly held first place in January, 1931, before settling into second place, where they finished the season.

At the start of the 1931–32 season Smythe believed that only one or two changes were needed in order to have a Stanley Cup-winning team. He brought in Dick Irvin as coach, drafted Frank Finnigan from the now-defunct Ottawa Senators, and brought Harold Darragh from Boston.

"The Maple Leafs," said Frank Selke, "were more than a good team: they were a grand team, and the fireworks were provided by the Kid Line, truly a sight to behold. When Irvin sent them out on the ice, the fans teetered on the edges of their seats, and an electric tension seemed to permeate the entire auditorium. There have been other great forward lines in hockey, but none could match the frenzy that greeted the Kid Line in the mid-thirties."

The Kid Line profited from a rule change permitting forward passing in the enemy's zone. Primeau mastered the new form by skating over the opposition blue line and luring the defenseman toward him while Conacher and Primeau outflanked the foe. At the last possible second Primeau would skim a pass to one of his mates, who would have an unimpeded shot on goal.

Those who watched the Kid Line in action were awed by the razzle-dazzle of the trio. One such fascinated spectator was General John Reed Kilpatrick, later president of the New York Rangers, who observed that "when they get near our goal, my heart stops beating."

Meanwhile the heartbeat of every Toronto sports fan seemed to accelerate as Smythe helped to engineer a remarkable project, the building of Maple Leaf Gardens, hockey's showplace of the continent.

"Our town is first rate," said Smythe, "and our opponents are big-league players, playing in big-league buildings. We owe it to Toronto, to our players, and to ourselves to build a new hockey rink that all Canada can be proud of."

Nobody disagreed with Smythe about the need for a new rink. Everything about Mutual Street's building was passé. It held only 8,000 seats with room for some 1,000 standees, obsolete in comparison to such structures as the 16,000-seat Chicago Stadium and the 13,000-seat Olympia in Detroit.

The need for a new building was one thing, but the financing of it was still another. Times were grim in 1929, when Smythe launched the idea for an arena. Financial ruin was everywhere as the Depression set in. "Wall Street Lays an Egg," shouted the headlines, and money was nowhere to be found. Smythe estimated that it would cost 1.5 million to build Maple Leaf Gardens.

The scarcity of money notwithstanding, when Smythe made up his mind, his decision was irrevocable. A major factor in his thinking, oddly enough, was pure economics. The Maple Leafs really couldn't make a good buck at Mutual Street, and if they couldn't do that, it was next to impossible to pay off stars such as Clancy, Day, and the Kid Line. More irksome still was the fact that teams playing out of the major United States arenas threatened to pay more money, causing dissent among the Toronto skaters.

Another critical factor working for Smythe was the emergence of Foster Hewitt, whose electrifying radio broadcasts from high in the rafters at Mutual Street were glamorizing and popularizing the game. Smythe was quick to recognize Hewitt's broadcasting genius and urged him to become a part of the Maple Leaf Gardens operation. In time the two hammered out an agreement whereby Foster Hewitt Productions would have rights to broadcast events from Smythe's rink. Thus Hewitt's permanent liaison with the

Maple Leafs and Smythe was sealed before the new arena was begun.

Late in 1929 Smythe conceived a souvenir hockey program, edited by Selke, which was published early in 1930 for the patrons of Mutual Street Arena. The program detailed plans for Maple Leaf Gardens. Hewitt helped to promote it on one of his broadcasts, suggesting that fans mail a dime to the hockey club for a copy and learn about Toronto's hockey future. Reaction was overwhelmingly positive. This convinced Smythe he should begin selling stock in his new venture. The Depression notwithstanding, the gamble was hugely successful.

It was Smythe's intention to have the arena completed in time for the 1931–32 season, an optimistic projection to say the least. For one thing, there was still the matter of pushing stock sales in the fall and winter of 1930, when the Depression was hitting hardest, and for another, time was against such speedy construction even in the best of times.

Before winter had set in, the site had been cleared of its original structures, and a wasteland remained at Carlton and Church Streets. Frank "Buzz" Boll, one of Smythe's young hockey prospects, was hired as "nightwatchman." Selke recalled that Boll was stocked with a cord of wood, a shack, a stove, and a baseball bat to ward off intruders.

That winter Smythe hit the low point in his slough of despond when he learned that his group had fallen approximately $200,000 short of cash in order to complete the last phase of the project, the actual construction. But Selke entered the picture and personally saved the day.

An accomplished electrician, Selke had been active in the Allied Building and Trades Council of Toronto while carrying out his numerous other duties. He got a brainstorm. Why not persuade the various workers who would be engaged in constructing Maple Leaf Gardens — most of whom were unemployed because of the Depression — to accept twenty percent of their paychecks in Maple Leaf Gardens stock?

Although they were at first reluctant, Selke was able to convince his fellow tradesmen that they would be making a wise long-range investment if they accepted his plan.

After Selke had won the backing of labor, Sir John Aird, President of the Canadian Bank of Commerce, volunteered a $25,000 stock investment; soon other directors jumped onto the Maple

Leaf Gardens bankwagon. Selke, Smythe, industrialist J.P. Bickell, and friends had finally turned things around in the right direction, and Thomson Brothers, a Toronto construction firm, began work five months before the 1931–32 NHL schedule was to begin.

Working sometimes in three eight-hour shifts, the men employed 540 kegs of nails, 950,000 board feet of lumber, 750,000 bricks, 77,500 cement bags, and assorted other equipment. Smythe has said that Thomson Brothers took a loss in building the arena, but they certainly lost no time. On November 12, 1931, the Chicago Black Hawks were scheduled to play the Leafs in the Queen City, and on that night Maple Leaf Gardens was finished, ready for its customers. Foster Hewitt was in place in his observation booth, the Gondola, fifty-four feet above ice level.

By the time Chicago and Toronto players lined up for the opening faceoff on opening night, Smythe believed that he had done all he could to produce a winner. His young players, particularly the Kid Line, had matured into stars; he had obtained King Clancy, a move that Foster Hewitt regarded as one of the best ever made by any man on any team, and he had an arena that made every player thirst for victory. He had everything except a good coach.

Art Duncan had been a splendid hockey player and a noble citizen. He broke into pro hockey with Vancouver in 1916 as a forward, enlisted in the army, played for the famed 228th Sportsmen's Battalion, and eventually served heroically overseas. In time he came east to play, and he did so commendably, first for Detroit and then for Toronto, before Smythe appointed him coach.

It was Selke's theory that Duncan lacked the insatiable enthusiasm for hockey that marks the brand of galvanic coach that the Maple Leafs required at the time. After the club had gone without a win in its first six games at its new ice palace, Smythe decided to replace Duncan. The choice was of utter importance because continued defeat would give Maple Leaf Gardens a disastrous beginning. Dick Irvin, one of the most adroit coaches in the NHL, had just been fired by the Black Hawks, even though he had led Chicago to the 1931 Stanley Cup finals. An indefatigable battler, Irvin was precisely the type of individual Smythe wanted. The Leaf boss lost no time in securing him.

Easy-going Art Duncan had allowed his players to get out of shape, and by early December the Maple Leafs, with a few conspicuous exceptions, were fat and flabby. A martinet without peer,

Irvin launched a Spartan training program that brought results almost overnight, and by Christmas week the Leafs were in first place.

The Maple Leafs' success in the 1931–32 season resulted in increasingly larger crowds at Maple Leafs Gardens and the conviction that Smythe had pulled off the impossible. His arena was the sensation of the league — 13,000 fans jammed Maple Leaf Gardens on March 5, 1932 — and the Toronto club battled the Canadiens for first place right down to the final weeks of the season. While the Canadiens perished in the preliminary playoff rounds, the Leafs and Rangers made it to the finals.

Whether the 1931–32 Maple Leafs were better than any Ranger club is a moot question, which frequently has been argued in Toronto's favor. The Kid Line was at least equal to New York's Cook Brothers-Boucher combination; Chabot was superior to Roach in goal; Clancy and Horner were better defensemen than New York's starters, Johnson and Heller; and Toronto had superior substitutes such as Bailey, Gracie, Finnigan, Blair, and Cotton.

Before the opening faceoff the finals took on a weird aspect. New York was scheduled to host the opening match of the best-of-five series and the second contest as well. But a Ringling Brothers/Barnum and Bailey Circus was slated to move into Madison Square Garden on April 7, the date of the second game, so the Rangers suddenly found themselves without a rink. Both teams finally agreed to play the match on neutral Boston Garden ice, and the series got underway.

The Rangers had one thing going for them — the luxury of a week's rest. The Leafs still were frazzled from their semi-final encounter with Maroons. Despite hostile Ranger faithful, Smythe's kids produced like old pros, with Busher Jackson leading the way on the strength of a hat trick.

More than 12,000 fans turned out in Boston to see the out-of-town finalists, and they left astounded by the Kid Line's antics. The same could be said for Ranger goalie John Ross Roach, who gave up two goals to Conacher, two to Clancy, and one each to Jackson and Cotton in the 6–2 Maple Leafs win. Toronto goalie Chabot, who had feuded on-and-off with his old boss, Lester Patrick, seemed to be rubbing it into Lester with some of the best netminding of his life.

On the night of April 9, 1932, 14,366 fans turned up at Maple

Leaf Gardens, fully expecting the final kill of the Rangers. They were not disappointed.

Right from the start Chabot outgoaled Roach, and that developed into the most important single factor in the decisive match. Irvin skated his second line, Bailey, Blair, and Cotton, against the Cook Brothers and Boucher. It was an interesting but not entirely successful venture. Boucher scored a hat trick for the Rangers, and Bun Cook also scored for the line. Blair got two, and Bailey got one, which meant the New Yorkers came off from that match-up one goal to the good.

The difference, however, was in the substitutes. Busher Jackson, Frank Finnigan, and Bob Gracie scored one goal apiece, giving Toronto a total of six to the Rangers four. Thus the Toronto Maple Leafs won their first Stanley Cup. Sometimes called the "tennis" series, it was an emphatic triumph — three straight wins, with scores of 6–4, 6–2, 6–4.

This team's *joie de vivre* and off-ice antics led to their being called the "Gashouse Gang," hockey's answer to the Gashouse pranksters of Dizzy Dean's St. Louis Cardinals. It was the era of the Marx Brothers, who set a style on the movie screen that was adopted by the Leafs' humorists, Hap Day, King Clancy, Harold "Baldy" Cotton, and Charlie Conacher. On one occasion, when Cotton persisted in grumbling to his linemates, especially room-mate Conacher that he wasn't being passed the puck enough, Conacher lowered him, by his ankles, from a twentieth-floor window of New York's Hotel Lincoln (now called the Royal Manhattan).

The Leafs had hoped to repeat their Cup-winning performance of 1932 the following season. Perhaps in an effort to will it they even went so far as to sit for a team photograph — with the Stanley Cup! Unfortunately, at the end of the day the Leafs were out of the money — Boston defeated Toronto in the final — and the Leafs' 1933 "Stanley Cup Champions" photo must remain a mild embarrassment to the club.

Early in the 1933–34 season tragedy struck in the form of the infamous Eddie Shore–Ace Bailey incident. Shore was hockey's toughest, meanest, most-feared player. In the course of his career his body was skewered in so many places more than 900 stitches were required to hold it together. His back, hip, and collarbone were fractured, both eyeballs were split open, every tooth was knocked out of his mouth, and his nose was broken fourteen times.

His jaw was cracked five times, and his ear was once almost severed by a sharp skate. Bailey, once the league's leading scorer, was a stickhandling artist, respected around the league.

Accounts of the events of the night of December 12, 1933 at the Boston Garden vary. Some eyewitnesses recalled that Shore had been tripped by Clancy, others that he had been checked by Horner. In any case, when Shore picked himself up from the ice he wanted revenge. Livid, he charged Bailey from behind. The impact of the blow was so severe Bailey took a backward somersault resembling a gymnast's trick. His head cracked against the ice. Frank Selke, Sr. recalled: "Bailey was lying on the Leaf blueline, with his head turned sideways, as though his neck were broken. His knees were raised, legs twitching ominously. Suddenly an awesome hush fell over the arena. Everyone realized Bailey was badly hurt. Horner tried to straighten Bailey's head, but his neck appeared to be locked. Red skated over to Shore, saying, 'Why the hell did you do that, Eddie?'

"Shore, little realizing how badly Bailey had been hurt, merely smiled. His seeming callousness infuriated Horner, who then hit Shore a punch on the jaw. It was a right uppercut which stiffened the big defense star. As he fell, with his body rigid and straight as a board, Shore's head struck the ice, splitting open. In an instant, he was circled by a pool of blood about three feet in diameter."

At that moment, the Bruins, as one, vaulted the boards and charged at Horner, but teammate Charlie Conacher rushed to Horner's side and the two held their sticks in bayonet position. "Which one of you guys is going to be the first to get it?" Conacher demanded. The Bruins suddenly conducted an orderly retreat to assist Shore and to see if Bailey was still alive.

For nineteen minutes Bailey lay unconscious while doctors worked frantically over him. An ambulance was summoned to rush him to the hospital, where he teetered precariously on the brink of death. He had suffered a cerebral concussion with convulsions, and he appeared incapable of recovery.

A day after the injury two brain surgeons operated on Bailey, thinking he had suffered only one concussion. After the initial surgery, however, they discovered he had suffered two, and a week later another operation was performed. Few had hope for Bailey, and the Toronto management made plans to have Bailey's body shipped back to Canada. From the time Shore first regained consciousness in the Boston dressing room he seemed a marked man. Editorials clamored for his scalp. He was reviled from coast to coast. Demands were made to bar him from hockey forever. In the event of Bailey's death, criminal prosecution was suggested.

Fortunately, in about two weeks' time Bailey recovered, although he would never play hockey again. This led to the Ace Bailey Benefit game, at Maple Leaf Gardens, February 14, 1934 — the league's first all-star match. It was an emotional evening. The Gardens was packed to capacity when Bailey stepped onto the ice to present special sweaters bearing his name to each of the players. "Ace could scarcely see the great men before him," wrote Ron McAllister, "because of the tears of honest pride that trickled down his face."

The players skated up to Bailey one by one and shook his hand as the crowd bellowed its appreciation. Eddie Shore was introduced last, and the Gardens erupted with wild applause when Bailey and Shore shook hands at center ice.

What goes up must come down, and so it was with the world champion Maple Leafs. Their descent was a long and gradual dip, rather like a balloon moving down to its mooring. With Ace Bailey gone from the lineup, the Maple Leafs were knocked out of the 1934 Stanley Cup playoffs in the opening round by the Detroit Red Wings.

The crumbling of a sports dynasty can inevitably be attributed to faults along the trading path. After winning the 1932 Stanley Cup, Smythe made two highly questionable moves, which helped to accelerate the eventual collapse of Toronto.

His first mistake was the 1933 trade with the Canadiens that brought goalie George Hainsworth to Toronto in exchange for the very capable Lorne Chabot whose temperament conflicted with Smythe's.

Chabot played only one season for the Habs; then he went with Howie Morenz to Chicago, where he replaced Charlie Gardiner. There he played the best goal of his life, winning the Vezina Trophy with a 1.83 goals-against average and earning a nomination to the first all-star team. Coincidentally, both Hainsworth and Chabot retired in 1937, each after playing fewer than a dozen games that season.

Smythe made another mistake, in his handling of Bill "Flash" Hollett, a native of Sydney, Nova Scotia, who showed up at the Maple Leafs' Kingston, Ontario, training camp in 1933, looking for a spot on the Toronto defense. Hollett impressed everyone but Smythe with one destructive bodycheck that sent King Clancy to the ice. "If they don't sign you to this team," Clancy told the kid later in the dressing room, "look me up, and I'll see that you're placed somewhere in the NHL."

Flash was sent to Buffalo in the minors, only to be recalled after the Shore-Bailey affair, when Red Horner was suspended. Upon Horner's return, Hollett was traded to Ottawa, but he returned to the Maple Leafs the next season. Smythe should have realized the youngster's vast potential then. He scored ten goals and sixteen assists for twenty-six points, best among NHL defensemen.

Smythe remained unimpressed, and he dropped Flash back to Syracuse the next fall. Hollett played for two weeks, broke his hand, and persuaded Smythe that he was dispensable. A week later he was sold to the minor-league Boston Cubs, from whom he graduated to the Bruins. He played seven splendid seasons for Boston.

Despite the label, Toronto's Kid Line was no longer comprised of kids. Injuries continued to hobble big Charlie Conacher, and speedy living was beginning to take its toll on Jackson. After Detroit defeated Toronto in the 1936 Stanley Cup final, Joe Primeau decided to call it a career. Smythe realized that once again the time had come to rebuild, and the question on everyone's mind was not whether he would succeed — that was taken for granted — but who the next Maple Leaf superstars would be. One of his most significant acquisitions was a goaltender named Walter Broda.

They called him "Turkey Egg" in the wheat country that surrounds Brandon, Manitoba. During a history lesson an instructor told his class that an English king was given that nickname because of the huge freckles covering his face. Since nobody had more freckles than Broda, after the history lesson Walter was immediately hailed as "Turkey Egg." Eventually he was called just plain "Turk."

Originally a Detroit Red Wings prospect, Broda was eyed by Smythe who offered Red Wings general manager Jack Adams $8,000 for the untried netminder, a sizable sum in the middle of the Depression. Adams did not want to trade Turk to Toronto: he liked Broda, and he loathed the Maple Leafs. But there was the matter of economics — the $8,000 — and a deal was struck.

In training camp for the 1936–37 season Broda and the veteran Hainsworth battled for supremacy. Hainsworth never played better goal and by the start of the season no clear winner could be declared. Smythe — always the gambler — opened with Broda on November 5, 1936 at the Gardens, a 3–1 loss to the Cup-defending

Red Wings. Although he fizzled on an easy shot late in the game, Broda was buoyed by a Toronto newspaper article the next day which encouraged him to try to be able to "take the raspberry as well as the rhapsody."

Hainsworth started in the next game, against the New York Americans, and also flubbed an easy shot in the third period in a 3–2 loss. Back at the Gardens on November 12, Broda defeated Chicago 6–2, but Hainsworth was an ace the next night in holding the Hawks to a 1–1 tie at Chicago Stadium.

The contest between the freckle-faced kid from Brandon and the aging veteran had begun to assume major proportions. Toronto's dressing room was split down the middle, one faction supporting Hainsworth and the other, Broda. Smythe still didn't make a move in either direction. He started Turk on November 21 at home and lost 4–3 to the Boston Bruins. The next night found the Leafs at Olympia Stadium in Detroit, Broda's old stomping grounds. On a hunch Smythe started him again.

The Detroit fans welcomed Broda as if he were their personal hero. Once again Turk played more than a creditable game, but Toronto lost, 4–2. On the train to New York Smythe decided to revert to Hainsworth. His club was playing the Rangers on the night before Thanksgiving, and Smythe was worried. A wrist injury still aggravated right winger Conacher, and Jackson was not playing up to par. The constant hounding by both press and spectators about the goaltending situation also was conducive to migraines. Smythe knew that he had to make a decision as soon as possible.

Hainsworth inadvertently made it for him that night in Madison Square Garden: the old-timer allowed five goals in a 5–1 rout. When the game was over, Smythe called him into his office and said he was giving him his outright release. The venerable Hainsworth was claimed by his former club, the Canadiens, where he played four more games before retiring.

Broda accomplished his first shutout on January 2, 1937, a 0–0 tie with the Montreal Maroons. His first shutout victory took place on January 23, 1937, at Maple Leaf Gardens, a 4–0 win over the New York Rangers. He beat the New York Americans 5–0 on February 6, 1937, at Maple Leaf Gardens, his last shutout of his first year.

Turk finished that critical rookie year with a 2.32 goals-against average, fifth best in the eight-team league but so close to pacesetters Davey Kerr, Norm Smith, Wilf Cude, and Tiny Thompson that

Broda had proved he belonged with the best, at least for the moment.

On November 24, 1936, King Clancy announced his retirement. At that time Smythe was absorbed with ridding the Toronto club of its deadwood and infusing youth into all lines, offensive and defensive. The challenge was as formidable then as it had been when he first began to organize a winner in the late twenties.

Some of King's cronies stayed on but not for long. Charlie Conacher remained with the team despite his battered hulk. Apart from his subdued kidney problem, Conacher suffered a smashed shoulder, broken wrist, broken bones in the right hand, a broken left hand, and a broken collarbone.

"Charlie's problem," said a teammate, "is that he thinks he's the only battleship in the fleet."

Busher Jackson, the other cog in the Kid Line, Hap Day, Red Horner, and Frank Finnigan were the other throwbacks who managed to shove the Maple Leafs into the 1937 playoffs, a best-of-three round with the Rangers. New York routed the Leafs 3–0 at Maple Leaf Gardens in the first game, which was interrupted with brawls. The teams returned to New York for the second match, and this time Toronto held fast for a 1–1 tie through regulation time. When the teams skated out for sudden-death overtime, manager Lester Patrick replaced aging defenseman Ching Johnson with a curly-haired kid from Winnipeg named Walter "Babe" Pratt. In less than fifteen minutes the tall youngster scored the winning goal, and the Leafs were through for the year.

Smythe continued to peel away the old bark. He released captain Hap Day, who immediately signed with the New York Americans. Day's replacement was Rudolph "Bingo" Kampman, a man built along the generous dimensions of a Clydesdale stallion and who reputedly could lift a heavy table by clenching its top in his teeth. Kampman's claims were later verified and made economically sound by several bets with teammates and other interested parties.

Frank Finnigan, another oldtimer, packed up his skates for good and headed back to the Ottawa Valley, and Art Jackson was sold to Boston. With Hap Day gone Charlie Conacher became captain of the club, much to the delight of young Broda, who seemed to follow the veteran right wing wherever he went.

With Conacher captaining the team, Toronto galloped smartly ahead of the Canadiens, the Americans, and the Maroons in the

NHL's Canadian division, and by January 15, 1938, the Leafs had a firm hold on first place. But progress and pain were inseparable for Conacher. Rushed back to action, he suffered a shoulder injury, and then came close to collapse because of a combination of physical and nervous ailments. By the end of January the captain was ordered to take a sabbatical. Charlie didn't know it at the time, but he had played his last game for the Maple Leafs.

The departure of Conacher turned the spotlight onto Gordie Drillon, a 6'2", 178-pound (almost Conacher's size) right wing from Moncton, New Brunswick. His ability had suggested stardom while he was playing for Toronto's minor league affiliate in Syracuse.

Hefty and handsome, Drillon alarmed Smythe in one way: he seemed disinclined to fight, and that left Smythe wondering whether he could fill Conacher's skates. In his rookie year, 1936–37, Drillon scored sixteen goals and seventeen assists for thirty-three points in forty-one games. A season later he had established himself as a first-rate forward with twenty-six goals, twenty-six assists, and fifty-two points. He led the league in goals and points.

Unfortunately, Drillon had two raps against him: he was following the beloved Conacher, and he had a habit of scoring the kinds of goals that lacked spectator appeal. The public considered Drillon more lucky than skillful and tended to label his efforts "garbage goals." In fact, Drillon had worked long and hard at perfecting the tip-in.

Nobody dared to call the Maple Leafs "lucky" for finishing atop the Canadian division. Skeptics were convinced of Toronto's ability when the Leafs defeated the American division leaders, Boston, in a three-game first-round Stanley Cup playoff. The Leafs swept the series without a loss, and Gordie Drillon was the star, scoring the winning goal in both the second and third games.

The victory sent Toronto straight to the Stanley Cup finals, where the Leafs awaited the victors in other playdowns. Surprisingly the Chicago Black Hawks defeated the Canadiens two-games-to-one in the quarter-finals and then upset the New York Americans two-games-to-one in the semifinal round.

On April 12, 1938, when the underdog Hawks defeated the Leafs to take the Cup, Smythe — and the entire city of Toronto — was stunned to the core. This was to be the year of the Maple Leafs' second world championship, and they frittered it away to an obviously inferior team, inferior, that is, until the chips were down. Smythe wasn't going to stand still. He couldn't help but admire Chicago's gutsy Doc Romnes, who had tilted so frequently and so well with badman Horner. During the early part of the 1938–39 season Smythe sent Bill Thoms to Chicago and got the older Romnes in return. But that wasn't enough. The Toronto defense was vulnerable. Searching the league rosters for help, Smythe learned that the Red Wings were unhappy with their fourth-year NHL defenseman Wilfrid "Bucko" McDonald. Shortly before Christmas, Jack Adams sold McDonald to the Maple Leafs, and Toronto acquired one of its most colorful players since King Clancy.

In the 1939 quarter-finals, Broda explored new heights of perfection, shutting out the New York Americans 4–0 and 2–0 in successive games, and the Leafs catapulted into the Stanley Cup semifinals against the Red Wings. He kept Detroit from scoring through the fourteen-minute mark of the second period before Marty Barry blitzed a shot past him. The once-maligned Broda had played 154 playoff minutes without allowing a goal.

Toronto won the first game, 4–1, thanks to Gordie Drillon's pair of goals. Drillon's performance was rather ironic since Maple Leaf Gardens fans had begun to display a great deal of antagonism toward the high-scoring forward. "They didn't like his lackadaisical style of play," said Ed Fitkin, "even though he was an opportunist around the net."

Detroit won the second game 3–1 (Drillon got the lone Toronto goal) at the Olympia, sending the teams back to Maple Leaf Gardens on April 1, 1939, for the last match of the semifinals. The Red Wings hurled their best shots at Broda and got past him four times, but Toronto matched that. The teams were to settle the round in sudden-death overtime.

With the overhead timer ticking into the fifth minute of the game, the chronically unpopular Drillon eased the puck onto his stick deep in his own territory. The Red Wing backcheckers tried to zero in on him as he accelerated at the Leaf blue line, but his fierce strides carried him past one red shirt after another. By the time he had crossed the Detroit line, Drillon was skating like a man possessed, determined to erase the criticism once and for all. His shot was flawless, hitting the twine at 5:42, and the crowd in Maple Leaf Gardens roared their approval. But their love was not to be permanent.

Drillon had carried the Leafs into the finals against Boston, but he would need help if the Leafs were to capture the Stanley Cup, especially since the Boston Bruins were highly motivated for the series. The Bruins also boasted a young goaltender from Eveleth, Minnesota, who already had earned the nickname "Mister Zero." Not even Drillon could solve Brimsek, and Boston won the Stanley Cup four games to one in the best-of-seven series.

While Broda and Drillon were important cogs in the Toronto machine another Leaf, acquired in the thirties, would prove supreme and, more than any other Leaf, engineer the successes of Toronto's first truly golden era, the forties. His name was Sylvanus Apps, and he would become the heart of the Maple Leafs.

The original "All-Canadian Boy," Apps was born in Paris, Ontario, a small town near Stratford. A graceful skater with long, powerful strides and dazzling bursts of speed, the 6', 180-pound center was described as "a Rembrandt on the ice, a Nijinsky at the goalmouth." At seventeen, he had entered McMaster University in Hamilton, on a scholarship, majoring in political economy. A football and track and field star, he represented Canada in pole vaulting at the 1934 British Empire Games in London, England, and placed first. When approached by Smythe he advised the Leaf honcho that he wanted to complete his university education and compete in the 11th Olympiade in 1936 before he would consider the NHL. He had another concern as well — "In my circle," he observed, "professional athletes were not looked upon as the right sort."

After the Olympics, in Berlin, Germany, where he vaulted to sixth place in the world before 100,000 spectators (including Adolf Hitler), Apps returned to Paris and contemplated hockey and advanced education. At a summer meeting with the young superstar Smythe was able to put enough incentives in place to make a career with Toronto worth Apps's while.

Irvin put Apps at center between Busher Jackson and Gordie Drillon. Although veteran Jackson no longer was noted for his diligence, the two younger players would remain on the ice for long hours after regular workouts, perfecting Drillon's "secret weapon," the tip-in shot. Apps was vital to the play since he was required to deliver the pass. Drillon, of course, was to get credit for the goals, but as Bill Roche pointed out, "The serious-minded Apps was the one who proposed that they do the experimenting."

The results came immediately, and by mid-season Apps was hailed as shoo-in for rookie of the year. "He's a better player than

Howie Morenz was at the same age," said Detroit Manager Jack Adams, who always was grudging in his acclaim for a Toronto player.

Syl finished the season with only ten minutes in penalties, but, more important, he scored sixteen goals and twenty-nine assists for forty-five points, second to Dave "Sweeney" Schriner of the Americans. Apps had missed the scoring championship by only one point. In the balloting for the Calder Trophy, given to the season's top rookie, Apps polled seventy-nine out of a possible eighty-one votes and easily won the award.

Thanks to Syl's crisp passes, Drillon led the NHL in scoring during the 1937–38 season, with twenty-six goals and twenty-six assists for fifty-two points. The unselfish Apps finished second again, scoring twenty-one goals and twenty-nine assists for fifty points. The next season he lead the Leafs in scoring and with every passing month reached new levels of stardom. His performance in the 1940's would realize Smythe's long-awaited dream.

1940 TO 1949

THE 40's   ANALYSIS

The 1940's clearly favored the Leafs over the Canadiens. When the Nazis invaded Poland in September, 1939, Conn Smythe boasted a formidable, if not championship, team at Maple Leaf Gardens. The Canadiens, by contrast, were in a state of disrepair and disarray.

In the 1942 Stanley Cup finals the Leafs dropped the first three games before roaring from behind to win the next four to take the Cup, the first team in sports history to rally from such a deficit in a championship series. Between 1947 and 1950 they became the first team in NHL history to win three consecutive Stanley Cups, thereby becoming professional hockey's first legitimate dynasty.

Montreal's emerging dynasty took shape in the midst of the war. Credit belongs to coach Dick Irvin, the young Maurice "the Rocket" Richard, who would become the Babe Ruth of hockey, and a big, gifted, ambidextrous goaltender named Bill Durnan. What should have been — based on talent — the first NHL dynasty never fully matured. Montreal's Stanley Cup win in 1944 should have been followed by another a year later but the Habs were foiled by a makeshift Toronto club with a patchwork lineup. Despite Richard, Durnan, and other stars such as Toe Blake and Elmer Lach, the Canadiens fell prey to an ulcerated rookie goalie, Frank McCool, who led the Leafs to an unexpected Stanley Cup with no less than three shutouts.

When the Habs rgained the Cup a year later, there was reason to believe that Irvin had the armament for the expected dynastic run. But no one, least of all Irvin, could have anticipated the spontaneous combustion that developed on the Leaf roster when Smythe mixed a bunch of eager youngsters with veterans like captain Syl Apps and Turk Broda. Even after Apps retired in 1948 the Leafs continued winning and closed the decade with their third-straight Stanley Cup in April 1949.

Montreal's principal asset was a small, unobtrusive front-office type named Frank Selke, Sr. The former aide to Smythe in Toronto, Selke moved to the Canadiens in the late 1940's and began a major reshaping of the organization. His most decisive

---

and far-reaching move was to construct a farm system that extended across Canada from the back-alley rinks of Montreal's French-speaking east end to the windswept prairie ponds of Regina. The result would not pay dividends until the early fifties, which meant the Habs would remain second-fiddle to the Torontonians until after yet another Maple Leaf championship.

MONTREAL: THE ROCKET'S RED GLARE

There was no evidence at the time to suggest any renaissance in the Canadiens' fortunes but at the start of the 1942–43 season a second Golden Era was dawning with the arrival of two seemingly awkward hockey players — goalie Bill Durnan and right wing Maurice Richard.

Insightful scouting and judicious trading had enabled the Habs to begin the 1940's with a formidable defense and an attack that was more than adequate. But the club's weak underbelly was goaltending. Paul Bibeault had won the job from Bert Gardiner, who was then traded to Chicago. Coach Irvin decided to give the tall French-Canadian the entire 1942–43 season to prove himself. Bibeault played all fifty games for Montreal and finished up with a less-than-stellar 3.82 goals-against average.

For the 1943–44 opener, Bill Durnan was in the nets. Durnan had starred with the Kirkland Lake Blue Devils when they won the Allan Cup in 1940. Surprisingly, he had remained unsigned by the pros. His debut with the Canadiens was reminiscent of George Hainsworth's many years earlier. Like Hainsworth, Durnan was an English-Canadian from Ontario who had supplanted a French-Canadian. The crowd wasn't terribly enthused about that, particularly because Bibeault was now playing for, of all teams, the Toronto Maple Leafs.

It took Durnan approximately an hour to persuade the capacity crowd that *Les Canadiens* had not made a mistake. Although he permitted two goals and the game ended in a 2–2 tie, his goaltending was so spectacular that the critical Montreal audience could offer no legitimate complaint. "He won the respect of his teammates and fans alike," observed one writer. Three nights later, he limited the Rangers to a single goal; the Canadiens triumphed, 2–1, and both Durnan and the Habs were off and running to one of the most extraordinary seasons any team has ever enjoyed in the NHL.

Durnan's life was made a lot easier by a tall French-Canadian defenseman, Emile "Butch" Bouchard, who had learned his hockey on the sidewalks of Montreal, not far from the Forum. After a season at Providence, in the American League, he was signed to a Canadiens contract.

In his first game against the Toronto Maple Leafs, Butch was confronted by the slick-skating Sweeney Schriner. The Leaf forward tried an assortment of head and stick feints but Bouchard held his ground like a seasoned pro. The one-on-one challenge became an obsession with Schriner, but, each time, Butch stopped him cold. With each rebuff, Toronto coach Hap Day became more and more frustrated. "Listen, Sweeney," he demanded, "next time you get into Canadiens territory, go around the other side."

Schriner accepted the advice and on his next expedition toward the Montreal goal he skated face-to-face with the veteran Red Goupille standing in his tracks, and scored easily. "At that time," noted a Toronto observer, "Bouchard became a marked man."

When Montreal visited New York on January 9, 1944, *le bleu, blanc et rouge* boasted an arresting 19–2–3 record and the New York *World-Telegram* ran a headline: "LES CANADIENS — WONDER TEAM OF THE ICE SEASON." In the accompanying story, the *World-Telegram* hockey critic observed:

What makes them go? In a phrase, their wonderful balance. They have the league's most effective goalie, a rugged defense, and three forward lines which mount a sizzling attack, and also backcheck faster and in more robust fashion than any other threesomes.

The first line of Phil Watson, Murph Chamberlain, and Ray Getliffe is two-way dynamite when they have the puck, or when the other side has it. Watson very likely stands next to Bill Cowley of Boston among the league's centers. Chamberlain and Getliffe are crack shots, particularly the latter, and both have that rare forward line ability to dish out the bodychecks. The trio forms the roughhouse line. There's not a weak spot in the lot, and that's the main reason *Les Canadiens* lose a game only about once a month.

By late January it was apparent that they had no challengers, and on February 26, nearly a month before the season's end, the Habs clinched the championship with a 10–2 victory at Boston.

When the season ended on March 19, the Canadiens had amassed a record-breaking thirty-eight wins, seven ties, and only five losses. Their margin over second-place Detroit was twenty-five points. They had scored a league-leading 234 goals and permitted only 109, thus giving Durnan, with a goals-against average of 2.18, the Vezina Trophy in his rookie season.

With such a redoubtable record the Canadiens appeared destined to romp through the playoffs as unchallenged as a lion in the African plains. Their first-round opponents were the Toronto Maple Leafs with onetime Canadien Paul Bibeault in goal. The Leafs stunned Montreal with a 3–1 defeat in the opening game at the Forum, but the Canadiens regained their composure and easily swept the series, winning the next four games in a row. Meanwhile, the Black Hawks wiped out the Red Wings in five games and skated onto Montreal ice April 4 hoping for an upset. The Chicago club had finished in fourth place, thirty-four points behind the Habs, but the Hawks realized that the brief best-of-seven series was conducive to an upset.

Their hopes were immediately dashed in the first game as the Canadiens thoroughly bedazzled the visitors with a 5–1 win. Montreal captured the second game, 3–2, and then moved on to the Windy City where they wrapped up the series with 3–2 and 5–4 decisions and Montreal's first Stanley Cup success in fourteen years.

Nobody was particularly surprised at the outcome of the series, nor was there anything unusual about the Canadiens' romp through the season, once it became obvious that they were the class of the hockey world. But there were several raised eyebrows over the play of Joseph Henri Maurice Richard. "Richard has the speed of Howie Morenz," said one sportswriter, "but hardly his daring." That line was a classic of poor judgement.

"Maurice Richard," summed up a writer for the Toronto *Star Weekly* magazine, "was the most exciting athlete I have ever seen. So much has been written about Richard that for me to offer a flood of new praise would be roughly equivalent to a Ph.D. candidate announcing he is going to prove *Hamlet* is an interesting play."

The young Richard was considered fragile by NHL experts, but after a series of setbacks in amateur hockey, he was invited to skate with the Canadiens in 1943. The slick-haired kid had little trouble making the NHL team in his first try, but he was overshadowed by such new Montreal additions as Gordie Drillon, who had been obtained from Toronto, and Dutch Hiller from Boston.

Irvin inserted Richard on a line with the veteran Tony Demers and young center Elmer Lach. The line clicked immediately and Demers scored two goals as the Canadiens won their opening game from Boston, 3–2. The result was especially appealing to one of the game's linesmen — Aurel Joliat.

Irvin had theorized that Lach was the ideal center for Richard but he wasn't so sure about left wing. He finally decided that Toe Blake would be worthy of an experiment on the unit, and in no time the line was made — for keeps. The trio, soon to be named "the Punch Line," finished one-two-three (Lach, Blake, Richard) in scoring on the team, with Richard collecting thirty-two goals and twenty-two assists for fifty-four points in forty-six games.

He was, however, buried in fifteenth place on the scoring list and certainly wasn't regarded with the same awe as his two linemates. That is, not until the first round of the Stanley Cup playoffs against Toronto. In the opening game Richard was held scoreless by the Maple Leafs' expert checking forward, Bob Davidson. But in the second game, on March 23, 1944, Davidson's most determined efforts proved feeble against Richard's towering performance.

Maurice scored three goals in the second period, breaking a scoreless tie, and added two more in the third period. The final score was Richard 5, Toronto 1! The last time a player had scored five or more goals in a Stanley Cup match was in 1917 when Bernie Morris scored six against the Canadiens for Seattle.

After disposing of Toronto, the Canadiens challenged Chicago and, onced again, Richard dominated an entire game. The Montrealers defeated Chicago, 3–1, on April 6 in the second game of the final round and Richard scored *all three* goals. Just to prove it was no fluke, Maurice practically single-handedly saved Montreal in the fourth and last game of the series after Chicago had mounted a 4–1 lead after two periods.

Richard's second goal of the game tied the match, 4–4, sending it into sudden-death overtime. Then his pass to Blake set up the winning goal, and minutes later, Richard, Blake, and Lach were sipping champagne from the Stanley Cup. In his first full season in the NHL Richard had set two major-league records: one for scoring five goals in a single playoff game (a modern record), and another for amassing twelve goals in the playoff series.

Next season, with only a few exceptions, the Canadiens iced virtually the same team they had when they won the Cup in April. A key addition was Ken Mosdell, a tall, rangy forward who had just been released from the armed forces. The Punch Line remained intact and began the season with the same syncopated attack that had stirred the fans in '43–'44. Richard broke from the post like an overzealous thoroughbred. His scoring was becoming so prolific that opposing coaches started mapping specific strategies to stop the Rocket, on the theory that if you could blockade Richard, you could beat the Habs.

There was no longer any question that Richard had orbited into a very special position among the galaxy of hockey stars. Hy Turkin, of the New York *Daily News*, dubbed him "the Brunette Bullet," and added that his sidekick, Lach, was a "sandy-haired stickhandling Svengali." For the first time in Richard's career he was being favorably compared with such Hall of Famers as Howie Morenz and Aurel Joliat. "He may prove to be one of the great players of history," suggested sportswriter Joe King:

> Those who saw Morenz will remember him for his flashing straightaway speed and his boundless daring. He was an arrow whizzing through the defense. He did not know caution. No momentary gap in the defense was too small for him to attempt.
>
> Richard is extremely speedy, but he is not the breathtaking adventurer that Morenz was. He is on a different pattern, with more guile in his makeup . . . Maurice makes much more use of the change-of-pace, the trickery of speed and stickhandling than did Morenz. Richard swoops around the defense, while Morenz dared the guards to stop him dead-on.

Ranger manager Lester Patrick, who was in a position to know, said Richard was more a copy of Jack Laviolette than of Morenz. *Daily News* columnist Jim McCulley referred to Montreal as "Richard & Co." And, needless to say, Maurice reinforced his reputation on each visit to New York.

With four games remaining in the season, *Les Canadiens*, snug in first place, invaded Madison Square Garden and routed the Rangers, 11–5. Banging two shots past goalie Ken McAuley, Richard lifted his goal-scoring total to an astonishing forty-eight in only forty-seven games. "McAuley," observed Hy Turkin, "acted shell-shocked."

He scored number forty-nine on March 15 with only two games remaining in the schedule. In the next-to-last game, against the Black Hawks on Forum ice, the Canadiens triumphed, but somehow Maurice was thoroughly blanked. That left only one more match, the final game of the season at Boston Garden. This time Richard came through in a 4–2 win over the Bruins and finished the season with fifty goals in fifty games.

Having defended their first-place championship with ease, the Canadiens now turned to the business of defending their hold on the Stanley Cup. Toronto's Maple Leafs, the robust third-place finishers, would be the opening-round opposition and it didn't take very long for Conn Smythe's outfit to prove they had come to play.

Leaf coach Hap Day once more assigned Bob Davidson the thankless job of manacling Richard and this time Davidson succeeded. Toronto upset Montreal, 1–0 and 3–2, in the first pair of games on Forum ice and Richard was completely neutralized. Although Montreal won the third game, in Toronto, by a score of 4–1, Richard was held scoreless. The Leafs captured the fourth game of the series with a 4–3 win and Richard finally scored. He then exploded for four goals in the fifth game, in which Toronto was routed, 10–3. Richard's inflationary output created the mirage that Montreal was about to dispose of the upstart Leafs, but when the teams met on March 31 in the sixth game, Richard was nullified and Toronto came away with a 3–2 win, stunning Montreal with elimination.

The fact that Toronto went on to win the Stanley Cup hardly consoled the Canadiens' front office. But Irvin was quick to guard against a panic shake-up and decided to launch the 1945–46 season with virtually the same lineup that he had used the previous season. There was one very significant addition, Ken Reardon. A boisterous prospect who had quit hockey to join the armed forces, he had returned to Montreal and Irvin immediately invited him to training camp where the gutsy defenseman became a fan favorite.

The Canadiens clinched the league championship on March 14, 1946, and gamboled along the rest of the route as individual players fattened their averages and collected the usual rewards. Durnan won the Vezina Trophy for the third consecutive year and was now regarded as superior even to Vezina himself. Blake, who received only one minor penalty all season, was awarded the Lady

Byng Trophy, for combined ability and gentlemanly conduct, and the Canadiens prepared for another march to the Stanley Cup, fully aware of the previous year's disappointment.

Paced by the Punch Line, they prevailed over Chicago and then Boston, to win the Cup, the sixth in the team's history.

The single most significant event in the history of the Toronto-Montreal rivalry occurred at the start of the 1946–47 campaign when Frank J. Selke was named manager of the Canadiens. Selke's move had everything to do with his relationship to Conn Smythe.

When Smythe went overseas to serve with the Canadian Armed Forces in World War II, it was Selke who ably filled the breach and guided the roster-riddled Toronto sextet. However, one of Selke's smartest moves in Toronto led to his downfall as a member of the Leaf hierarchy and his "deportation" to Montreal.

The *coup de grace* was rooted in a decision Selke made in 1944 while Smythe was overseas. At the time the Leafs had signed Frankie Eddolls, a young defenseman who had learned his hockey in Verdun, not far from where Rocket Richard had played his junior games. Dick Irvin had seen Eddolls play and was impressed. Since Dick was on speaking terms with Selke, he mentioned that he wouldn't mind having the Montreal lad in the Canadiens' system.

Selke's mind was turning. He knew that Montreal had the rights to a tenacious center playing in nearby Port Colborne, Ontario. "We'll let you have Eddolls," said Selke, "if you give up Ted Kennedy."

The proposal was intriguing and perplexing to both sides and very nearly foundered on the rocks of uncertainty. At last, the parties agreed to the swap and Ted Kennedy put on the royal-blue-and-white uniform of the Maple Leafs. In time, young "Teeder" became the darling of Toronto hockey fans, one of the most proficient centers in NHL history, and captain of the Leafs.

There was only one thing wrong. In his haste to complete the deal, Selke neglected to obtain the green light from Smythe who happened to be in war-torn France at the time. When the vitriolic Smythe finally learned about the trade, he made nearly as much noise as the cannons that were booming around him. He promptly cabled Maple Leaf Gardens demanding that the deal be erased and Eddolls returned to the Toronto fold. This, of course, could not be arranged, and when Smythe was so advised he blasted off again to no avail.

"The deal spelled *finis* to my usefulness as assistant to Conn Smythe," Selke later reflected in his autobiography.

The wisdom of Selke's decision would be underlined in years to come. Eddolls eventually became a member of the Canadiens but only as a mediocre defenseman soon traded to the Rangers. Kennedy was eventually voted into the Hockey Hall of Fame.

Smythe's return to Toronto at war's end generated open warfare at Maple Leaf Gardens. He publicly roasted Selke for the Leafs' demise in the 1945–46 season, overlooking the fact that Toronto had annexed the Stanley Cup in the previous season. Smythe still rankled over the Kennedy deal, and the Major, a stern advocate of discipline, inspired Selke to resign from the Maple Leaf organization in May, 1946. By autumn, Selke had obtained a job with Montreal.

In his first months as managing director of the Habs, Selke had little to worry about. Montreal opened the 1946–47 season at home with a 3–0 triumph over the Rangers, and the Punch Line appeared to have more verve than ever. The Rocket scored two goals and his linemates, Lach and Blake, dazzled the New Yorkers with their footwork.

Under Dick Irvin's guidance, the Canadiens had distilled a combination of accurate shooting, hard skating, and the kind of roughhouse deportment one would expect in a Pier Six brawl.

But the Leafs didn't accept punishment without retaliation. Early in February, 1947, the Canadiens and Leafs erupted in one of the most acrimonious feuds in their long history. It started when Toronto forward Don Metz collided with Elmer Lach and sent the Montreal center sprawling to the ice. Examination later revealed that Lach had suffered a fractured skull and would be lost to the team for the rest of the season. Metz, who received a minor penalty, argued that the check was clean and that he should not have been penalized. The Canadiens sought retribution. Hostilities escalated when Toronto and Montreal sportswriters entered the fray, toeing the hometown lines.

Whatever their pugilistic skills, the Canadiens proved to be better hockey players and relentlessly pulled away from the second-place Leafs. Richard, who had led the league in goals-scored, but never in total points, was in a neck-and neck battle with Max Bentley of the Black Hawks late in the season. The Hawk center led the Rocket by a single point as the Canadiens took to the ice against the Bruins at Boston and Bentley went up against the Rangers in New York in the last games of the regular season.

Richard assisted on Johnny Quilty's goal in the second period and added another assist late in the final period, but Bentley received an assist early in the third period at New York and then scored, himself, a few minutes later. Richard was edged by a single point, 72–71, although he finished the season with a league-leading forty-five goals.

If it was any solace to Richard, he helped his Canadiens to a 4–1 series win over the Bruins in the semifinal round while the Maple Leafs eliminated the Detroit Red Wings. Even before the final began, the rival coaches were at each other's throats with Irvin verbalizing like never before. He hadn't forgotten the Metz-Lach incident and, uniquely, introduced it as an essential factor in the eventual outcome of the Cup final.

"Irvin appeared in a strange new role when he prophesied that the outcome of the series rested solely in the hands of Providence," reported a Toronto columnist. "White-faced, he told Toronto newspapermen that if the accident which Elmer Lach suffered playing against the Leafs earlier in the season was only an accident, the Leafs would win the series. If, on the other hand, the injury was deliberate, Providence would intervene and *Les Glorieux* would win the Stanley Cup."

Providence certainly appeared to be on Montreal's side in the opening game. The Canadiens thoroughly wasted the Leafs, 6–0, commanding play in every period. Irvin was reportedly urging his team to win the second game "for Elmer" and had stirred the Habs to the boiling point.

Blood was spilled in the first and second periods of the second game. Toronto blood. Early in the game Richard slashed Vic Lynn, sending him off the ice with a cut over the eye. Late in the second he slashed Bill Ezinicki's face with his stick, cutting the Toronto player's head wide open.

Referee Bill Chadwick banished Richard from the game with a match penalty and the Canadiens disintegrated before the angry Leafs who went on to a 4–0 win. NHL president Campbell reviewed the episode and levied a one-game suspension against the Rocket as well as a $250 fine. Toronto writers immediately chastised Irvin for setting the tone of the contest and added a few choice barbs for Richard. Montreal writers were divided in their comments. Some criticized the Rocket for losing his temper; others blamed the referee for not cracking down on the Leaf players who were fouling Richard before the incident.

As if the Canadiens didn't have enough trouble, they were now being confronted with a quote attributed to goalie Durnan, supposedly uttered after the opening game. He had allegedly asked: "How did the Maple Leafs get into the playoffs?"

Selke maintained that the normally diffident Durnan would never have uttered a remark so likely to irritate the opposition. But a Montreal writer carried the quote and it soon spread like a forest blaze across the pages of the Toronto dailies.

With each game, Durnan was finding it more and more difficult to stop the puck. Toronto smashed four pucks past the perennial Vezina Trophy-winner and handled the Canadiens, 4–2, in the third match. Selke slammed the door of the Habs' dressing room in the face of Canadian Press hockey writer Fraser MacDougall and refused to permit any Toronto newsmen to enter the subdued locker area.

Richard was back in the Canadiens' lineup for the fourth game of the final, but the Leafs held him in tight check as they outplayed Montreal and won the game in sudden-death overtime on a goal by captain Syl Apps. One Montreal player benefited from the game and that was Bouchard whose leg was cut and required sixteen stitches to close the wound. In those days all NHL players were covered by insurance policies that provided a stipend for any stitch they incurred in action. "That came to eighty bucks for me," said Bouchard. "I'll buy a couple more hives for my bee farm."

The belated Montreal resurgence began on April 17 at the Forum. Led by the Rocket, who scored twice, Montreal defeated Toronto, 3–1, to pull within a game of tying the series. The feeling in the Canadiens' camp was that the worst was over. They would return to Maple Leaf Gardens, mop up the Leafs, and return to Montreal for the playoff clincher.

This line of thinking appeared to be confirmed before the game was half a minute old. Buddy O'Connor stole the puck from a Leaf defenseman and cleanly beat Turk Broda in the Toronto net. The time was 0:25 of the first period and the Habs seemed on their way to a rout. But the younger Leafs failed to crumble as one might have expected, and battled Montreal on even terms until Vic Lynn scored for Toronto at 5:34 of the second period.

The score remained tied well into the second period when the man who was once Montreal property, Ted Kennedy, fired a long, low shot past Durnan. Montreal fought gamely for the equalizer, but the Leaf defense was impenetrable and Toronto won the game, 2–1, and captured the Stanley Cup.

Oddly enough, it was Selke who deserved as much credit for the

Leaf victory as anyone. The nucleus of the Toronto team was composed of youngsters he had help sign or discover while he was pinch-hitting for the absent Smythe. There was no consoling the bitter Irvin. His claim that only a Montreal victory would prove Don Metz had wronged Elmer Lach had boomeranged and there was nothing to do but return home and brood about next year.

Montreal had placed four players — Durnan, Richard, Bouchard, and Reardon — on the NHL First All-Star Team. In addition, the Rocket captured the Hart Trophy as the league's most valuable player. But those close to the team, especially the astute Selke, realized that the Habs were in trouble. Deep trouble. True, they had four All-Stars and some effective players of near-All-Star caliber. But they were woefully weak in bench strength. The question was simple. Could Selke rebuild fast enough to offset the crumbling dynasty?

Because of ignorance or their own selfish interests, many outsiders insisted the Canadiens were the team to beat. "They'll be more of a powerhouse than they were last year," predicted Conn Smythe. But the Toronto overlord overlooked the fact that Durnan was being troubled by his right knee which underwent an operation during the summer. An unhealthy Durnan usually meant underperforming Canadiens. An added problem was Richard and Bouchard's refusal of Selke's contract offer, causing dissension in the ranks. Some Montrealers were displeased with Selke's decision to deal Frankie Eddolls and Buddy O'Connor to the Rangers. Even in Toronto, the wolves were on Selke's trail: "If we didn't know that Selke and Irvin were temperate men," wrote a Toronto columnist, "we would have been forced to believe that Frankie Boucher had engineered that particular deal after the Montrealers had been entertained at Hogan's Irish House for several hours. For, in return for O'Connor and Eddolls, the Rangers gave up Joe Bell, Hal Laycoe, and George Robertson. All three of them are now languishing in the minors."

The obituary notices were a bit premature. By November, 1947, the Habs appeared to be serious playoff contenders. They resumed hostilities with the Leafs on November 6 when Ken Reardon and Vic Lynn slugged it out for three minutes. In that same contest Richard was hit so hard by "Wild Bill" Ezinicki that the Rocket crashed into the door to the Leafs' bench, knocking it off its hinges.

Still bothered by his ailing knee, Durnan was bombed, 9–1, by the Bruins in mid-November and began hearing catcalls from the formerly loyal Forum fans. A week later Cal Gardner of the

Rangers collided with the Montreal goalie, opening a gaping wound over Durnan's eye. He was pulled from the game and replaced by young Gerry McNeil.

"The Canadiens won't finish in the first four," declared Ranger coach Frank Boucher, in what was the most outspoken critique of the Montrealers. "The other clubs are just stronger than them; that's all." Boucher's prediction was bolstered by the performance of ex-Montrealer Buddy O'Connor, who was leading the Rangers in scoring, and Frank Eddolls, who had become a first-stringer, and a good one, on the New York defense.

As the schedule reached the homestretch in early March, 1948, however, it appeared that the Rangers, who had embarked on a perilous seven-game winless streak, would fold completely and allow the Canadiens to squeeze into a playoff berth. But the Habs couldn't regain enough momentum and New York finally won a game and clinched fourth place in the final week of the season. The Canadiens' only consolation was that Lach beat out O'Connor for the scoring championship by a single point. "The collapse of the Canadiens," said one respected analyst, "can be blamed not on Selke but on the failure of the reserves developed by his predecessor, Tommy Gorman."

The big story of the 1948–49 season was an offer made to Selke by the Toronto Maple Leafs. Conn Smythe astonished the hockey world by dispatching coach Hap Day to Montreal with instructions to obtain Maurice Richard's contract. "Maple Leaf Gardens has never been close with a buck," said Day, "and I have explicit instructions to meet any price mentioned for Richard's services. We consider Richard the greatest right wing in the major league, if not the greatest player."

The *Globe and Mail* followed suit by publishing a fanciful photograph of Richard wearing a Maple Leaf jersey, captioned "Wouldn't He Look Good in a Sweater Like This?" Selke was not amused: "All the money in Toronto wouldn't buy him," he assured. Irvin then underlined the point: "It's propaganda. All this is merely an attempt to upset my boys on the eve of the game."

Selke might have been tempted by the reported six-figure offer but there were other considerations. "The Rocket is rooted among the predominantly French population," Selke explained. "Even if I suggested, even in fun, that the Rocket might go, the fans would tear down the Forum, brick by brick. The only time you'll ever see Maurice in a Leaf uniform is in that artist's conception in the *Globe and Mail*."

Selke's retort offered the kind of assurance Montreal fans needed. The Montreal *Star* printed a photograph of the Rocket with the caption "He's Still With Us, Folks." Selke then offered to purchase the contracts of any or all of Max Bentley, Bill Ezinicki, Harry Watson, or Garth Boesch of the Leafs.

Puck-shocked and despondent, Bill Durnan had threatened to retire before the 1948–49 season, but Selke was successful in persuading him to stay on. The big goalie was never better and on March 7, 1949, recorded his fourth-straight shutout, for a total shutout skein of 283 minutes, as the Canadiens defeated Boston, 1–0. The lone goal was scored by Rocket Richard!

Although Toe Blake had retired to become coach of the Valleyfield Braves of the powerful Quebec Senior League, the two-thirds Punch Line still boasted the Rocket and Elmer Lach. The pair played well through the season and helped Montreal to a third-place finish and the right to face league-leading Detroit in the first round of the playoffs.

Thanks to the young Gordie Howe, Ted Lindsay, Sid Abel, and a well-rounded bench, the Red Wings had become the new class team of the NHL. They were also tough, and they proved it in the opener when Lach left the game with a broken jaw after colliding with "Black" Jack Stewart of the Detroit defense. Even without Lach, the Canadiens extended the Red Wings to seven games before bowing out. Detroit lost to Toronto in the final when the Leafs won their third-straight Stanley Cup.

The Habs' performance over the decade had been respectable, although in the second half of the forties they had been thoroughly outclassed by Toronto. As the new decade dawned, however, they were on the eve of their greatest era ever, an era of absolute hockey supremacy.

TORONTO: THE
GOLDEN YEARS

The Maple Leafs' performance in the 1940's contrasted sharply with that of the Canadiens. Whereas the Habs often failed to play to their potential, the Leafs frequently exceeded expectations during the war years and immediately thereafter. That Toronto was championship-bound was evident as early as 1940. In April of that year, they reached the finals but were eliminated by the Rangers, four games to two. It was the third time in a row that Toronto had gone to the last round but failed to come home with the Stanley Cup.

Perhaps Toronto's setbacks were due to ill luck, perhaps to some intangible factor. Smythe couldn't be sure, but he had a rare opportunity to find out if coaching was the weakness. Prior to the start of the 1940–41 season, Dick Irvin was offered the job of manager-coach of the Montreal Canadiens. He received Smythe's permission to negotiate with the Habs, and eventually accepted an offer. Smythe selected Hap Day as the new coach of the Leafs.

There was an immediate change for the better under Day. He helped Turk Broda smooth out some hitherto rough edges. He prescribed handball as a tonic for sharpening the goalie's reflexes. On the ice during practices he insisted that Broda face the shots without his goalie stick. "It was a bruising form of practice," recalled Broda biographer Ed Fitkin, "but the Turk was a willing worker and was improving under such unusual treatment.

Broda's lessons were complemented by a psychological boost. Smythe sold longtime Broda threat, backup goalie Phil Stein, to New Haven. It was a clever ploy, and it inspired Turk to the best goaltending of his career. For the first time in the history of the club, it appeared that the Leafs might have a Vezina-winner.

But first, Broda would have to beat out Frankie "Mister Zero" Brimsek of the Bruins as well as Detroit rookie Johnny Mowers. The three of them tenaciously stayed in the running through the end of February, but Broda elicited most praise because of his marked improvement.

"He wasn't flopping," said Fitkin in his book *Broda of the Leafs*. "He was better on rebounds. His timing was sharper, and he had more confidence . . . He was always 'on' the puck, barking instructions to defense mates or lagging forwards in his high-pitched voice. He had his heart set on the Vezina."

But so did Brimsek and Mowers. What was worse — for Broda

— Apps was seriously injured, out of play for the season, leaving Toronto without its most dependable backchecking forward. His absence was sorely felt. Where once Broda had had a comfortable eight-goal lead on his foes, he now watched his defenses sag. With two games left in the season, Mowers went ahead by one goal while Brimsek remained one behind. Smythe had also offered Broda a $1000 bonus for a Vezina win; now, that too seemed to be evaporating. In their last two games of the season the Leafs were to play Chicago, on March 15, 1941, in Toronto, and the next night the Hawks in Chicago Stadium. The Bruins were scheduled to meet the Red Wings on March 16 in Detroit and again on March 18 in Boston.

Broda played the best hockey of his life, beating Chicago 7–1 at home and then shutting out the Hawks 3–0 in Chicago. Thus he had allowed a total of ninety-nine goals-against for a 2.06 average. The onus now fell on Mowers and Brimsek, who would face each other in back-to-back games.

In the opener, in Detroit, the clubs played a 2–2 tie, which meant that Brimsek's goals-against total had climbed to 101. He therefore was eliminated from the Vezina race. It was then Mowers vs Broda. The Detroit rookie had a total of ninety-eight goals against him — one less than Broda — with one game remaining. If he could prevent the Bruins from scoring, he would have the Vezina in his first NHL season.

Normally Broda would have remained at his Toronto home to listen to the radio broadcast of the match, but since the Maple Leafs were destined to play the Bruins in the first round of the playoffs, Turk and the rest of his teammates were sitting in Boston Garden on the night of March 18. Some fans immediately detected Broda and adopted him as their hero of the evening. They assured him that their favorites would annihilate the Red Wings and guarantee Turk his Vezina trophy and $1000 bonus. Broda wasn't so sure.

After only fifty seconds in the first period, Jack Crawford, the helmeted Boston defenseman, moved the puck out of the Bruins' zone. He detected an opening in the Detroit blueline corps and penetrated farther than he had expected, finally hurling a hard shot at Mowers. The young Detroit goalie lunged at the blur of black rubber, but it was too late. Crawford had scored, and Broda had at least a tie for the Vezina.

But Mowers and his Red Wings tightened up, preventing the Bruins from getting even close to a second goal in the first period.

Having regained their poise, the Wings were even more effective in the second period, and it appeared that Mowers just might hold off the Bruins for the rest of the game.

The third period began, and Bruins manager Art Ross dispatched the line of Eddie Wiseman, Roy Conacher, and Bill Cowley to the ice. This unit, more than any other, had a special motivation for helping Broda. The kid brother of Charlie Conacher, Roy was a close friend of the Toronto backstopper during the off-season and was determined to help him on this night. Soon after the faceoff Conacher got his stick on the puck and sent a pass to Wiseman, who quickly lateraled to arch-playmaker Cowley. This time Cowley shot instead of passing — and fooled Mowers completely. Broda had his Vezina.

In the first playoff round Toronto and Boston went the limit, Boston taking it on a goal by Mel "Sudden Death" Hill. (In an interview late in his life, Hill remarked that the nickname had stuck with him through the years, but noted that at his advanced age the handle was a bit unsettling.) Coach Day could not hide his feelings. "This was a marvelous hockey team, and it deserved a better fate," he told reporters. "I'm afraid this is the biggest disappointment of my hockey career." It was little comfort to Day that the Bruins, extended to the limit by Toronto, marched into the Stanley Cup finals and whipped the Red Wings in four-straight games.

One of the more depressing aspects of Toronto's defeat was that it was likely to be Conn Smythe's last chance to see a Stanley Cup-winner for some time. World War II had been underway for more than a year, and Smythe was known to be anxious to serve in the Canadian Armed Forces once more. During the off-season he enlisted in the army and was commissioned a major in the 30th Light Antiaircraft Battery, which he had mobilized.

The departure of Smythe meant that Frank Selke would become acting manager; the Maple Leafs would remain in capable hands. With the sting of the playoff defeat behind them, Selke and Day went about strengthening the vulnerable parts of the roster. Their target was the New York Americans, a franchise teetering on the brink of collapse and therefore willing to talk trade.

Talk they did. When it was over, Toronto had acquired right wing Lorne Carr to team up with Sweeney Schriner, his old New York Americans teammate. The Leafs had given up Red Heron, Gus Marker, Johnny O'Flaherty, and Nick Knott. Now Day had two formidable lines, starting with Apps, Drillon, and Davidson and rounded out with Schriner, Carr, and Billy "the Kid" Taylor. His third unit was comprised of a hot group of spares that included Nick and Don Metz, Pete Langelle, Hank Goldup, and Johnny McCreedy. Turk Broda was redoubtable in goal, and the defense consisted of McDonald, Kampman, Reg Hamilton, Wally Stanowski, and Jack Church. If any of the defensemen were injured, Selke would telephone his Hershey, Pennsylvania, farm team and request young Bob Goldham, one of the best propsects in the minors.

The Leafs were not to be denied. In the spring of 1942 they engineered the greatest turnaround in a championship series in NHL history when the Red Wings, who had eliminated the Canadiens, met Toronto in the Stanley Cup finals.

"Don't underestimate this Detroit club," warned Smythe on the eve of the series. "They can skate, and they're going to run at us. Unless we match them check for check and stride for stride, we're going to be in trouble."

Right from the opening faceoff, Adams sent his speedy skaters on their mission: toss the puck in and dash after it, forecheck the Leafs into errors. "It was not pretty hockey," said Stanley Cup historian Henry Roxborough, "but it was effective."

It was so effective that the normally poised Toronto skaters fumbled their way around the rink like battle-weary warriors. The Red Wings' harrassment tactics worked on two levels, physical and mental. Tough Jimmy Orlando handed out several thudding bodychecks and sent young Goldham bleeding to the bench after clobbering him on the head with his stick. Don "the Count" Grosso scored twice for Detroit, and the jubilant Red Wings skated off with a 3–2 upset triumph.

Toronto fans were transfixed as they watched Detroit skate away with a 4–2 win in the second game. Grosso again scored twice, and teammates Mud Bruneteau and Jim Brown each tallied once. The beleaguered Leafs were able to get goals from Schriner and Stanowski, but the big guns of Apps and Drillon were strangely silent. Even worse, the usually reliable Bucko McDonald was proving to be especially vulnerable on defense against the Wings' new skate-and-run style.

On April 9, 1942, Motor City fans flocked to the Olympia to see whether what they had heard and read about their club was on the level. At first they thought it all was a joke. Toronto's Lorne Carr put two shots past goalie Mowers in no time at all, and the Leafs appeared to be in control for the first time in the series. Then the Wings skimmed the puck into the Toronto zone, and the Leafs' rearguard began falling over themselves trying to keep up with the Detroit sprinters. Before the period had ended, Jerry Brown and Joe Carveth had been set up for goals by Detroit defenseman Eddie Bush. The fact that center Sid Abel had retired with a badly bruised cheek seemed to inspire them to even greater efforts.

Bush proceeded to set up goals by Pat McReavy and Syd Howe; then he added one himself, and the underdog Motor City sextet suddenly found themselves favored to capture the playoffs in an incredible four-straight games. It was easy to understand the logic behind such talk. The usually reliable Drillon had been completely defused and had gone for seven games without scoring. Needled by Bush and Orlando, Broda played his worst game of the series, and McDonald, the former Red Wing, was skating in mud on the Toronto defense. "You got the idea," wrote Vern DeGeer in the Toronto *Globe and Mail*, "that it was all over but the shouting."

Quitting in the face of defeat had never been Day's style, and he was not about to start. He cooly pondered the situation, seeking answers to the question of why his machine wasn't functioning the way it should. At last he thought he had the solution, but to be sure he phoned Smythe, who was stationed in Petawawa, Ontario. Smythe endorsed the plan, as did Selke, although it was very possibly the most daring plan ever tried in a championship sports series — anywhere.

Day benched his ace sniper, Gordie Drillon, and veteran defenseman Bucko McDonald. That in itself was startling enough, but he then revealed that they could be replaced by the most unlikely players imaginable. Drillon's substitute was Don Metz, kid brother of Nick Metz, who had scored only two goals all season and who had not played for about two weeks. McDonald was replaced by raw rookie Ernie Dickens, who had played only ten NHL games in his life.

In Detroit the move was interpreted as panic. Every correspondent covering the series predicted a quick demise for the Toronto club, and an Olympia record of 13,694 fans turned out to see the Red Wings do the honors.

First Mud Bruneteau and then Sid Abel scored for the Red Wings, and with the game more than half over Detroit held a commanding 2–0 lead. Mowers seemed to have the Wings' net boarded up for the night, and the fans could almost taste the Stanley Cup champagne. There was only one problem: the Maple Leafs forgot to quit.

Toronto needed one goal to ignite their frozen attack, and they finally got it at 13:54 of the middle period when Bob Davidson took relays from Langelle and McCreedy to beat Mowers. They were beginning to warm up, and within two minutes they were hot. Taylor moved the puck to Schriner, who lateraled to Carr. Carr brought the score to 2–2, and it stayed that way through the end of the second period.

The Leafs' rally seemed to stimulate the Red Wings to new strength in the third period, and despite Broda's courageous display, Carl Liscombe lifted Detroit into the lead again at 4:18 of the third. The screams of delight that reverberated around the Olympia were frightening; the fans believed that Liscombe's goal had applied the *coup de grace* to Hap Day's skaters. But the Leafs seemed to possess a persistence that would not tolerate defeat. Apps roared into Red Wings territory and delivered a smoking shot that beat Mowers. Then with seven minutes and fifteen seconds remaining in the period, Apps and Don Metz collaborated on passes to Nick Metz, who fooled the Detroit goalie. Broda held fast, and Toronto pulled off a 4–3 triumph.

To an extent, Detroit had sown the seeds of its ultimate series defeat in the fourth game. Not long after Nick Metz had scored what was to be the game's winning goal, Wings defenseman Eddie Wares was handed a misconduct penalty by referee Mel Harwood. Instead of accepting the decision, Wares ignored Harwood's command and then insulted the official by handing him a hot water bottle he obtained from the Detroit bench. Wares eventually skated to the penalty box but not before Harwood had added a fifty-dollar fine to his sentence.

By then Jack Adams was livid, and virtually exploded when Harwood gave Detroit another penalty for having too many men on the ice. Grosso was designated to serve the penalty, but he too chose to antagonize Harwood, dropping his gloves and stick in front of the embattled referee. Harwood replied with a $25 fine.

The game finally continued to its conclusion, and all would have been well had Adams not decided to resume hostilities with the referee. The Detroit boss leaped over the boards and charged at Harwood, pummeling him until linesmen Don McFadyen and Sammy Babcock intervened — accompanied by the local police. One spectator taking all this in with consummate interest was NHL

President Frank Calder. Calder fined Wares and Grosso $100 each, and Adams was suspended indefinitely.

Few could guess precisely what effect Adams's suspension would have on the Red Wings. The Detroit high command decided that veteran Ebbie Goodfellow, no longer useful as a player, would coach the team in Adams's absence. The question was whether Detroit could recapture the momentum lost at the Olympia.

The answer was supplied by the principal in Day's experiment, Don Metz. Metz scored a hat trick, driving the Leafs to a 9–3 shellacking of the Wings. Thus Toronto was down only three games to two, but the sixth match was slated for Olympia Stadium, and the Red Wings were ready to do just about anything to settle the issue on home ice.

Broda's defiant stand in the first period deflated Detroit, and before the second period was fifteen seconds old, Don Metz had done it again; Toronto was in the lead. Insurance markers followed from Bob Goldham and Billy Taylor. The Leafs, who only a week earlier had been teetering on the brink of elimination, had pulled themselves into a 3–3 tie in the series.

Still, the Red Wings, like the Leafs, had one more shot at the title. On April 18, 1942, 16,240 spectators, a Canadian hockey attendance record at the time, crowded into Maple Leaf Gardens to see the winner take all.

At first, it looked as if Toronto might fall just short. Syd Howe put Detroit ahead 1–0, and Toronto's attack suddenly fizzled as it had in the first three games of the set. At one point goalie Mowers blunted Toronto's shots with his team two men short, and Detroit skated out for the third period guarding the 1–0 lead.

The Leafs needed a break, and they got it early in the third when referee Bill Chadwick whistled Jimmy Orlando into the penalty box for two minutes. Coach Day sent the Schriner line out for the power play instead of Apps and the Metz brothers. "Sweeney was a big man," wrote Charles Coleman, "a fast skater and very nimble in his play."

Never was Schriner more nimble than he was in front of the Detroit net with his team on the brink of defeat. Sweeney awaited the pass, but the puck rolled to him on its side. Schriner backhanded the puck past a startled Mowers to tie the score. The Maple Leafs were alive again!

In the next two minutes the Red Wing forwards attempted to puncture the Maple Leafs' blueline corps, but Day's "substitutes" came through nobly. Rookies Ernie Dickens and Bob Goldham would not be breached, and Don Metz checked zealously on the forward line.

A whistle was blown, and Day changed squads. He sent young center Pete Langelle on left wing with veteran Bob Davidson and Johnny McCreedy on the right side. Immediately they stormed into Red Wing ice, McCreedy leading the way with a shot on Mowers. The Detroit goalie moved far out of his cage to deflect the drive, but the puck rebounded back into play, and Mowers was stranded away from the gaping net. In a desperate lunge the Detroit defense tried to cover Mowers's abandoned net, but Langelle pounced on the puck like a leopard seizing his prey and smacked it into the cage.

When the thunderous roar of the audience had diminished, Turk Broda knew that it was his game to win. The Maple Leafs were closer to the Stanley Cup than they had been in ten years. Joe Carveth, Carl Liscombe, and Gerry Brown of Detroit's first line tested the Turk with shrapnel, but Broda displayed the brand of goaltending that was to earn him a reputation as the most dependable money goalie in NHL history. After one sortie Turk punted the puck ahead to his defense as Schriner picked up speed at center ice. Sweeney took the pass and scored for the second time in the game. With less than five minutes to play Toronto was ahead 3–1.

One man more than any of the thousands in the arena fixed his eyes on the clock as the Maple Leafs battled to retain the lead. It was Conn Smythe, who had been granted permission by his army superiors to leave the Petawawa military base in order to watch his team in their most critical battle ever.

Ed Fitkin described the last seconds: "Pandemonium broke loose on the ice and in the stands at the final bell. Every player on the Leaf bench leaped over the boards and rushed out on the ice to grab and hug a teammate, while the crowd roared with the ecstasy of the moment . . . the moment they had waited ten long years to witness." Never before, and never since, has a team lost the first three games of a Stanley Cup final and then pulled itself together to take it all.

Months after, hockey experts analyzed the arresting Toronto triumph. "If the Red Wings had maintained their composure," wrote one critic, "there is no question that they would have kept the edge on Toronto and won the Stanley Cup. In big-league hockey a 'cool' club often can defeat a superior team that panics."

To this day, critics have theorized just how long Smythe's

hockey dynasty could have prevailed with such young stars as Broda, Apps, Stanowski, Goldham, and Taylor, to name only a few. But World War II had already involved the United States, and several members of the Maple Leafs left for battle overseas. In the meantime it was the job of Day and Selke to keep the Leafs afloat in a turbulent NHL.

Following their leader, Conn Smythe, one Maple Leaf after another enlisted in the armed forces: Johnny McCreedy, Bingo Kampman, Don and Nick Metz, Ernie Dickens, Bob Goldham, and Wally Stanowski. Others were soon to come. But Broda was still in the nets, and Mel Hill, the clutch-scoring playoff ace, was obtained when the New York Americans folded. Then there was Syl Apps.

"Apps," said the New York *World-Telegram*, "is hockey's greatest star." Nothing that Syl did on the ice that season could dispel the accolade. The captain was ably abetted by Sweeney Schriner, Billy Taylor, Bob Davidson, and Lorne Carr. Babe Pratt, the rollicking Ranger defenseman, was obtained in a deal with New York, and the Leafs, with Day and Selke in command, were off and running for another Stanley Cup. Apps, of course, led the way. Rangers manager Lester Patrick spoke of him as a potential successor to the great Morenz.

The Leafs didn't run away with the NHL pennant in 1942–43, but they did manage to remain at or near the top by mid-season. Apps had scored twenty-three goals in twenty-nine games and appeared a shoo-in to break every league record. But on the night of January 30, 1943, the Bruins visited Maple Leaf Gardens, and fate struck down the captain at the peak of his career. Completing one of his patented headlong rushes, Apps crashed into the goalpost and seriously broke his right leg, midway between the knee and ankle. He was finished for the season, and when he recovered, he enlisted in the Canadian Army.

Without Apps the Leafs were a shadow of their former team. They finished in third place, eight points behind league-leading Detroit, and were dismissed from the semifinals in six games by the Red Wings, who proceeded to win the Stanley Cup in a succinct four-game sweep of the Bruins.

The Leafs desperately needed help at center ice and got it from young Ted "Teeder" Kennedy, originally of Port Colborne, Ontario, who had come from the Canadiens in the Frankie Eddolls trade. Kennedy played only two games at the end of the 1942–43 season. He set up one goal in a 5–5 tie against the Rangers in New York but played a mediocre game against the Bruins in Boston. He had been suffering a groin injury and was benched for the play-offs. "To keep up his morale," said Selke, "I had him sit with me, and I was dumbfounded by his mature observations on the game as it progressed. I remember telling sportswriter Ed Fitkin that I thought we might have acquired a superstar."

As was so often the case, Selke's genius rang true. Kennedy became a Toronto regular but almost by default. The armed forces had claimed Taylor, Schriner, Apps and Broda, but Selke had promoted other solid youngsters such as forward Gus Bodnar and defenseman Elwyn "Moe" Morris. "It appears," said Hap Day, "that we have reached the *Children's Hour* in the NHL."

The coach prophetically added: "We may be short on ability, but I think we're going to be long on action."

Most of the action was on the Toronto roster cards. When Broda went to war, Selke scraped the bottom of the goaltending barrel and came up with Benny Grant, who had last played goal for the Leafs as a substitute between 1929 and 1932! Grant eventually was replaced by Jean Marois, who, in turn, was replaced by Paul Bibeault. As part of a league-wide effort to help the feeble New York Rangers, Bucko McDonald was sent to Manhattan.

The Leafs played sensationally in their 1943 opener against the Rangers at Maple Leaf Gardens. From the moment the puck was dropped, Toronto took control and worked up an attack. The puck darted across the ice into the Rangers zone, where rookie Gus Bodnar beat goalie Ken McAuley. Fifteen seconds into the game the Leafs already had a goal. Bodnar's score was a record for the fastest goal ever scored by a rookie, and it signaled a superb year for Toronto. Ted Kennedy closed out the Maple Leafs scoring that night, and Toronto won 5–2.

Kennedy's perseverance and grim determination arrested the attention of many spectators in Maple Leaf Gardens, but none was more attentive than John Arnott, a service station operator who had become a fixture at the Gardens with his penetrating cheers directed toward Pete Langelle.

During a lull in the action Arnott would develop a slow cre-scendo, imploring, "C'monnnn, P-E-T-E-R!" But when the stylish Langelle joined the army, Arnott decided to shelve his cheer for the duration of the war, until Peter returned. Then one night during the 1943–44 campaign Arnott became enthralled with young Ted Kennedy.

Just before a particular faceoff involving Kennedy, a booming voice was heard across Maple Leaf Gardens. "C'monnnn, T-E-E-D-E-R!" A new hero was christened in Toronto.

Although Kennedy had been well schooled in hockey basics by his mentor, Nels "Old Poison" Stewart, he was weak in one department: skating. His strides were labored, almost painful to watch, and he often seemed to be moving like an express train with one set of brakes locked into its wheels. He finished his freshman season with twenty-six goals and twenty-three assists for forty-nine points in a year in which inept goaltending made high scoring relatively easy. Lorne Carr led Toronto with thirty-six goals and thirty-eight assists for seventy-four points, finishing third in the league, precisely where the Maple Leafs landed — behind Detroit and first-place Montreal.

Most unfortunate, from the Leafs' perspective, was the fact that they would face Montreal in the first playoff round; the Habs had compiled an awesome thirty-eight victories, only five defeats, and seven ties during the regular season.

It should not go un-noted, however, that while the Leaf wartime teams were often rags-and-patches collections of aging journeymen and untried rookies, the Montreal roster stayed pretty much intact. During the war years, and subsequently, the Canadiens came under considerable criticism for what was charged as their under-participation in the war effort. Much of French Canada had avoided both World Wars, and even the vaunted Punch Line was able to remain intact against greatly diluted opposition. The year the Rocket scored fifty goals in fifty games, the likes of Apps and Broda were away in Europe, fighting a war.

In the 1943–44 semifinals, Montreal defeated Toronto, 5–1. Maurice Richard scored all five goals, a league record. The Canadiens went on to sweep the series, 2–1, 4–1, and finally, 11–0. "You can't expect kids to beat grownups," Day concluded when it was over. In the finals, the Habs swept Chicago, four games to none.

Selke immediately began wheeling and dealing in the Smythe tradition, and in the process built the nucleus of a postwar Toronto dynasty. Nobody realized the strength of Toronto as the 1944–45 season began. Selke lured Sweeney Schriner out of retirement, adding punch to the attack, but he still had a job to do in goal. Bibeault, who had been "loaned" to the Maple Leafs under the curious NHL wartime regulations, was the natural choice, so Selke tried to swing a deal with Montreal. The Canadiens would agree only if Toronto would throw in Gaye Stewart and Bob Goldham when they were ushered out of the army. Selke rejected the offer, sending Toronto scouts all over Canada in search of a goaltender. The ultimate choice was Frank McCool, a tall, skinny Albertan. Not only was McCool nervous, he was assailed by chronic ulcers.

Again with his eye on the future, the industrious Selke traded Don Webster and George Boothman to Buffalo in the American League, for a young right wing named Bill Ezinicki. Notorious for his devastating bodychecks, Ezinicki had starred for the Oshawa, Ontario, Generals, Canada's Memorial Cup (Junior league) champions in 1944. Meanwhile the war was winding down in Europe and Asia, and several early enlistees, among them Nick Metz, Wally Stanowski, and Johnny McCreedy, returned home. Conn Smythe returned also — on a hospital stretcher.

Smythe never shirked trouble, especially when he believed that it was his duty to confront danger. During World War I he had spent fourteen months in a German prison camp. While the Leafs pursued pucks during World War II, Smythe was heading his 30th Antiaircraft Battery, which, after last-minute training in England, moved across the English Channel with the Allied forces invading Normandy. A month after the British-Canadian forces had established a beachhead near Caen, France, Smythe's battery was guarding a bridge. A German bomber swooped over the area and dropped a spotter flare. Unfortunately, the flare missed its intended target and landed on an ammunition truck.

Aware that his troops faced immediate slaughter if the ammunition exploded, Smythe dashed to the scene in a valiant effort to extinguish the blaze. He was a moment too late. The truck erupted in a cacophony of blasts that rocked the countryside and sent shrapnel flying. Smythe hurled himself to the ground, but a huge chunk of burning metal tore through his body and buried itself near the base of his spine.

Smythe was rescued by a medical corpsman and given immediate attention. Finally, he was shipped to England, where he lay in a hospital bed, vascillating between life and death. Medical science was in his favor, and Smythe hung on until the healing processes prevailed. In time he was sent back to Canada, his back encased in a cast, and a long recuperative period in store. By March, 1945, he was back at his post in Maple Leaf Gardens, ready for another assault on the Stanley Cup.

Smythe spent his "recuperative" period trying to strengthen the

Leafs. He offered $25,000 to the Canadiens for Rocket Richard and said that he would add a $1,000 bonus for the person who could arrange the deal. His bid was, of course, rejected. He then attempted to secure Bruin Milt Schmidt and Ranger Neil Colville, both of whom were still wearing khaki. Again he was turned down, and the Leafs finished the season a respectable third but twenty-eight points behind first-place Montreal, which had lost only eight games in the fifty-game schedule. Significantly, Toronto had handed them five of those defeats.

It was believed that Toronto's Achilles heel would be goaltending. "Ulcers" McCool had finished the season with a mediocre 3.22 goals-against average, although he did win the Calder Trophy. By contrast, Bill Durnan of Montreal had an impressive 2.42 goals-against mark. "McCool's performances had been spotty," wrote Henry Roxborough in *The Stanley Cup Story*. "There were many observers who believed that goalkeeping was Toronto's weak spot."

The opening game of the Toronto-Montreal series, at the Forum on March 20, 1945, would tell the story.

Ulcers notwithstanding, McCool performed as if he had ice-water in his veins. He thwarted the Canadiens without allowing a goal through the final minutes of the third period. However, Durnan had matched him save for save, and it appeared that sudden-death overtime would have to settle the tilt.

It was then that the Montreal brass realized they had erred in dealing Ted Kennedy to Toronto. As the end of regulation time approached, Bob Davidson blasted a shot at Durnan, which ricocheted off a Montreal defenseman's leg and onto Kennedy's stick, fifteen feet in front of the goalmouth. Teeder wheeled around and struck the puck on his backhand. The shot found its mark with only twenty-two seconds remaining in the period. Toronto startled the hockey world with a 1–0 victory. Ulcers McCool scored a shutout in his first playoff game.

In case anyone at the Forum believed that McCool's performance was a fluke, he came back two nights later and stood the Canadiens on their heads once more. The Leafs won 3–2.

The panic in Montreal was well founded. Not only had the Canadiens lost two-straight games at their home rink, but the fabulous Rocket Richard, who had scored fifty goals in fifty regular-season games, had been thoroughly blanketed by the industrious Bob Davidson. Rocket was to be shut off the scoreboard once more in the third game, at Maple Leaf Gardens, but Elmer Lach of the Punch Line tallied once, and three Canadiens substitutes scored. Montreal won 4–1.

The fourth game went into sudden-death overtime tied at 3–3. More than twelve minutes of the extra session had elapsed when referee King Clancy conducted a faceoff deep in Montreal territory. Gus Bodnar took the draw for the Maple Leafs, and Murph Chamberlain faced off for the Canadiens. Bodnar was facing the Montreal net when the puck dropped to the ice. In that split-second the Toronto center swung his stick and drove the puck behind Durnan. The time was 12:36; Toronto led the series three games to one.

Only once did the fabled Montreal attack assert itself; in the fifth game at the Forum. Richard broke free from Davidson and scored four goals, leading the Flying Frenchmen to a 10–3 victory, which might have destroyed McCool's nerves. But Frank was superb when the clubs returned to Toronto on March 31. He nursed a 3–2 lead into the game's final minutes and then was aided by an unexpected twist of luck.

Fewer than forty seconds remained when the Rocket sped down the right alley and bombed a heavy backhand shot at the Toronto goal. It was heading for the far corner, and McCool daringly hurled his body in front of the drive, but failed to trap the puck, which rebounded off his pads and rolled out to Toe Blake, who had been following the play.

There was nobody between Blake and the wide-open net — just a six-feet-by-four-feet opening and empty ice. But the Montreal winger didn't realize there was nobody behind him, and afraid of being stick-checked from behind, rushed his shot, flinging the puck over the cage. McCool scrambled into position and held fast until the final bell sounded. Toronto won the series, four games to two.

The Leafs' victory lifted them into the Stanley Cup finals against an efficient Detroit club, which had finished the regular season fifteen points ahead of Toronto. Smythe was unimpressed. "We'll win the Cup," he asserted, "because we've got too good a fighting club to lose." Others in the Toronto camp wondered whether McCool's ulcers could stand the stress of the finals.

The game plan, as devised by Smythe, Selke, and Day, was to concentrate the Bob Davidson-Mel Hill-Sweeney Schriner line against Detroit's best shooters. It had worked against the Habs.

Even in his wildest dreams Smythe couldn't have imagined that it would work so well. Toronto won the first two games, at the Olympia, 1–0 and 2–0, and returned to Maple Leaf Gardens, where McCool came up with his third-straight shutout, 1–0. Frank McCool thus became the first goaltender in NHL history to produce three consecutive shutouts in Stanley Cup play. "It doesn't look like the puck ever is going to go in for us," snapped Jack Adams.

Indeed it didn't for a grand total of 188 minutes and 35 seconds before ex-Leaf Flash Hollett beat McCool at 8:35 of the first period of game four. The Leafs, within a win of the Stanley Cup, counterattacked. Kennedy scored a hat trick and put Toronto ahead early in the third period, but the Red Wings weren't finished. Sparked by rookie left wing Ted Lindsay, Detroit rallied for a 5–3 win.

If the Leafs were worried, they didn't show it until after the fifth game, in which Detroit came out on top 2–0. The Wings had pulled to within one victory of tying the finals. At the end of regulation time, the sixth game was scoreless, and moved into sudden-death overtime. Both McCool and Detroit goalie Harry Lumley practiced the art of netminding to perfection that night, and it was only a bizarre bounce of the puck that decided the contest.

Seconds after the clock had ticked off the fourteenth minute of overtime, Harold Jackson of Detroit blooped a high shot into Leaf territory; it bounced off the pre-plexiglass wire netting, far out of the range of the goal. Calm to the point of unconcern, McCool awaited the response of his teammates with a new attack.

It never came. The puck had struck the netting at a crazy angle and was sprung back into play with unusual force, falling in front of the net. Detroit's Ed Bruneteau was there, and easily pushed the puck past McCool.

A new specter rose before the Leafs. They now faced the possibility of the very humiliation they themselves had foisted on the Wings in 1942 — four losses after three wins in a Cup final. Day promised his team that if they gave the same effort they had in the previous game, the championship would be theirs. Toronto came through with goals by Mel Hill and Babe Pratt, and sterling goaltending by McCool, in a 2–1 triumph. The Leafs had won their third Stanley Cup.

In the 1945–46 season Toronto was beset by problems, especially in goal. Ulcers McCool, a playoff sensation only a year earlier, became the goat of the Maple Leafs. His average soared to more than 3.60, and Smythe was tempted to give the pads back to

Turk Broda, a rusty but willing army veteran. On the night of February 3, 1946, at Madison Square Garden, the Rangers, doormat of the NHL, rallied to score six against McCool in a 6–6 tie. When it was over, Frank McCool was NHL history. Broda played the last fifteen games of the season in a lost cause.

McCool's exit followed the departure of Teeder Kennedy, out for the season with a cut tendon. Kennedy had played poorly until being sidelined, and critics had begun to carp that he was merely a wartime phenomenon who couldn't cut the ice with the returning big leaguers. "It was," said Frank Selke, "the unhappiest year of my long connection with the game."

Selke, who had so industriously cultivated a farm system that soon was to bear fruit for the Leafs, became the target of Toronto darts. "When the Maple Leafs were having their long run of successes," recalled Selke years later, "nobody bothered to credit me with any great part in the triumphs.

"But now when we failed to make the playoffs for the first time, I was naturally selected to be the goat . . . Conn Smythe had me on the carpet publicly and in the press. He was adamant; it was my selection of reserve material that led to the team's downfall . . . I tried to explain to him that our veterans had now aged to a point where they could no longer play good hockey on successive nights."

Selke resigned as assistant manager of the Leafs in May, 1946, and became managing director of the Montreal Canadiens. The baton was back in Conn Smythe's hands, and everyone concerned with NHL hockey wondered whether he would make or break the Leafs without the assistant who had served him so faithfully and so well.

Having regained his energy and recuperated from his war wounds, Smythe was determined to make up for time lost in the army. He dispatched his scouts to all points in Canada, searching for new talent. Smythe himself went on innumerable expeditions and talked with friends in all walks of hockey. Many of them gave him tips that resulted in the acquisition of new skaters.

Rabbit McVeigh, a star with the old New York Americans, put him on to Vic Lynn, a burly left wing skating for Buffalo, in the American League. When a Montreal sportscaster suggested that Garth Boesch was the best defense prospect in Western Canada, Smythe checked the tip and wound up signing the Saskatchewan wheat farmer. Then there was Howie Meeker, from New Hamburg, Ontario, who had survived a grenade blast at his feet during the war and showed the kind of right wing speed Smythe liked. And "Bashin'" Bill Barilko. A nineteen-year-old defenseman from Winnipeg named Jim Thomson was signed along with Gus Mortson, a defenseman from Kirkland Lake, Ontario. Together they would soon be known as the "Gold Dust Twins." Joe Klukay, the "Duke of Paducah," had been spotted earlier, and he was put under lock and key.

Already in the cast were captain Syl Apps, Teeder Kennedy, Harry Watson, the Metz brothers, Gaye Stewart, Bud Poile, Bodnar, Ezinicki, Goldham, Stanowski, and Broda. "We want a hard, agressive team," said Smythe, "with no Lady Byngers."

Smythe knew what it was to be defeated occasionally, but that didn't mean he would tolerate it and he instilled the same feeling in his players. "They are the worst team in the league for holding, tripping, and interfering," snapped New York coach Frank Boucher.

Sometimes Smythe showed his players what he meant: for example, the night when a Detroit fan hurled a chair at one of Smythe's defensemen, Gus Mortson. Smythe leaped up, hobbled down the aisle, and tossed a left, and a right, and another left at the fan, and that was that.

The Toronto Maple Leafs followed Smythe's lead and fought and won in a way few hockey teams ever have. They won the Stanley Cup in 1947, 1948, and 1949 — an unprecedented Stanley Cup hat trick — and again in 1951. The 1948 champions were considered the greatest of the four, but the nature and composition of the clubs were such that you have to talk about them collectively.

Smythe condoned the roughest tactics and exploded when his players were less than rough. Young defenseman Jim Thomson incurred Smythe's wrath for turning the other cheek in a Stanley Cup semifinal game against Detroit in 1947. "Nobody," Smythe warned, "pops anybody on the club without getting popped back. I'm not interested in hockey players who don't play to win. You can take penalties, but you gotta play to win."

Besides the ability to brawl with the best Smythe's men also made up for lack of conventional talents with sheer inventiveness. Barilko and Garth Boesch created the tandem "Maginot Line kneedrop." A split-second before an enemy would shoot, they would drop to their knees and block the shot. The technique later was copied by other league defensemen. Other style-setters were Nick Metz and Joe Klukay, whose penalty-killing tactics have yet to be excelled.

They were all part of the eclectic team that amazed the hockey world by winning the 1947 Stanley Cup. In 1946 the Leafs had finished fifth in the six-team league, and Smythe figured that it would take at least two years to rebuild. So he brought up a lot of youngsters and threw them in with a few veterans. "I should have figured it out years ago," Smythe said. "Youth is the answer in this game. Only the kids have the drive, the fire, and the ambition. Put the kids in with a few old guys who still like to win, and the combination is unbeatable."

It was something of a local joke in Toronto that the Leafs were able to win the Stanley Cup, yet they couldn't place a single player on the league All-Star team. They did have the rookie-of-the-year in right wing Howie Meeker, and center Syl Apps was a genuine hero in the Leafs' six-game upset of Montreal in the Stanley Cup finals. Still, it was true that the club didn't have a superstar, and as Toronto got ready for the 1947–48 season, Smythe knew that this vital factor could make the difference between a good Leaf team and a great one. His belief was solidified when Toronto stumbled through the opening month.

Smythe knew which player he wanted, but getting him was something else. Max Bentley was the man, a wiry center who skated like a dream, shot like a bazooka, and had led the NHL in scoring the previous two years. Toronto already had two fine centers in Apps and tough, tenacious Ted Kennedy, but Smythe felt he needed Bentley if he were going to create the superteam of his visions.

Bentley's club, the Black Hawks, was in last place and seemed ripe for a proposition, but the Chicago manager, Bill Tobin, was a hard bargainer. Smythe finally had to offer five players before Tobin gave in. It was an astonishing deal, described then as "the greatest mass trade in professional hockey history." Included in the package was the entire "Flying Forts" line of Gus Bodnar, Bud Poile, and Gaye Stewart. These three players, plus defensemen Bob Goldham and Ernie Dickens, were extremely popular, and Smythe had a lot of explaining to do.

Max Bentley was a rare bird on the Leafs — a fragile pacifist. He made an inviting target for opponents, but few were foolish enough to pick on him — unless they wanted to tangle with "Wild" Bill Ezinicki.

Ezinicki was not much bigger than Bentley, but he had sinewy arms and a body that bulged from daily weightlifting. He had a passion for free-skating that was surpassed only by his passion for bodychecking. He also had a passion for tape, winding reams of it around his knees and legs until they bulged grotesquely.

Ezinicki was adored in Toronto and despised everywhere else. The Red Wings charged him with deliberately injuring goalie Harry Lumley. Boston *Globe* writer Herb Ralby said, "Toronto has the leading candidate for the most-hated opponent in Ezinicki." In New York a woman in a front-row seat jammed a long hatpin in Ezinicki's derriere as he bent over to take a faceoff.

"Ezzie" was toasted by some of his most fearsome rivals. "He's a tough little guy," said Montreal's equally tough Ken Reardon, "but he's definitely not dirty. He can check and pester you and sometimes hurt you, and he can make you mad, but he's not dirty. Because he's short, he can hurt. Those low bodychecks of his enable him to throw his shoulder into your stomach."

His linemates were Boy Scouts by comparison, especially Syl Apps. "Apps is the cleanest player I've known," commented his coach, Hap Day. "He doesn't smoke. He never bends an elbow except to twist his stick over an opponent's wrist. The strongest language he ever uses is 'By Hum' and 'Jiminy Christmas.' " (One night Boston defenseman Flash Hollett extracted two of Apps's teeth by shoving the wooden shaft of his stick into Syl's mouth. The Leaf captain muttered, "By Hum, this has gone far enough," and leveled Hollett with a flurry of punches.)

Late in the 1947–48 season, Apps announced that he would retire after the playoffs. This was hard to believe: he was only thirty-three, physically fit, one of the NHL's leading scorers, the most popular hockey player in Canada, and apparently capable of reaching the 200-goal plateau early the next season.

Despite the heroics of Meeker, Lynn, Kennedy, Apps, Nick Metz, Klukay, and a new arrival — sniper Sid Smith — the balance wheel was Max Bentley. On the faceoff the Leafs would outmuscle their opponents for the puck and then skim it to Bentley, who would cradle it on his stick and feint his way through the opposition until he was within wrist-shooting distance of the goal. He'd then blur the puck toward the apprehensive netminder. "Max," said Detroit's Jack Adams, "comes close to being the greatest player in the game."

By late February, 1948, Bentley's line had scored forty-five goals, the Apps line had forty-three, the Kennedy line, forty-one.

There was a pattern to the Leafs' scoring. They'd fall behind in the first and second periods, then surge in the third. But despite their balance and power, they were closely pursued by the Red Wings.

Going into the final-weekend home-and-home series with Detroit, the Leafs held a one-point lead. That weekend may have been Toronto's most glorious forty-eight hours of the entire season. Not only did they win both games (5–3 and 5–2), but some individual kudos were earned as well. Broda had entered the series tied with Detroit's Lumley for fewest-goals-against average, but Lumley, suffering from a bad case of nerves, didn't play up to par. It was more than fitting that Broda should win the prize, for he had been the only Leaf voted to that year's All-Star team.

Even more heartwarming was Apps's performance. He had needed three goals to reach 200 for his career. It was a tall order to fill in such high-pressure matches, but Apps got goal number 198 in the first game and scored a hat trick the following night.

In the playoffs Toronto powered past Boston, four games to one, and Detroit, four games to none, to take the Cup.

Although it was Toronto's fourth Stanley-Cup win in seven years, Smythe's men couldn't contain their exuberance. After they had trooped into their dressing room, Broda was stretched over the knees of Bentley and Klukay and doused with a bottle of Coke by Meeker.

Laughing in the corner with pure childish joy was Bentley, the player who had lifted the Leafs from the realm of the great to the plateau of complete supremacy. Bentley, who as the age of sixteen had been rejected by the Montreal Canadiens, led the Leafs in scoring during the regular season and finished second to Ted Kennedy in the playoffs. "He's an even better player than I thought," beamed Smythe. "He gave us the third center we needed to give us the Murderers' Row of hockey — three twenty-five-goal centermen."

Next day, the triumphant Leafs stepped off the train to be hailed by tens of thousands of Toronto fans. With the Queen's Own Rifles band leading the parade, Smythe and his troops rolled under a torrent of ticker tape in open cars from Union Station to City Hall, where another 10,000 fans cheered when Syl Apps was introduced. It was the last time Apps would be seen as a Maple Leaf; he stuck to his retirement decision, as did Nick Metz.

Kennedy was named captain, but without Apps and Metz the Leafs finished fourth in the 1948–49 season and appeared to be doomed against the Bruins in the Stanley Cup semifinals. Instead, they routed Boston in five games, setting up a rematch with Detroit in the finals. The Wings had finished first over the regular season, a full eighteen points ahead of the Leafs. But when the Wings faced Toronto, they again disintegrated. The Leafs won in four-straight.

It was Toronto's third Cup in three years, an NHL record. As William Houston observed in his magnificent *Inside Maple Leaf Gardens:* "The Maple Leafs were a glittering national treasure, as Canadian as prairie wheat fields and lonely northern lakes. They symbolized excellence and a winning tradition. In English Canada, they were the country's most popular team, in any sport."

As the 1940's drew to a close, hopes were high for the new decade. A rugged young Leaf defenseman was emerging as the team's next superstar, a blond adonis with Hollywood good looks. His name was Bill Barilko.

1
9
5
0

TO

1
9
5
9

THE 50's   *ANALYSIS*

Try as they might the Leafs never were able to repeat the superb roster replacement process that enabled them to win five Stanley Cups in the 1940's. However, the brilliant acquistion of Max Bentley in 1947 enabled manager Conn Smythe to work with a solid center-ice nucleus into the new decade. The bad news was that the Leafs three-Cup dynasty ended in 1950 in a bitter and controversial seven-game semifinal.

Thanks to 1940's Stanley Cup heroes Bentley, Howie Meeker, and Harry Watson the Leafs regrouped in 1951, regaining the Cup on the strength of four overtime wins in the five-game final. Montreal won the other game, also in overtime, on a Rocket Richard goal.

Whether the Leafs could have continued their assertive play will eternally remain a moot point because everything changed with the disappearance of 1951 playoff hero Bill Barilko. The defenseman, who scored the sudden-death Cup-clinching goal in 1951, was lost in a plane trip over the northern Ontario bush. Barilko had literally been the heart of Toronto's championship team and was irreplaceable. His death — neither the crashed plane nor Barilko's body were discovered for eleven years — directly resulted in the plummeting of the hockey club. From 1951–52 almost to the end of decade the Leafs were an unmitigated disaster.

The Canadiens' machine was not fully revved up until Montreal's vast farm system began producing prodigies and once the talent stream moved from a trickle to a flow it seemed unending. The first spate of young Hab aces included Doug Harvey, Dickie Moore, Jacques Plante, and Bernie "Boom Boom" Geoffrion.

The first tangible proof that the Canadiens would become dominant occurred in 1953 when they outlasted a stronger Red Wings club (Detroit was upset by Boston in the semifinals) to reach the finals where they ousted the Bruins in five games.

Despite the victory, Montreal lacked the overall depth to keep pace with the Red Wings. The Habs lost the Cup to Detroit a year later and would not regain it until two critical moves were made.

The first was Selke's relentless pursuit of the prodigious Jean "Le Gros Bill" Beliveau in the hope of persuading him to abandon the wealth of the Quebec Senior Hockey League for the glory (but not much more cash) of the NHL. It took a while but Selke eventually succeeded and the addition of Beliveau lifted the Canadiens up to Detroit's elite class.

Then, following the infamous Richard Riot of 1955, precipitated by Richard's suspension for striking a linesman, Selke blamed coach Irvin for contributing to the Rocket's volatility and replaced him with Toe Blake. The final piece was in place.

Blake not only harnessed Richard's winning fury but coaxed him into playing some of the best hockey of his life despite the Rocket's advanced age. To say the Canadiens had a powerhouse in the 1955–60 period would be roughly equivalent to describing the Concorde Jetliner as fast. Overloaded with future Hall of Famers such as Richard, his kid brother "Pocket Rocket" Henri Richard, Geoffrion, Beliveau, Moore, Harvey, and Plante, the Canadiens won Stanley Cups from 1956 through the end of the decade.

Meanwhile, the Leafs were bouncing from the twin poles of mediocrity and ignominy. No amount of managerial help seemed to work and the once-productive farm system kept turning out duds like Barry Cullen, Brian Cullen, and Hugh Bolton. The Leafs' downward spiral was finally reversed by a thoroughly unlikely character with a shining bald pate. George (Punch) Imlach who had never played in the majors, was as unknown as Selke and Blake had been famous and has spent his entire playing/coaching and managerial career buried in the minors. Not only that but Imlach had to execute an undercover *putsch* to remove existing bosses Howie Meeker and Billy Reay. That done, Imlach was in complete control of the club, short of actual ownership. The results were immediate and arresting.

The 1958–59 Leafs had no business making the playoffs. Yet by sheer force of personality and a good mix of youth and experience, Imlach prodded, cajoled, and insisted that his team would do the impossible. Yet with only two weeks remaining Toronto was nine points behind a strong New York Ranger team featuring such future Hall of Famers as Andy Bathgate, Harry Howell, Gump Worsley, and Bill Gadsby.

Over a period of fourteen days the Leafs kept winning and the Rangers kept losing until the final night of the season when Montreal obliged by defeating New York at Madison Square Garden while the Leafs won at Detroit. Nobody knew it at the time but a new era was being ushered in as a new decade was arriving. It would be known as the Imlach Epoch and would restore the lost dignity of the Maple Leaf hockey club.

MONTREAL:
HOCKEY'S GREATEST DYNASTY

Elmer Lach, who had considered retirement, returned for the 1949–50 season, and the Habs showed no inclination for anything less than a contending spot. Nor did they reveal any lack of fire despite the retirement of Murph Chamberlain. If anything, Ken Reardon appeared to attempt to compensate singlehandedly for Chamberlain's departure. In November of 1949 he collided with Cal Gardner, breaking the Leaf centerman's jaw in two places. Few observers believed it was an accident. Then in February of 1950 he collaborated with Montreal sportswriter Vince Lunny on an article that appeared in *Sport* magazine. Throughout the piece Reardon referred to his running feud with Gardner. "I tried to smash Gardner in the face with my stick," said Reardon, alluding to one of their eruptions, "but his stick broke in the first exchange of blows and he held the butt end in front of his face as a protector. I was going to smash him to pieces, but the other players intervened. I was so determined to swing at him full force that I never thought of jabbing the end of my stick into his mouth. I could have done it easily."

"Someday," the article went on, "the Canadiens' wild Irishman is going to carve Gardner into little pieces and it will take a brave man to restrain him." The article spoke of Reardon as a man "who intends to pursue his course of intended action even at the risk of being expelled from the league."

Reardon again was quoted: "I am going to see that Gardner gets fourteen stitches in the mouth. I may have to wait a long time, but I'm patient. Even if I have to wait until the last game I ever play, Gardner is going to get it good and plenty."

As soon as the magazine hit the stands, league president, Clarence Campbell had a copy of it delivered to his office. He summoned Reardon to his Montreal headquarters and later revealed that the Hab defenseman had acknowledged the magazine statements attributed to him. Not long after that, Campbell announced an unprecedented fine. Reardon would have to post a $1,000 cash bond with the league "for his good conduct in the future." Reardon would be entitled to petition for its refund when he retired. The president added that he thought Reardon was sincere in telling him that the Reardon-Gardner feud was over.

The regular season ended on a pleasant note for the Canadiens when they clinched second place. They defeated Chicago, 4–0, on the final weekend of the season, and Durnan had the rare delight of receiving an assist after passing the puck ahead to the Rocket who, in turn, scored a goal. At the conclusion of the game the thirty-five-year-old goaltender said he was "getting tired" and planned to retire at the end of the season.

Durnan's decision was reinforced by the Canadiens' dismal effort in the first round of the playoffs against New York's fourth-place Rangers. Durnan faltered behind a weakened defense and Richard was overshadowed by Pentti Lund of the Rangers who suddenly developed into a potent scorer. The New Yorkers swept the first three games before Elmer Lach scored an overtime goal to temporarily save Montreal in the fourth match. In that same contest Durnan was replaced by young Gerry McNeil who played a commendable game.

Irvin decided to go with McNeil again in the fifth game which was scoreless until the fourth minute of the third period. Then the Rangers opened the floodgates and poured three goals past McNeil, winning 3–0. When it was over Durnan sat on his dressing-room bench, his eyes welled with tears. "Rangers," he kept repeating, "couldn't do anything wrong; couldn't do anything wrong."

Durnan wasn't the only member of the old guard to throw in the towel. Pugnacious Ken Reardon, bothered by an old back injury, conferred with Selke prior to the 1950–51 season and announced he was finished. "Reardon is convinced he should withdraw from active play while he is still in one piece," said Selke. Durnan was replaced by McNeil, a very efficient but somewhat nervous netminder while Reardon's job went to a baby-faced defenseman who was to become one of the greatest in NHL history. His name was Doug Harvey.

In the meantime, Richard was fulfilling all the rave notices as hockey's greatest goal-scorer. "He can shoot from any angle," said goalie Frank Brimsek. "You play him for a shot to the upper corner

The immortal Georges Vezina, Montreal's first super goaltender.
CourtesY Hockey Hall of Fame.

Two of Toronto's more legendary sports figures were Maple Leafs founder Conn Smythe (right) and venerable trainer Tim Daly (left) in their younger days. COURTESY HOCKEY HALL OF FAME.

Nicknamed "the Black Cat," Johnny Gagnon starred for the Canadiens on a line with Aurel Joliat and Howie Morenz. COURTESY HOCKEY HALL OF FAME.

Les Canadiens earned the nickname The Flying Frenchmen because of the Stratford Streak, alias Howie Morenz. Courtesy Hockey Hall of Fame.

Following the death of Howie Morenz, a benefit game, featuring NHL
stars was held. Detroit Red Wings manager Jack Adams (first row, center)
coached one of the clubs. Toronto's Charlie Conacher stands behind
Adams. COURTESY HOCKEY HALL OF FAME.

Leaf immortal Charlie Conacher, right wing on
Toronto's fabled "Kid Line" of the 1930's.
COURTESY HOCKEY HALL OF FAME.

Toronto goalie Walter "Turk" Broda goes through an artificial "save" routine for the cameraman. COURTESY HOCKEY HALL OF FAME.

Leafs-Canadiens action in the 1940's. Toronto's rushing defenseman Wally Stanowski cradles the puck inside the Habs zone. COURTESY HOCKEY HALL OF FAME.

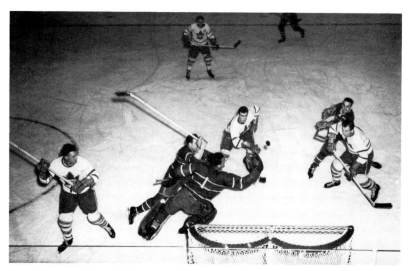

Canadiens goalie Bill Durnan reaches for the flying puck as Leafs (left to right) Ted Kennedy, Tod Sloan, and Joe Klukay await the rebound. Max Bentley (top) is point man on this power play in 1948 action. COURTESY HOCKEY HALL OF FAME.

Two of hockey's best-ever goalies: Billy Durnan (left) and Turk Broda. COURTESY HOCKEY HALL OF FAME.

Two perspectives on Leaf Bill Barilko's 1951 Cup-winner against the Habs. The newly discovered photo (below) reveals Barilko's reaction as well as those of Maurice Richard (center), Butch Bouchard (left), and goalie Gerry McNeil. COURTESY HOCKEY HALL OF FAME.

Once a hated Toronto opponent in the early 1940's, Harry Lumley later became a Leaf goaltender in 1952. The 1950's became an era of Leaf frustration unparalleled until the Ballard years. COURTESY HOCKEY HALL OF FAME.

Jacques Plante stops a drive from Toronto forward Ron Stewart. Jean-Guy Talbot moves in for the rebound. COURTESY HOCKEY HALL OF FAME.

Jacques Plante was the first NHL goalie to make a practice of leaving his net to trap the puck along the boards. Bob Pulford of Toronto attempts the intercept. COURTESY HOCKEY HALL OF FAME.

Frank "the Big M" Mahovlich storms the Montreal goal as Jacques Plante makes a kick save. Doug Harvey defends for the Habs. COURTESY HOCKEY HALL OF FAME.

Goalie Jacques Plante makes a jumping save as Toronto's Eddie Shack (left) and Dick Duff (9) converge on the Montreal goal. COURTESY HOCKEY HALL OF FAME.

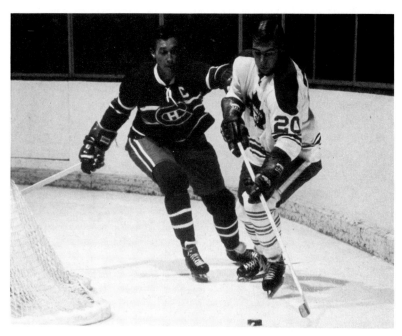

Two top centers, Jean Beliveau and Bob Pulford of Montreal and Toronto, respectively, battle for the puck. COURTESY HOCKEY HALL OF FAME.

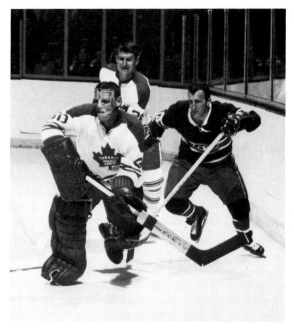

Leaf goalie Terry Sawchuk clears the puck as Montreal forward Claude Provost and Toronto defenseman Allan Stanley come up from behind. COURTESY HOCKEY HALL OF FAME.

Ken Dryden, Montreal's scholar-goaltender, makes a save with Habs captain Henri Richard in the background. COURTESY HOCKEY HALL OF FAME.

The last of the legendary Canadiens superstars, Guy "the Flower" Lafleur.
COURTESY HOCKEY HALL OF FAME.

One of the team's all-time greats, Darryl Sittler clashed with Leaf GM Imlach and tore the team captain's "C" from his jersey in frustration when pal Lanny McDonald was traded to the Colorado Rockies. COURTESY BRUCE BENNETT STUDIOS.

Hard-hitting Wendel Clark was made Leaf captain before the start of the 1991–92 season. COURTESY BRUCE BENNETT STUDIOS.

Much of the Habs' hope for a Stanley Cup in the 1990's rests with netminder Patrick Roy. COURTESY BRUCE BENNETT STUDIOS.

and he wheels around and fires a backhander into the near, lower part of the net."

"When Richard breaks on one defenseman," said Boston's Murray Henderson, "there's no telling what he'll do. If he gets his body between you and the puck, you just can't get at it. He cradles the puck on the blade of his stick, steers it with one hand, and wards off his check with the other. Strong? That guy is like an ox, but he sure doesn't look it."

Even then few but his closest friends were able to understand the brooding Richard personality. True, the Rocket had learned to speak English, but when he was around the rink he rarely betrayed a smile.

At home Richard was no more ebullient. "He roams around the house muttering to himself," revealed Lucille Richard, his affable wife. "He gets mad and stays that way until he gets a goal. And even a goal, or a cluster of them, won't make him happy unless the Canadiens win. When he's in a surly mood, all he does is eat. He keeps me busy broiling steaks and frying pork chops."

Author Vince Lunny, who had great insight into Richard, added, "His nerves are as taut as trout lines. If he had to keep the tension bottled up within himself, he'd probably blow up. Luckily, hockey is a physical contact sport which provides a release for the nervous tension that twists his stomach into knots and threatens a nervous breakdown."

On one occasion, after serving a five-minute major penalty in Detroit, Richard scored three goals on his next shift, returning to the bench only when the hat trick was complete. Montreal won the game 3–2.

Another time, he walked into the dressing room and approached Irvin. "Dick," he said, "I feel pretty bad, so don't give me too much ice tonight. This afternoon I moved to another apartment and I couldn't hire a truck. My brother and I carried everything on our backs."

Irvin planned to use the Rocket for spot duty that evening, but once the game began, Richard asked to take his regular turn. He went on to score five goals against the Red Wings! "I wonder," said Irvin, "what you'd have done if you weren't tired?"

In the 1951 semifinals, against the powerful Detroit Red Wings, Richard was dominant, scoring two overtime winners and completely outperforming his new arch-rival, Gordie Howe, as the Habs took the series in six games.

But Richard alone couldn't cope with the Toronto Maple Leafs in the finals. Every game in the series went into sudden-death overtime. Toronto won the opener, 3–2, on a goal by Sid Smith. The Rocket scored the second-game winner. Toronto won the next two, setting up a climactic fifth-and-final match.

The Habs were leading, 2–1, with less than a minute left in the third period when Toronto's Ted Kennedy and Max Bentley combined to feed a pass to Tod Sloan. Goalie McNeil couldn't cope with Sloan's shot and the game, once more, went into sudden-death.

Irvin hoped the Rocket would come through for him as he had earlier in the game when he scored the opening goal in classic Richard fashion. "He had only Jim Thomson between him and the goal," recalled Dink Carroll, of the Montreal *Gazette*. "Thomson may have been an All-Star defenseman, but they all looked alike to Richard in those circumstances. He went around Thomson like a hoop around a barrel, pulled goalie Al Rollins out, and fired the puck into the empty net."

That, however, wasn't enough, and when the first overtime began, the Richard line lost the puck to Harry Watson of Toronto. He passed the puck to Howie Meeker inside the Canadiens' zone and the crew-cut right wing cut behind the Montreal net before sliding a crisp pass toward the blueline. Leaf defenseman Barilko saw it coming and dived headfirst at the puck, swinging his stick in the same motion. While Barilko was still hanging in mid-air the puck sailed over McNeil's right elbow and into the net.

(A previously unpublished photograph of this most famous of Leaf goals was discovered recently in the Hockey Hall of Fame archives by authors James Duplacey and Joseph Romain and reproduced in their Leaf photo history, *Toronto Maple Leafs: Images of Glory*. See photo insert.)

In the Montreal dressing room the consensus was, "Wait 'til next year." This, of course, was an old refrain except that, under Selke's deft maneuvering, "next year's" were becoming more and more attractive to Montreal fans. The essential reason was that the Habs' farm system had begun to transport several excellent prospects to the big club and there was more help on the way. One of the first arrivals was Bernard Geoffrion, a brash young right wing with a stunning shot who had learned his hockey within trotting distance of the Forum. Even more promising was Jean Beliveau, a huge skater who was playing amateur hockey in Quebec City. With

Geoffrion and Beliveau in the fold, there would be lusty and lively days ahead.

Because of the farm system recruits, Richard, and the strength McNeil displayed in goal, Selke looked ahead confidently at the team's prospects for the decade. He described his goalie as "the best in the business," despite some excellent work by Al Rollins in Toronto and Terry Sawchuk in Detroit, and argued that McNeil had proved his mettle in the playoffs.

"He outgoaled Sawchuk, Rollins, and Turk Broda at every turn," remarked Selke. "Losing out in our bid for the Stanley Cup was a bitter pill to swallow, but we think that we've found something more valuable than the Stanley Cup. That something is an outstanding goaltender." Selke's assessment would prove overly optimistic.

In 1951, the Canadiens began making overtures to pry Jean Marc Beliveau, the pride and joy of Quebec City away from the Quebec Aces of the Quebec Senior League. Opposition to their efforts were formidable — opposition from the Aces, even opposition from Quebec City businessmen-politicos who threatened that the Forum's beer license would be revoked by the provincial government in Quebec City if Montreal didn't lay off Beliveau. The Habs' biggest single obstacle, however, was the wily George "Punch" Imlach, coach of the Aces, who was able to short-circuit Montreal's lobbying for two years.

While Beliveau was still a distant dream, the Canadiens were getting by offensively on the continuing excellence of Rocket Richard and the coming-of-age of Bernie Geoffrion.

Nicknamed "Boom Boom" because of the reverberation of his stick hitting the puck and the puck hitting the end boards (although it often went directly into the net), Geoffrion had many of the incendiary qualities of Richard. "Remember," the Boomer would say, "the Rocket always was my idol when I was a kid in Montreal. When Maurice doesn't score he's not happy and he doesn't want to speak to anyone. I'm the same way."

But the Geoffrion character had one ingredient that was missing in the Richard psyche, a flamboyant sense of humor. For the most part Rocket was a quiet, introverted sort even when life was agreeable, but when Geoffrion was scoring easily he became an opera-singing clown who led the Canadiens' laugh parade. He began delighting teammates late in the 1950–51 season after scoring 103 goals in fifty-seven Montreal Junior League games. Like

Beliveau, Geoffrion was under great pressure to turn pro with the Canadiens and he resisted until there were only eighteen games remaining in the 1950–51 schedule. Geoffrion realized that the Calder Trophy for rookie of the year was given to players who had skated in twenty or more games. By waiting until there were fewer than twenty games in the '50–'51 schedule he thus became eligible to win it the following season.

When approached by Selke, Geoffrion laid the facts on the line: "I'll lose my chance for the Calder. It's too late in the season to catch up with the other guys."

The Boomer was no fool. He opened the 1951–52 season with two goals, including the winner, against Chicago in a 4–2 Montreal victory and immediately established himself as the newest Canadiens hero. For Geoffrion it was relatively easy. Not only was he an excellent young prospect but he had recently married Marlene Morenz, the attractive blonde daughter of the late Howie Morenz.

"I was a figure skater at the time," Marlene remembered, "and was practicing at the Forum for an ice carnival.

While I was doing a spin I missed a piece of cardboard on the ice and took a bad spill. As I looked up, deeply embarassed, I noticed this fellow laughing his head off. I was furious and was still furious after the show when a knock sounded on the dressing-room door. It was my brother [Howie Morenz, Jr.] who wanted me to meet a friend of his from junior hockey. It turned out to be the same fellow who had been laughing at me. And that's how I met Boomer. Soon we were all laughing.

A few miles away, at a local Montreal rink, another Richard was beginning to look like a future Hab prospect. This was fifteen-year-old Henri Richard, the Rocket's kid brother. Some critics cautioned that it was premature to foresee the NHL for Henri. Unlike Maurice, Henri was small and showed no signs of filling out. Besides, another of the Richard brothers, Jacques, had failed after suggesting some of the Rocket's ability. "Jacques," said Baz O'Meara of the Montreal *Star*, "didn't have the same drive as his famous brother, nor the tenacity to make the big-time. On the other hand, Henri has hockey player's legs, a very good shift, and if he listens to his older brother he might become a star."

In time Henri would join Maurice on the same line. In the

meantime Irvin sought a left wing to round out the abridged Punch Line. Both Maurice and Elmer Lach had sprung ahead in the scoring race, first with Bert Olmstead on left wing and later with Dickie Moore, another Montreal-bred youngster with all the mustard Richard possessed.

As he had himself predicted, Geoffrion had become the foremost rookie-of-the-year candidate but more than the numbers, it was the manner in which he was scoring that was meaningful. Geoffrion, although he may not have realized it at the time, had become a hockey revolutionary. Instead of using the traditional forehand wrist shot or the backhand, Geoffrion would draw his stick back like a golfer and slap the puck. The result was the "slapshot" which would eventually be adopted by most of the league's leading scorers and would dramatically change the face of the game.

The forte of the slapshot was the extraordinary speed Geoffrion generated, harder than anything the NHL had seen, including the bullet-shooting Charlie Conacher of the early thirties. Toronto coach Hap Day, who played with Conacher on the Maple Leafs, had no qualms about putting the Geoffrion shot in proper perspective.

"It's definitely harder than anything Conacher shot," said Day. "I watched Geoffrion closely on the play. I saw him draw the stick back, but I never saw the puck until it bounced off the goalpost. It's the first time I never saw the shot I was looking at."

Geoffrion alone wasn't galvanizing the Canadiens. Nor was Dickie Moore. A speedy youngster named Paul Meger was shining on the forward line along with Dick Gamble. Young Tom Johnson and Doug Harvey offered goalie McNeil formidable protection on defense. "We like Moore," said Jim Vipond in his *Globe and Mail* column. "He's a chippy operator who mixes with the toughest and still knows how to stickhandle and skate his way to the opposition net. He's not unmindful of Milt Schmidt as he leans forward in gaining top speed. These Montreal kids are making the customers forget Maurice Richard."

But the Rocket wouldn't let anyone forget him. Recovered from a stomach ailment after a Florida vacation, he returned to Maple Leaf Gardens on March 19, 1952, to aid the Habs in their second-place battle with Toronto.

Montreal won the game, 3–0, which enabled them to beat out Toronto for second place and it was Richard who proved the catalyst with one of his displays of pure fury on ice. "The Rocket's goal was typical," wrote Gord Walker in the *Globe and Mail.* "On a two-man break in the second period, Lach was covered by Jimmy Thomson. He still got over a perfect pass to Richard who appeared to be blanketed by Jimmy Morrison. Yet the Rocket somehow got his stick around and zipped the puck into the net."

Richard's histrionics had already become too numerous for most fans to remember. Some rooters preferred to recall the goals he scored. Others remembered the fights, and still others pointed to the obscure episodes that made Maurice so unique.

"The impact Richard had on the Canadiens," said Peter Gzowski, "and through them on the rest of the league, seems to me beautifully summed up in one incident that occurred in Toronto.

It was the time that, soaring head over heels as the result of an artful Maple Leaf check, Richard shattered the "unbreakable" Herculite glass that had just been installed in Maple Leaf Gardens around the top of the boards. No one had nicked it before, and only Eddie Shack has broken it since, which was unfair, since Shack hit a faulty piece. Richard put the heel of his skate through it, and there was something perfect about it being the Rocket, the epitome of recklessness, of untrammeled fire and fury and abandon on the ice, who did it.

Few players ever upstaged Richard. One of those who did was Gordie Howe, and the Red Wing immortal managed to pull the surprise on "Maurice Richard Night" at the Forum. As the presentation was coming to an end, Richard headed for the sideboards when Howe called out, "Hey, Rocket!" As Richard turned, Howe pulled off his leather gauntlet and extended his hand. For a brief second the Forum crowd hushed as the two archfoes shook hands at center ice. "It was a sort of genuinely unrehearsed spontaneous gesture that caught the big crowd completely by surprise," said Elmer Ferguson. The crowd remained silent for another moment and then burst into a thunderous ovation.

The Canadiens finished in second place during the 1951–52 season and went up against the fourth-place Bruins in the Stanley Cup semifinal. Richard scored twice in the opener, a 5–1 Montreal win. Rookie-of-the-year Geoffrion notched a hat trick in game two, a 4–0 Hab victory. The Canadiens were stunned when the Bruins swept the next three games, but rallied and took the next two,

Richard scoring the series-winning goal. The goal itself was a classic.

Blond Bill Quakenbush, one of the most experienced and intelligent defensemen in the NHL, skated backward on the Bruin defense, prepared to meet the ominous challenge, for Richard was now in full flight, his eyes blazing madly, his destination known to all. Quakenbush was traveling at about ten miles per hour in reverse as Richard bore down on him with more than twice that speed. Quakenbush hurled his black-shirted body at the Canadien ace, but it was as if he were checking a phantom.

Nevertheless, Quakenbush had done his job quite well, for he had forced Richard to take so circuitous a route along the right side that the Rocket appeared to have taken himself right out of the play. "He looked to be too deep for a shot," said Baz O'Meara of the Montreal *Star*, "but then he suddenly did a deft cut to the left."

A right-handed shot playing right wing would have been cradling the puck too far to his right to release a threatening drive, but Richard, the anomaly, was a left-handed shot. Thus, the puck was on his left side, closer to the net, as he barreled past the flailing Quakenbush. "Sugar" Jim Henry, both eyes blackened from previous injuries and barely recovered from a broken nose, guarded the right corner of the net, allowing Richard nothing but the "impossible" angle shot to the far left corner.

Almost atop Henry's bulky goal pads, Richard finally released his drive. It was low and hard and Henry never managed to see, let alone touch, the puck. "One minute I was facing him" commented the Bruin netminder, "waiting for the shot; the next he had whizzed by and the puck was in the net."

The ovations that traditionally greeted Richard goals had the impact of a thunderclap. This time, however, the din shook the very foundations of the ancient Forum. The goal was all the more remarkable in that earlier in the game Richard had been in a partial coma after a devastating Leo Labine bodycheck.

Reactions to the goal were as surprising as the score itself. Elmer Lach, who had been sitting on the bench watching the Rocket in orbit, leaned forward onto the sideboards and fainted. Art Chapman, manager of the Buffalo hockey club, was watching from the press box and simply stood mouth agape after the red light flashed. "Only Richard could score like that," he said later.

"He is like Babe Ruth was," said Irvin. "He adds that little extra flourish to everything."

"That little flourish" gave Montreal the winning goal, although Billy Reay added another one into the empty net with less than a minute remaining to give the Habs a 3–1 victory. When the final siren wailed, reporters searched for the proper adjectives to describe Richard's achievement Veteran journalist Baz O'Meara, summed it up this way:

In all his storied, starry career, Richard has scored some of the most spectacular goals of hockey history. No player has ever matched him as a thrill-producer. No one has come close to him for versatility of execution. Of all the goals credited to him, none ever excelled that gamewinner against Boston . . . None ever drew a greater ovation, more gasps of admiration, because it was scored under the pressure of pain.

The pain had not entirely dissipated when Richard settled onto the bench in Montreal's joy-filled dressing room. His father, Onesime Richard, walked in and put his right arm around his son's shoulder and hugged him. No longer able to control the emotion that welled within his battered frame, the Rocket broke down and cried.

Decimated by injuries, the Canadiens were no match for the Red Wings, who were well rested after their four-game sweep of the Maple Leafs. The Detroit sextet swept Montreal in four consecutive games to win the Cup, although some observers argued that Detroit benefited from the officiating throughout the playoffs. "The Wings can put the best seven men on the ice of any team in the league," said Toronto's managing director, Conn Smythe in a barbed reference to what he perceived as biased officiating. Irvin agreed. Bitter to the end, Irvin refused to congratulate the winners and slammed the dressing-room door in the face of Detroit reporters.

Irvin's grumpiness and the general depression in the Montreal dressing room was not reflected by the even-tempered Selke. He realized that his plans were jelling and that only a few more years were required before his rebuilding job would be complete. In the meantime, he bathed in the fading sunlight generated by such veterans as Bouchard and Lach. Although Elmer had vowed to retire a few seasons earlier, he appeared at the 1952–53 training camp with the same vigor he had displayed as a rookie, and continued to excel through the campaign.

Paced by Lach, Richard, and the energetic youngsters, Montreal finished second behind Detroit and went into the playoff semifinal a heavy favorite to defeat the fourth-place Black Hawks. But Chicago was not the traditional doormat of yesteryear. They presented a creative coach in Sid Abel and a superb but underrated goaltender named Al Rollins, previously of the Leafs. This still should not have presented a problem for the Habs, except for an unexpected development — goalie Gerry McNeil became overwrought with nervousness and was a major disappointment in the series.

Before Irvin could grasp hold of the situation Chicago had advanced to the lip of victory in the semifinal round with a 3–2 advantage in the best-of-seven series. With an ironic twist of strategy, Irvin suddenly benched McNeil — much in the manner he had replaced Durnan years previous — and inserted Jacques Plante, an unusual goaltender if ever there was one.

In his spare time, Plante had a hobby of knitting toques, the French-Canadian wool caps worn by his ancestors. He was confident to the point of being cocky and betrayed a bizarre goaltending style that would soon be copied by other netminders around the league. It was Plante's idea that he could assist his defensemen by roaming out of his cage, formerly a strict taboo, and behind the net when the pucks were caromed off the boards and skidded behind his cage. By doing so, Plante was able to control the puck and pass it off to a teammate, while scrambling back to his goal crease before any shots were taken.

All this was well and good and terribly fascinating, but for the adventurous and unconventional Plante to experiment with the Canadiens in the playoffs and on the brink of elimination was something else! But Irvin had made a commitment, and Plante was his goalie. Jacques the Roamer immediately went into the nets and stopped the Black Hawks cold. He foiled a breakaway early in the fifth game, and with that impetus the Canadiens won two-straight games and captured the first round.

Meanwhile, the Bruins had stunned the league-leading Red Wings with a four-games-to-two upset in the other semifinal round, and qualified to meet Montreal for the Stanley Cup. After building up a 3–1 lead in games, Montreal clinched the Cup when the Rocket passed the puck to Lach in a sudden-death overtime with the score tied, 0–0, and Elmer converted the pass for a goal.

The success of the Canadiens, as well as the Maple Leafs and Red Wings, was soon to boomerang on them in a rather perverse manner. In the early fifties it had become apparent that the Bruins, Rangers, and Black Hawks were suffering attendance setbacks that were exacerbated by great deficiencies in player personnel, although the Rangers, under the guidance of Frank Boucher, were building a formidable farm system.

Pressure from the three losing cities was finally felt in the NHL hierarchy, which responded by creating a draft system. Selke contended that the new draft was aimed at diluting his dynasty. He fought the draft on the grounds that Montreal should reap the rewards of its hard-earned success. In a significant display of altruism, Selke sold highly regarded young Ed Litzenberger to the Black Hawks for only fifteen thousand dollars, although the crack forward was worth more than four times that amount. It was that same Litzenberger who was instrumental in Chicago's march to the Stanley Cup in 1961.

One of the prime reasons for the "Curb-the-Canadiens" movement was Selke's own triumph in signing Jean Beliveau for the 1953–54 season. Unlike previous contract agreements, the Beliveau negotiations were conducted in the same atmosphere of excitement that might have greeted the signing of the North Atlantic Treaty. *Le Gros Bill* was accompanied by an accountant and an attorney and came away with one of the largest salaries in hockey history, unlike Maurice Richard who entered the league earning coolie wages and with virtually no fuss or fanfare.

Beliveau's premiere was widely trumpeted throughout the league. His decision to stay in Quebec had merely whetted the interest of hockey fans throughout the NHL, and they came out in extraordinary numbers to see what he was all about. At first glance, he suggested that he would be the most overrated flop since the aluminum hockey stick!

Beliveau was the antithesis of Richard, Geoffrion, and Moore. His long strides suggested that he was not really trying very hard and his phlegmatic disposition was in stark contrast to the volcanic teammates surrounding him. Even worse, Beliveau displayed no thirst for fighting.

Every low-salaried skater from New York to Chicago was determined to get a piece of Beliveau and many of them succeeded. He suffered a cracked fibula after being heavily checked in Chicago shortly after the start of the season and was sidelined a total of twenty-six games for assorted injuries during the season. But Beliveau had a good sense of history and realized that his teammate, Richard, had endured a similar spate of injuries when he broke into the league. "If my career turns out like the Rocket's," he said, "all of this will really be worthwile."

Occasionally, Beliveau offered cause for favorable comment. His stickhandling ability suggested that he had an invisible string linking the puck to his stick blade, and his shot was hard and accurate. "The playing of Beliveau," commented Canadian novelist Hugh MacLennan, "is poetry in action."

But Beliveau's production left him overshadowed by his teammates' histrionics, which were abundant in 1953–54 and not all that positive either. Clearly established as a star, Geoffrion found himself assailed and assaulted just like Richard. The Boomer's boiling point was equally low and in November, 1953, he was fined $250 for charging referee Frank Udvari.

Some observers marveled at veterans like the Rocket and Lach. Others raved over the kids, and still others marveled at the raw intensity with which the Habitants approached the game.

"Before every game," said television commentator Bud Palmer, "they must put in thirty minutes of silence. They just sit there, backs to the wall, and their heads are down, as if in prayer."

Nevertheless, the Red Wings remained the class of the league and proved it in a stirring Stanley Cup final with the Habs. The teams went down to a seventh and final game that was decided on a rather innocent long, soft shot by Tony Leswick, of Detroit. Goalie McNeil, who had made a brief comeback with the Canadiens, appeared to have it in hand when defenseman Doug Harvey attempted to deflect it out of danger. Harvey managed to get only a piece of the puck and it caromed off his left glove and into the net behind the startled netminder.

That was enough for McNeil. He permanently retired after only four full seasons in the NHL and never fulfilled the promise Selke had held for him when he hired McNeil to replace Durnan. The great Lach also retired, but neither of the older players would be terribly missed. Plante would be an excellent replacement in goal, and the front line was fortified with the likes of Richard, Beliveau, Moore, Bert Olmstead, and Floyd Curry.

"One of the most remarkable facts about the team — and a tribute to Frank Selke's talent-seeking abilities — has been the way it has been able to refresh its strength from new, young players whenever a group of older ones begins to disintegrate," wrote Peter Gzowski.

Yet the balance wheel of the dynamo that was *Les Canadiens* remained the galvanic Rocket. Late in the 1954–55 season it seemed that, finally, Richard would win the league scoring championship, the title for most total points in the regular season. Then in one of the most astounding administrative blunders of his career, league president Campbell suspended Richard for the remainder of the season — and the playoffs — after an incident in Boston. Until the suspension the Canadiens had been expected to nose out Detroit and win the league championship. "Without Richard," wrote Selke in *Behind the Cheering* "the team had lost its soul. Our boys were certain that, in one fell stroke, they had lost both the league championship and the Stanley Cup."

On St. Patrick's Day, 1955, a Thursday, the Habs and Red Wings were to meet in the third-last game of the season. Montreal fans had become increasingly incensed over Campbell's actions and by game time the city was verging on riot. Foolheartedly, Campbell insisted on attending the game where, despite a protective ring of attendants, he narrowly escaped assassination. A tear-gas bomb exploding in front of Selke's box diverted attention. Campbell seized the opportunity to escape.

Soon, the fire chief ordered the Forum evacuated. The game was called off, forfeited to the Red Wings. Outside, bands of vandals tossed bricks and other debris at the Forum, at passing trolley cars, and at automobiles. Newspaper kiosks were set alight and burned down. Roving bands proceeded east along Ste. Catherine Street, smashing store windows and looting at every turn. The rioting continued into the night, eventually dissipating of its own accord.

By next morning the Richard Riot was headline news around the world. The New York *Times* gave it page-one coverage as did other distinguished dailies. In Montreal the Rocket himself went on TV and radio, pleading with the community to accept Campbell's decision and to look forward to his return the next season.

Richard's plea became a balm to all as Montreal fans turned once again to the business of the pennant race. The Canadiens regained enough equilibrium to defeat the Rangers on Saturday night, but lost to Detroit on Sunday and had to settle for second place. The Hab fans, however, were more distressed that the Rocket would lose the scoring race. Caught in the middle of this was Geoffrion, who had preferred that his idol, Richard, take the title but nevertheless was obliged to try to help the team win the pennant. By the end of the last game of the season, in Detroit, Geoffrion had overtaken Richard and won the scoring championship. Richard was runner-up. Beliveau finished third.

Dick Irvin, who was uncertain about his hockey future in Montreal, and, unknown to Selke, suffering through the first stages of bone cancer, had been irritable through the season and was blamed by Selke for unnecessarily inciting Richard through the season. Soon after the final game, Selke summoned his old friend, Irvin, into his office and informed him that he could remain with the team in "another job," but not as coach. He also made it clear that he would not object if Irvin decided to take the Black Hawk coaching job, which he knew Irvin had been considering.

Irvin, one of the all-time-great NHL coaches, considered Selke's proposal and announced that he would move on to Chicago. Selke had inherited Irvin when he made the switch from Toronto to Montreal in 1946. Now, for the first time, he had the challenge of selecting a new coach for the Habs.

Surely, there was an abundance of qualified coaches to choose from, but the task of controlling the Canadiens was something special. No team in the NHL had such a distillation of French — and English — Canadians. Selke would have to find a man who, like Irvin, would be able to maintain harmony in the club. On top of that, he required a personality who could command the respect of aces such as Richard, Beliveau, and Geoffrion and who could follow in Irvin's difficult footsteps as a winner. A big winner.

One rumor had it that Selke would be obliged to select a French Canadian. One suggestion was Butch Bouchard; another was Roger Leger, both former players and both well respected in the French-speaking community. Others speculated that Billy Reay, though not a French Canadian, would wind up with the job. Several of the Forum directors were partial to Reay and he was the only choice seriously in the running for the job along with the favorite, Hector "Toe" Blake.

"The Old Lamplighter" had studied coaching well in the Quebec Senior League. He was partially French Canadian and he was admired by all the players, particularly Richard. Kenny Reardon, who had moved up to a key front-office position with the Canadiens, was a strong advocate of Blake, and ultimately the opinions of Selke and Reardon prevailed. On June 8, 1955, the signing of Blake was officially announced before a standing-room crowd at the Forum, and the Canadiens were ready to become the greatest team in hockey history.

Toe Blake eventually wielded a dictator's baton over the Canadiens, but at first he ruled like a benevolent despot. This was easy because the players, to a man, respected Blake, and vice versa. The pivotal personality on the team was the Rocket. He went out of his way to assure the Canadiens' hierarchy that he backed Blake to the hilt, and he meant every word of it.

Now it was up to the Old Lamplighter to produce. All the ingredients were there: a young competent goaltender, a strong, inelligent defense, and the most explosive collection of scorers in history. It was simply a matter of stirring them to the proper boil without creating the fire hazard of previous years. Richard Riots were to be avoided at all costs.

"Blake and Selke were trying to give the Rocket all they had by way of a tranquilizing program," said author Josh Greenfeld. "They started giving him de-pep talks long before the season began. They pointed out to him that he was thirty-five years old, that he did not have to carry the emotional burden of victory alone, that he still would be treated with sufficient respect by the other players around the league even if he went a little easier on the roughhouse, and that the important thing was not one game, not one fight, but to lead the team to a Stanley Cup victory."

The Canadiens' organization, not to mention the city of Montreal, was still smarting from the black eye it had received from the St. Patrick's Day disaster. A unique community spirit seemd to engulf the team right from the start of training camp in nearby Verdun, Quebec. "I could see immediately," said Blake, "that we would have good harmony in the club. The boys were greatly disappointed with the way they'd finished the last two years. One year a bad goal beat them, the next year a bad fuss. They were determined they were not going to let anything beat them this time, least of all themselves."

The major roadblock would be provided by the Red Wings. Fortified by the Production Line of Sid Abel, Alex Delvecchio, and Gordie Howe, an excellent bench, and good goaltending, Detroit seemed as powerful as ever. To dethrone them would be a major accomplishment and would required adroit manipulation of lines, right down to the third unit. And that was as much a key to the success as anything. When the Beliveau line or the Richard line was exhausted, Blake had the good fortune to call upon Floyd "Busher" Curry, one of the essential unsung heroes, Claude Provost, and a very capable rookie, Don Marshall.

His scrubs, such as defenseman Jean-Guy Talbot and Bob Turner, were good enough to be first-liners on almost any other team, which was a credit to Selke's superb farm system. It was indeed a galaxy that dazzled nobody more than it did Blake. "I couldn't help be amazed once we started holding our first work-outs," said Toe. "I was glad I was as young as I was. Otherwise I would have been killed. All those great shots. The puck was flying around with such speed I thought I was in a shooting gallery."

It is impossible to project just how the 1955–56 Canadiens would have reacted to Dick Irvin, but one can surmise the results would not have been as positive as they were with Blake. Irvin was confounded with a ramshackle Black Hawk team in October, 1955, but he managed to give them an aura of respectability although they failed to make the playoffs. The condition of his health was worsening and by the start of the 1956–57 season had deteriorated to a point where he had to be given a sabbatical. He died in May, 1957.

The memory of Irvin had lingered on when Blake took over as Montreal coach. Toe's success at Valleyfield in the Quebec Senior League was well known to management, but it hardly made an impression on the rank-and-file fan who had as many doubts about Blake as Toe himself. "I was nervous," the rookie coach allowed. "I felt I had to produce with a club like that. So much potential. And it was a big test for me. But the Rocket went out of his way to help me. So did Kenny Mosdell and Floyd Curry and Butch Bouchard.

"Sometimes it's tough to coach players you once had as team-mates. But these fellas went out of their way to make it easy for me. Even from the beginning we were like one big happy family."

This was virtually a miracle because Blake's Canadiens boasted a number of extroverts who bordered on egomaniacs. One of them was Plante who eventually collided with Blake one time too many. But that was later. Geoffrion was very much a team player but also a clown, given to renditions of Pagliacci in the dressing room, television singing appearances, and occasional dashes of brag-gadocio. The Rocket remained basically an introvert and a loner while Beliveau exuded a princely humility that endeared him to practically everyone.

Normally, a hockey team splinters into small groups of players after each game. With the exception of Richard and Plante, the Canadiens would travel *en masse* to the movies, a tavern, or a restaurant.

One might have suspected that the Rocket would be jealous of the Young Turks grabbing the spotlight from him, but the opposite was true. He went out of his way to make life comfortable for *Le Gros Bill* and was quick to praise the big youngster. "He gets along with everyone," said Richard, "and he's the best center I've seen since I've been in the league."

Still another young center captured the Rocket's attention as much as Beliveau. Henri Richard, only nineteen years old, was invited to training camp for an audition. This was a rudimentary procedure with the Canadiens. After a week or so of scanning the youngsters the high command would then distribute them to any one of several farm teams. Certainly a kid straight out of junior hockey and as small as Henri was not going to crack the varsity.

At first Henri was named "Flash" but this soon was changed to "the Pocket Rocket" as he displayed less and less inclination to be dropped from the varsity. This disturbed management because everyone agreed that at least a year in the minors would be most beneficial to young Richard.

Merely for experimental purposes Blake inserted Henri at center with his brother and Dickie Moore at left wing. Whenever he stepped on the ice Henri controlled the play, dashing around the rink with his lilting hop-steps. The appearance of his kid brother seemed to galvanize thirty-five-year-old Maurice while Moore complemented the line perfectly with his tough checking and superb shooting. It was no contest. Henri Richard made the team on his first try.

"He's a little small yet," said Blake, "but with his speed we keep telling him not to try to go through the big opposition defensemen, just go around them.

Henri's arrival enabled Blake to compose a second line of Beliveau, Geoffrion, and Olmstead while mixing Mosdell, Curry, Marshall, Provost, and Jackie Leclair in varying combinations for his third unit. "I'm lucky I was a member of that team," recalled Beliveau. "We had everything. We had great scoring, we had great checking, we had great goaltending. And we had great blending, the ideal combination of experienced veterans and good young rookies. And also great team spirit."

Experts varied in their opinions of the final standings for 1955–56, but Dick Irvin had no qualms about rating his former team: "They should win the championship by ten games!" Blake agreed: "If we finish anywhere but first I'll feel I've done a very bad job. If things go right, yes, we should win by ten games. But any hockey man will tell you that in hockey things don't always go right."

The gears didn't mesh perfectly for Blake. His club was baffled by an uncommon number of injuries. Yet whenever one ace was sidelined another filled the breach to play just as well. As the Canadiens approached the midpoint in the season, they were already six games in front of the pack. The Rocket was having another splendid season and just about everyone hoped that this time he would win his long-coveted scoring championship. But he would be deprived of this honor by Beliveau who, ironically, was adopting some of Richard's old belligerence.

Up until 1955–56 Beliveau had become known as "Gentleman Jean" because of his abhorrence of rough and dirty play. As a result, the league bullies punished him severely. Just before Irvin left Montreal, he persuaded Beliveau that he had better fight back if he wanted to survive in the NHL jungle. Beliveau began retaliating in 1955–56. His penalty minutes mounted alarmingly but his scoring totals jumped just as quickly.

"Like the other great players Jean smartened up when he saw the opposition getting the better of him," said Irvin. "He'll never be the type to go around looking for trouble, but now he can be as tough as anybody."

Selke was a very happy man at the start of 1956. There was no longer any doubt that he had chosen wisely in Blake. The Rocket was turbulent, to be sure, but managed to maintain decorum at the right time, and his prize catch, Beliveau, had become the talk of hockey.

"Big Jean is great," said Black Hawk manager Tommy Ivan, "because he takes the direct route. No long way around for him. He has the size and the weight to hold his own. He's tremendously strong, a beautiful skater, a superb stickhandler, strictly a team man and with a perfect sense of playmaking. He'd be a star on any hockey club."

He was, significantly, different from Maurice Richard in one area. "Jean doesn't have the desire to score that Maurice has," said Blake.

This was meant more as an analysis than criticism. "With Maurice," said Selke, taking the issue a step further, "his moves are powered by instinctive reflexes. Maurice can't learn from lectures. He does everything by instinct and with sheer power. Beliveau, on the other hand, is probably the classiest player I've ever seen. He has a flair for giving you his hockey as a master showman. He is a perfect coach's hockey player because he studies and learns. He's moving and planning all the time, thinking out the play required for each situation. The difference between the two best players in the game today is simply this: Beliveau is a perfectionist, Richard is an opportunist."

The Rocket and *Le Gros Bill* formed two-fifths of the most devastating power play, the five-man charge when the enemy is shorthanded, in hockey history. Doug Harvey and Boom Boom

Geoffrion were stationed at the left and right "points" near the blueline. Beliveau, Richard, and Bert Olmstead played up front with Olmstead doing the major digging in the corners for the puck. "Of all the players," Blake once observed, "I don't think Olmstead received all the credit he deserved."

More often than not, Olmstead would head for the boards to fetch the puck. If he fed it to Harvey, the hyperrelaxed defenseman would calmly look around and thread-needle a pass to someone near the net. Or, if everyone was covered, he'd skim it across the ice to Geoffrion whose potent shot was the fright of every goalie. For purposes of variety or deception the Boomer might feed the puck to Beliveau or Richard stationed closer to the net.

Statistics underlined the potency of Montreal's power play. The Canadiens scored twenty-five percent of their goals on it, a fact that terribly distressed their five opponents. At a meeting convened after the season, the NHL voted, against Montreal's opposition, to change a rule terminating a minor penalty at the scoring of a goal. The rule was specifically aimed at curbing the Canadiens' awesome power. "When they're playing that power play right," said the oft-critical Blake, "it is a beautiful picture to watch."

Finding a flaw in this armament was virtually impossible. The best critics could do was charge that Selke's dreadnought was too old a club to last long. "They can say what they want," the manager replied. "When our old men stop producing we'll bring up younger fellows who will start producing." He would then unveil charts indicating that the Canadiens had strings on some ten thousand players on 750 teams across the continent. Launched in 1946, Selke's farm system was bigger than the farm systems of all other NHL clubs combined.

There was no need for replacements in 1955–56. By the end of January, Montreal's lead was substantial, but three games with the hated Red Wings loomed on January 29, February 2, and February 4. The loss of all three or even two of three games could have induced a panic, a slump, and lost of first place.

The teams played a 1–1 tie in the first game at Detroit. The Rocket and Beliveau scored in the second match, giving Montreal a 2–0 win. In the third game *Le Gros Bill* scored twice and the Canadiens won, 2–1. They now sported a fifteen-point lead and, for all intents and purposes, the battle for first place was over.

A year after his suspension the Rocket was virtually canonized in Montreal. A French-Canadian record company pressed a disk in his honor, as well as one for Geoffrion, and an English outfit came up with a hillbilly version of the St. Patrick's Day riot called "The Saga of Rocket Richard." His goals received as thunderous a response as ever, and from time to time, when Gordie Howe visited the Forum, the crowd would boo whenever Howe carried the puck.

Conversely, the Forum faithful took a dim view of Geoffrion, as good as he was. They resented the fact that he had wrested the scoring championship away from Maurice while the Rocket was under suspension, and they generally made life miserable for the normally ebullient Boomer. Geoffrion was so despondent about the negative reaction that he seriously considered retiring before the 1955–56 campaign.

"It was not my fault the Rocket was suspended," Geoffrion would say in defense of his position. "I couldn't deliberately not score. So I was sick of the whole thing. Even thinking about hockey made me throw up. I wanted to get away from hockey. But then before practices began Beliveau and Richard visited me. And they urged me to stay in the game."

Plante was another eccentric. Some people contend that he was a hypochondriac. Others noticed that he did, in fact, suffer from asthma and in cities such as Toronto he would divorce himself from the team and stay at a select "nonasthmatic" hotel. At the time, Blake didn't mind that. "Starting that season," said the coach, "and for five years, he was the greatest goalie the league has ever seen."

Interestingly, the Habitants' defense was not all that tough in the Murder, Inc. sense of the word. They didn't have to be. With the forwards outskating the opposition at every turn, the defensemen were mobile enough to outwit the enemy with brainpower and speed without resorting to violence.

The foundation of the defence, Harvey, had only one "flaw." He was so laconic in style, so calmly sure of himself, that he executed plays of extreme complication with consummate ease. Lacking the flamboyance of Eddie Shore or other Hall of Fame defensemen, Harvey was slow to receive the acclaim he deserved. But by 1955–56 it had become apparent that he was superior to Shore in many ways. "Doug Harvey was the greatest defenseman who ever played hockey — bar none," said Blake. "Usually a defenseman specializes in one thing and builds a reputation on that, but Doug could do everything well."

Not far behind Harvey in all-around ability was Tom Johnson, himself a well-coordinated puck-carrier and a solid man behind

---

the blueline. "It took everybody a long time to know that Johnson was as good as we knew he was," said Blake. In 1970 Johnson was inducted into the Hockey Hall of Fame.

With this abundance of stars Blake was careful not to introduce any bizarre stratagem that would disrupt the team. Under Irvin, the Canadiens had become renowned for what was known as "Firewagon Hockey," which, as the name implies, accented the rush, rush, rush until the enemy was run through the ice with exhaustion. Peter Gzowski said he preferred to describe the Canadiens' trademark as élan. "On the ice," he wrote, "the Canadiens swoop and gambol, skating like fury and burning with zeal; they are somehow romantic, like Scaramouche or Cyrano or Jean Gascon."

Blake was acutely aware of this quality. All he did was improve on Irvin's failing psychology. Everything else then fell perfectly into play. "Your style of coaching has to depend upon the players you have," said Blake, "because if you try to change the styles of your players, you're in trouble.

"If you're connected with so many superstars as I was, then you've got to let them go all out and let the defense look after itself. And, fortunately, I had a defense that could look after itself. But I told my team that four or five stars don't make a team. Everyone in uniform is important."

With Blake orchestrating his club to perfection, the Canadiens romped home first with ease — twenty-four points, or twelve games, ahead of Detroit. Four of the top seven scorers were Canadiens. Beliveau led the league with eighty-eight points while the Rocket was third with seventy-one, followed by Olmstead's seventy and Geoffrion with sixty-two. Beliveau, Richard, Harvey, and Plante were named to the First All-Star Team. Plante's 1.86 goals-against average gave him the Vezina Trophy. Harvey captured the Norris Trophy as the league's best defenseman and Beliveau was voted the Hart Trophy as the most valuable player in the NHL. The club set a record by winning forty-five games, losing only fifteen, and tying ten for one hundred points.

In the playoffs, the Habs eliminated the Rangers in five, then the Red Wings in five. The Canadiens had regained the Stanley Cup. Butch Bouchard, the tall captain, who was on the verge of retirement, accepted the trophy at center ice and then the champagne flowed. A day later, the citizens who the year before had been the shame of the NHL, proudly toasted their heroes with a thirty-mile parade through the city of Montreal.

"Perhaps to some Montrealers it was as if Bonnie Prince Charlie had become king," said Josh Greenfeld, "perhaps to others it was like the restoration of the Bourbon dynasty. But all of hockey-mad Montreal was happy — in any language."

It was more than that. The deafening cheers were an expression of retribution for the previous year's "crime" against the Rocket as well as a feeling of jubilation about the rosy future, what Canadiens publicist Camil Desroches called "those wonderful five years."

Armed with basically the same lineup as they had iced in 1955–56, the Canadiens won an unparalleled four more Stanley Cups in succession and finished in first place in six out of seven years! "I saw the old Canadiens with Morenz and Joliat," said Muzz Patrick, the Rangers' manager. "There's no comparing that team to this one. This Montreal outfit is many, many times better."

"Nobody seems to be able to skate with them, to shoot with them," said New York columnist Jimmy Powers, "and if, as happens, they have a bad night and get licked, it is an event." Such was the case until 1960, although the Canadiens were experiencing an inner upheaval of major proportions which would affect the team right up to the present.

While the Canadiens overran the NHL, Selke had surrounded himself with a loyal high command that included Ken Reardon, Toe Blake, and such minor-league operatives as Mickey Hennessy, Del Wilson, Frank Carlin, Sam Pollock, and Mike Kartusch.

At the top of the pyramid was Senator Donat Raymond, who scrupulously avoided interference with Selke's day-to-day operation of the Canadiens' empire. Both Selke and Raymond were getting on in years, and it was believed that sooner or later sucessors would have to be chosen. The obvious heir to Selke's throne was the popular cigar-smoking Reardon who was related to Senator Raymond through marriage. Reardon traveled extensively with the Montreal sextet and was often called upon as club spokesman in Selke's absence. He was a hockey man with insight and something of the same respectful legacy as a player that Blake possessed.

Finding someone to follow in Senator Raymond's footsteps would be another story. The Senator was a wealthy and distinguished French-Canadian with a genuine love for hockey and a passionate interest in *Les Canadiens*. When Senator Raymond began suffering from ill health, he confided to Selke that he preferred the next Hab boss come from the Molson family, one of the most respected and oldest in the province of Quebec. Selke acted as unofficial liaison between Raymond and Senator Hartland de Montigny Molson, who headed the Molson Brewery, one of Canada's largest makers of beer and ale.

Prior to the 1957–58 season the Molson family acquired the Canadian Arena Company with Senator Molson at the helm. Like Raymond, Molson had the respect of both the French- and English-speaking communities of Montreal. He was an avid sportsman and had served as a fighter pilot during the Battle of Britain.

Having a powerful organization such as Molson's Brewery behind the NHL club was unprecedented and it raised conjecture about whether the character of the Canadiens would change. At first there was no perceptible alteration in the team's image and structure. Selke remained at the controls, flanked by his trusted lieutenants. Undisturbed, Blake ran the team with his usual efficiency, although there were occasional signs that he was feeling more pressure as a winner than most coaches do as losers.

Conversely, the Rocket appeared more relaxed than ever and he, in turn, became almost beloved, if that's possible, in alien arenas throughout the league. When he scored a hat trick at Olympia Stadium in Detroit in October, 1957, he received a standing ovation. "It took sixteen years," said Detroit writer Marshall Dann, "but the time finally came when Rocket Richard drew more cheers than jeers in Detroit." The Rocket soon scored his five-hundredth NHL goal and said, "I'm dedicating it to Dick Irvin. He taught me everything I know about hockey."

Richard had leaped ahead of the scoring race in 1957–58 like a Kentucky Derby sprinter. By the second week in November it appeared that, at last, he would go on to win that elusive scoring championship. Then tragedy struck again. While playing against the Maple Leafs at Toronto on November 13, the Rocket tangled with defenseman Marc Reaume of the Leafs. It was an innocent collision, ironically different from so many of Richard's clashes with his foes.

As Reaume scrambled to his feet, his razor-sharp skate blade sliced between Richard's tendon guard and his stocking. Reaume pressed forward and in so doing, his blade cut into Richard's tendon, almost snapping it in half. The Rocket was carried into the Maple Leaf Gardens' hospital where Dr. Jim Murray administered fifteen stitches to the wound. "He was lucky," said Dr. Murray.

"Just a shade more and the tendon would have snapped. Had this happened it could very well have meant the end of his career."

Richard was thirty-six years old at the time of the mishap and it was freely predicted that this would be the end of the line for him, whether he recovered completely or not. But by February 20, 1958, Richard was back in the lineup and celebrated his return with two goals and two near-misses.

In the fourth game of the semifinal playoff round against Detroit, the Rocket celebrated his one-thousandth NHL game by scoring a hat trick. It pulled the Canadiens up from what appeared to be a 3–1 loss and guided them to a 4–1 series victory over the Red Wings. Between the Boomer and the Rocket, Montreal defeated Boston, four games to two, to win the Stanley Cup once more.

Selke's only concern for the future related to the 1958 NHL draft. Toronto did the most significant raiding and came away with Bert Olmstead, the tenacious and pestiferous digger who had lent so much support to Beliveau and Geoffrion. Any suggestions that Olmstead was over the hill were dissipated in future seasons, but neither Blake nor Selke appeared terribly concerned. They had designated tall, husky Ab McDonald to replace Olmstead and also promoted speedy Ralph Backstrom from their farm system to operate at center.

Over the years Backstrom would prove to be an effective big-leaguer but never the star his early press notices suggested. He won the Calder Trophy as rookie of the year in 1958–59 with eighteen goals and twenty-two assists, but he symbolized something about Montreal rookies that would plague the Canadiens to the present. By an unfortunate (although some debate the term) stroke of fate or genetics, some of the finest players to come up through the Canadiens' system happened to be small of stature and disinclined to the brutal warfare of hockey. Players like Andre Boudrias, Yvan Cournoyer, and Bobby Rousseau were among them — all worthies and stars in junior hockey but lacking that extra beef so often needed in the NHL. Backstrom was among the first and he managed to dazzle with his footwork in the early years although he never became a star. But by the spring of 1959 Backstrom's promise was so enormous that Chicago Black Hawks' owner Jim Norris offered Selke $135,000 for the young center. Selke's reply was an unequivocal "no."

Such affluence began to have an interesting effect on Montreal's crowds. They still reserved hoarse cheers for the beloved Rocket but success turned them, once more, into vocal critics. Perfection was expected at every turn, and when it wasn't accomplished, scapegoats were quickly found. One of the first was goalie Jacques Plante. Still the best in the league, "Jake the Snake" occasionally enraged spectators with his scrambles behind the net for the puck. Once, the play backfired on him. He missed the disk; an opponent retrieved it and shoved the rubber into the yawning cage before Plante could return to guard it. In November, 1958, Plante's goals-against average began climbing. "Worse than that is Plante's nervousness," snapped Blake.

Our home fans have been riding him and he's let it get his goat. It's affecting his work. He's got to get over it; after all he is a professional . . . The only way to shut up a guy who boos you is to play better. If you have a bad year, he'll boo all the more. This ought to make Plante fight back. Instead, he's getting worse. I realize that as a French-Canadian, Jacques is more emotional than a lot of guys. But Bill Durnan wasn't a French-Canadian and it got him. Same with Wilf Cude. Same with Gerry McNeil.

"I know what Plante is going through," said Durnan. "The only thing Jacques can do is hitch up his pants and let them boo."

The Blake-Plante tension was, perhaps, even more ominous than it seemed. Severe to a fault, the coach was down on his goaltender and was to become more and more disenchanted with Plante's behavior as the seasons progressed. Ultimately, it resulted in a rupture that never healed and Plante, not Blake, was sent on his way. Blake would have preferred it if Plante had displayed the uncompromising attitude toward the game that marked the personality of his buddy, the Rocket. Now there was a man! The elder Richard kept steaming along, completely recovered from his tendon mishap and as dedicated as ever. "He lives for only one thing in life," said Blake, "to score goals."

The Rocket returned to the lineup in time for the 1959 Cup final against Toronto. The Leafs managed just one victory, despite numerous perorations by Toronto general manager-coach Punch Imlach, and the Canadiens walked off with an unprecedented fourth-straight Stanley Cup victory.

TORONTO:
GOODBYE,
BILL BARILKO,
GOODBYE,
MAPLE LEAFS

It was believed that with a patch here and a patch there the Leafs would be quite capable of winning an unprecedented fourth-straight Stanley Cup. There would be problems, to be sure, and the biggest was Turk Broda.

The corpulent goaltender had celebrated his thirty-fifth birthday, and there was considerable doubt that he still had the reflexes to handle the firewagon hockey of the fifties. At first Broda allayed everyone's fears, and the Leafs marched into first place on November 1, 1949. But then a series of injuries decimated the lineup, and by November 30 the Leafs had gone six games without a win, tying only one match. It was then that Smythe declared what became known as hockey's "Battle of the Bulge."

"It's condition that's needed," said Smythe. "Nothing but condition. It if isn't Turk's fault, we'll find out whose it is."

Smythe's opening salvo in the battle was a demand that his players reduce their weight to specified limits. Broda, at 197 pounds was ordered to lose seven. To underline the seriousness of his offensive, Smythe promptly called up reserve goalie Gil Mayer from his Pittsburgh farm team. "We're starting Mayer in our next game," Smythe asserted, "and he'll stay in here even if the score is 500-to-one against the Leafs — and I don't think it will be."

This was the supreme insult to Broda, who except for a stint in the army had kept the Toronto net under lock and key, the old specter of backup goalie Phil Stein notwithstanding. But Smythe was unimpressed. On a Tuesday he gave Turk until Saturday to fulfill the weight demand. "I'm taking Broda out of the nets," Smythe said, "and he's not going back until he shows some common sense. Two seasons ago he weighed 185. Last season he went up to 190 — and now this. A goalie has to have fast reflexes, and you can't move fast when you're overweight."

Smythe's outburst reverberated across Canada and parts of the United States, and soon the Battle of the Bulge became a *cause célèbre*. Neutral observers regarded Turk's tussle with the scales as a huge joke, win or lose, but to the Toronto boss it was no joke. None of the Leafs was particularly amused either.

Toronto restaurant owner Sam Shopsowitz took an ad in the local papers, declaring, "For that *'Old* Broda' look, eat at Shopsy's." Another newspaper featured a caricature of Broda stopping eight pucks at once with the caption: "Just three weeks ago I was the best goalkeeper in the league. If I'd only eaten a few more king-sized steaks at the Palisades, I'd be fat enough to fill the whole net and they would never score on me!"

After a day of severe dieting Turk trimmed his weight from 197 to 193. Even so, by midweek Broda had still not reached the magic number, and Smythe dropped another bombshell, sending five players as well as cash "in five figures" to Cleveland for twenty-three-year-old goalie Al Rollins. According to hockey experts, Rollins was the best professional goalie outside the NHL. The acquisition of Rollins underscored the gravity of Broda's position. "I don't blame Mr. Smythe," Turk said, "I guess we had to learn the hard way."

After much effort and considerable unsolicited advice from well-wishers across Canada Broda was able to get his weight down to just under 190 pounds. In his first game back he recorded a shutout and went on to post a very respectable 2.45 goals-against average for the season, good enough for a Second All-Star-Team berth. His dieting teammates also got in line weightwise.

Going into the 1950 Stanley Cup semifinals against the Red Wings, the key Leafs were perceived to be Broda and Kennedy, and, to a lesser extent, clutch-scorer Bentley. Since the mid-thirties, when Detroit's Jack Adams and Toronto's Conn Smythe had waged war with one another, no love had been lost between the two clubs, and this contest continued the inglorious tradition.

One incident, more than any other, was pivotal. Late in the third period of the first game, as Toronto was coasting on a 4–0 lead, Gordie Howe attempted to check Ted Kennedy but narrowly missed and crashed headfirst into the boards. Unconscious, Howe was removed to hospital where at first there was some doubt he would survive. Although all the reports exonerated Kennedy of any responsibility for Howe's injury, the Leaf captain became the target of vicious Detroit physical and verbal abuse for the rest of the series.

At one point, the Wings' Lee Fogolin sent Kennedy rolling with a stick trip. When play halted, as Fogolin was en route to the penalty box, Ted Lindsay rushed up and crosschecked Kennedy back down to the ice. Toronto's Gus Mortson flew at Lindsay, and fights broke out all over the rink. The Leafs' Jim Thomson fell, about twenty feet out from the Detroit goal, and Leo Reise bludgeoned him across the head and shoulders with his stick. Thomson was momentarily defenseless as Reise slashed away. By this time Kennedy was on the other side of the rink, and Reise moved over to get in some more stick work, this time across Kennedy's shoulders.

Lindsay returned and rushed at Kennedy, his stick held high; then Abel came on, flailing with his fists. A fan grabbed Kennedy and held his arms as other Wings struck him. Broda, handicapped by thirty-five pounds of leg pads, trundled over to assist his teammate. Lindsay and Abel persisted in their determined efforts.

The series ultimately went to seven games, to be decided on Olympia ice where the Red Wings won, 1–0, on a sudden-death overtime goal by Leo Reise.

The final round between the Red Wings and the New York Rangers might have been anticlimactic except that it too went into overtime in the seventh game, during which Detroit won the Stanley Cup. Soon after the victory a statement was issued from the Detroit camp that the Maple Leafs' dynasty was dead. The Leafs were wounded, perhaps, but as events to follow in 1950–51 would prove, they were very much alive.

Conn Smythe was not overly depressed by Toronto's defeat. Moments after the Red Wings had won the seventh and final game of the 1950 semifinal series, Smythe walked into the Toronto dressing room and addressed his troops. "You've got nothing to be ashamed of," he said. "For four years you played like champions. That's quite a reign, and I'm proud of you all."

Yet Smythe knew that it was time for a change. Hap Day, who had won five Stanley Cups in only ten years as coach, was promoted to assistant manager. Gentleman Joe Primeau, the man who retired as a Toronto center on the night Turk Broda made his Maple Leafs debut, was appointed coach.

"If enough of our boys become men," Smythe announced on the eve of the 1950–51 season, "we will be a great hockey team."

The "boys" to whom Smythe alluded were goalie Al Rollins, Broda's stand-in; left wing Denny Lewicki, a Junior sensation; defenseman Hugh Bolton; and center George Armstrong. Smythe also was concerned about his favorite fat man. "Broda," said Smythe, "is like a man on a teeter-totter. When he's up, he can compete with the best. When he's down — well, he's down, and so is his goaling. The thing is, will he be up enough to do the job for us?''

For the first month of the season Broda was up more than he was down. By November 2, 1950, the Maple Leafs sat securely in first place and had gone nine games without a loss. The kids were coming through as Smythe had hoped, and there even were a few surprises. The best surprise of all was the acquisition of a forward named Tod Sloan. The Leafs had twice before rejected him because of his small size, but he had given up smoking and gained fifteen pounds. "Tod is his own boss," said Smythe. "He does what he likes with the puck. It took us a few years to discover that the best way to handle him is to leave him alone."

The Torontonians were hailed as the best team in hockey. "They have three front lines, each of which is better than Detroit's Production Line," said Rangers manager Frank Boucher. "And not only that but their passing is the best of any team since pre-war days. They've got the best power play I've seen in a long time."

The balance wheel of the power play was Max Bentley, the thirty-year-old center whose wrist shot terrorized enemy goaltenders. Max credited his off-season dairy work for his shooting success. "I milk eight cows twice a day," he explained. "Milking develops powerful wrists, and strong wrists generate powerful shots. Weight doesn't matter as long as the wrists are flexible and powerful."

As the season approached its regular-schedule conclusion with the Leafs a strong second, Smythe had plenty to smile about. His decision to alternate young Al Rollins with Turk Broda had proved to be a brilliant maneuver. In fact, as the Wings and Leafs entered the final weekend of the season, Detroit goalie Terry Sawchuk held a mere two-goal lead over Broda-Rollins in the Vezina Trophy race. The Red Wings had one remaining game — against Montreal — while the Leafs had a home-and-home series against Boston, starting on March 24 in Toronto.

The Canadiens beat Sawchuk three times, putting the onus squarely on Rollins's goalie stick. At Maple Leaf Gardens on Saturday, March 24, Rollins was superb. He stopped the Bruins cold until the last period, when Johnny Peirson beat him, and shut them out the rest of the way as Toronto whipped the visitors 4–1. The teams returned to Boston Garden on Sunday night with Rollins nursing a one-goal lead over Sawchuk in the Vezina derby.

"Rollins," wrote Hal Walker in the Toronto *Globe and Mail*, "must have felt like the man waiting in death row for the executioner before the final game."

But Al had won his last six games of the schedule, allowing only seven goals in that stretch. The question perplexing the hockey world was whether he could come up with a shutout against the Bruins on Boston's home ice. A crowd of 8,472 turned out to learn the answer.

"The Toronto team," wrote Walker, "was concerned only with one thing, keeping Bruin attackers from their boy's vital bastion. And this they did with a determined show of checking, rarely electing to move past center ice."

However, there were some Maple Leafs bent on scoring. Sid Smith, who entered the game with a total of twenty-nine goals, was eager to reach the coveted thirty-goal plateau. "I promise," said Teeder Kennedy before the opening faceoff, "that I'll set you up for it."

But neither team scored in the first period, and in the second the close-checking Leafs permitted Boston only one shot on goal. Rollins needed only twenty more minutes of shutout hockey to reach the Vezina.

For more than three quarters of the third period Rollins was flawless. Then at the seventeen-minute mark Kennedy skated over the Boston blueline and spotted Smith, who was partially covered by Boston defenseman Bill Quakenbush. "As he had promised he would," wrote Hal Walker, "Kennedy set him up with a neat pass, and Sid outbattled Quakenbush to get his stick on the puck and put it beyond goalie Jack Gelineau's reach."

When Smith had scored his thirtieth goal, defense was the only strategy concerning the Maple Leafs. Rollins was tested sharply by Peirson, but he stopped the Boston forward with a sliding stop and smothered the puck to prevent a rebound. That move deflated the Bruins, and the clock ticked away the remaining seconds until the siren ended the game. Rollins waved his stick in glee and was surrounded by teammates, who pounded his back as they stormed into the dressing room. It was now time for more important matters than the Vezina Trophy; the playoffs were upon them.

"This is a new deal," said coach Primeau. "What you accomplished during the season is all out the window. This is the final examination, and everyone must go all out."

The Bruins supplied the opposition for Toronto in the first round, and any indications that Boston would lay dead were dispelled in the opening game, at Maple Leaf Gardens. Not only did the visitors win, 2–0, but they also managed to dispatch Rollins to the hospital on a controversial play in which Boston forward Pete Horeck charged the Toronto goalie and tore his left knee ligaments.

Broda was rushed in to replace Rollins. "He has assumed the mantle of responsibility again," said Primeau. "We have to be the ball carriers this time. We have to go out there and play some hockey."

Barilko put Toronto ahead in the first period, but Peirson tied it in the second. Nobody scored in the third, and neither team could get a goal in the sudden-death overtime. Because of a Toronto midnight "Blue Law" the game was called after the first sudden-death overtime as a 1–1 tie.

The Bruins had believed that by knocking Rollins out of the series they had paved the route to the Stanley Cup finals. But old reliable Turk Broda needed only two games to regain his playoff form. He shut out the Bruins 3–0 then beat them 3–1 in Boston. "The Turkey," commented Joe Perlove in the Toronto *Star*, "merely has played like everybody who knows the Turkey expects him to play — just slightly better than sensational."

Toronto swept the series with 4–1 and 6–0 victories, and the Montreal Canadiens upset Detroit, to qualify for the finals against the Leafs. On the eve of the battle Smythe's former aide, Selke, remarked:

> I hope this series will be as clean and sporting as ours with Detroit, but unfortunately I doubt it. Those lurid games with a lot of socking, bloodletting, and penalties may get the passing attention and create temporary excitement, but over the long stretch it is the sort of hockey Canadiens and Wings played that is going to make a lasting contribution to the welfare of the game.

As the series unfolded, it turned out be more the way Selke had hoped. By any standards it was a Stanley Cup classic and the finest hour for many Maple Leafs, particularly defenseman Bill Barilko.

At first notorious for his bashing snake-hip bodychecks, Barilko had matured into a vigorous two-way player whose exuberance was matched by his ability. The man of the hour in this game, though, was Sid Smith. Smith opened the scoring against the Canadiens, and with the score tied 2–2 in overtime, Smith closed the scoring. But not before Barilko saved the day.

Just when it appeared that Rocket Richard had Broda beaten, Barilko dove in front of the shot and deflected it wide of the target. Then the Leafs carried the puck into Montreal territory. Canadiens defensemen Doug Harvey and Bud MacPherson appeared to have regained control when Tod Sloan swooped in on them and poked the puck free. Sloan slid a fast pass to Smith, who, in turn, rapped the puck past goalie Gerry McNeil at 5:51 of sudden-death.

The Barilko-Smith save was a tough act to follow, but the Rocket proved he could follow any act by putting a suden-death overtime shot past Broda in the second game, sending the teams back to Montreal tied at one game apiece.

In the third game Richard put Montreal into the lead only to have Sid Smith tie the score. For the third-straight game the clubs went into sudden-death overtime, with one difference: Primeau had benched Broda in favor of the younger Rollins. The move paid off handsomely.

Three times within the first four minutes of overtime the Canadiens pierced the Toronto defense, and each time Rollins was equal to the occasion. The third shot, fired by Ken Mosdell, was so blistering that it bounced behind Rollins, but Teeder Kennedy rushed in and cleared the puck out of danger. Eventually it moved into Montreal territory, where Sloan retrieved it. He put a short pass onto Kennedy's stick, and the captain beat McNeil at 4:47, putting Toronto in the series lead, two games to one.

"I was so weak when Teeder shot that winner," said Rollins, "that I couldn't holler, although I wanted to shout and shout."

Never before in the history of Stanley Cup play had there been four consecutive sudden-death overtime games, but that record was to be broken at the Montreal Forum on Thursday night, April 19, 1951. A goal by Canadien Elmer Lach tied the match at 2–2, setting up the extra session.

Once again Rollins blocked the Canadiens, and with five minutes of overtime gone, Max Bentley intercepted the puck from the Montreal defenders. At that moment Primeau ordered a line change, and left wing Harry Watson, just recovering from an injury, jumped over the boards and moved into high gear. He shoved the puck past defenseman Doug Harvey, retrieved it, and sped clear in on goalie McNeil. His shot from the left side flew past McNeil's outstretched left leg and into the webbing at 5:15. Toronto needed only one more win for the Stanley Cup.

As the teams prepared for the fifth game, at Maple Leaf Gardens, experts wondered whether it was possible for there to be still another overtime, "There are two schools of thought on tonight's game," wrote Al Nickleson in the Toronto *Globe and Mail.*

One is that the Leafs will break out for a decisive win in regulation time after battering down an early Montreal drive.

Another viewpoint is that the game will be just as close as the others, and there's fearful speculation among some followers that if it moves into overtime, that great opportunist Rocket Richard will do as he did a week ago . . . . There's a possibility, too, that neither team will triumph. Overtime could run into the Saturday night curfew and force replay of the game later, if necessary.

Feeling in the Montreal camp was remarkably confident under the circumstances. "The Canadiens are so confident they're going to win in Toronto," wrote Dink Carroll in the Montreal *Gazette*, "that they've neglected to bring anything along with which to break training in case they lose."

The Habs reinforced their pregame confidence by taking the lead twice. Rocket Richard opened the scoring. Then Tod Sloan tied the score for Toronto less than four minutes later. With Eddie Mazur of the Canadiens harassing him all the way from center ice, Sloan managed to beat goalie McNeil with a hard shot. But the Canadiens kept coming on in wave after wave. At 4:47 of the third period Montreal rookie Paul Meger captured a rebound from Doug Harvey's shot and beat Rollins.

Fortified with a 2–1 lead, the Canadiens had to tighten their defenses and hope that McNeil could repulse the Leafs' drives. As expected, the Toronto players stepped up their attack with enormous gusto and several times appeared to have the tying goal on their sticks.

"It began to look as if almost singlehandedly McNeil was going to beat them," said Dink Carroll. "How he stopped some of the shots they fired at him nobody knew, but stop them he did. There were times when he went to the ice and players of both teams, battling desperately, piled up in the crease. At the bottom of the pile would be little Gerry with the puck."

He baffled the Leafs until there was only a minute and thirty seconds remaining in the third period. The faceoff was deep in the Montreal zone. Strategists on both sides immediately went to work.

Joe Primeau took the big gamble. He ordered Rollins from the Toronto net and replaced him with Max Bentley, whom he stationed at the blueline alongside defenseman Gus Mortson. The four remaining skaters — Teeder Kennedy, Sid Smith, Tod Sloan, and Harry Watson — were placed in a line facing the goalmouth.

Dick Irvin countered with his most diligent defensive players: Ken Mosdell, Floyd Curry, Ed Mazur, Tom Johnson, and Butch Bouchard. Referee Bill Chadwick ordered the players to line up for the faceoff. The puck was dropped, and a wild scramble followed. Only three seconds had elapsed before referee Chadwick whistled for another faceoff.

Undecided about his strategy, Irvin sent Elmer Lach onto the ice to replace Mosdell; then he changed his mind and recalled Lach. Mosdell snared the puck from the faceoff and nearly put the puck into the open Toronto net, but back-skating Harry Watson intercepted it in time. With sixty-one seconds remaining, the faceoff was just outside the Montreal blueline. Day dispatched Rollins back to the Toronto goal with instructions to race for the bench if the Leafs pushed the puck into Canadiens territory. Teeder Kennedy won the faceoff and looped the puck to the boards, where players from both teams jammed heavily. Chadwick whistled a stoppage of play.

At this point Irvin committed the pivotal mistake. He removed his defensive aces and replaced them with Elmer Lach, Rocket Richard, and Bert Olmstead, his crack offensive unit. Lach skated opposite Kennedy for the critical faceoff.

Sitting in the stands, Canadiens managing director Frank Selke fidgeted as the players lined up on the ice. He remembered how he had fought to obtain Teeder Kennedy for the Leafs and how it ultimately had cost him his job in Toronto. He knew that Teeder was the best faceoff man in the business.

Kennedy dug his blades into the ice, riveting his eyes on the linesman's hand. The instant the puck hit the ice his stick flashed. The puck moved swiftly to the blueline, where Max Bentley trapped it and immediately skated in the direction of the Montreal goal. Lurching like a scared jackrabbit, Bentley finally decided there were too many bodies in front of the net to attempt a flanking movement. He shot the puck at the mass of legs and it bounced loose. Sid Smith, the Leafs' prime opportunist, snared the rebound and whacked a shot at McNeil. He beat the Canadiens goalie, but the puck hit the goal post and bounced free. It appeared that McNeil's luck would save him, but Sloan had forced his way to a point just outside the goal crease, and when Smith's shot caromed free, Sloan swiped the rebound past the beleaguered McNeil and tied the score with only thirty-two seconds remaining in regulation time.

"The balance of power paid off for Toronto," said *Globe and Mail* sports editor Jim Vipond. "The Leafs had strength in depth while the Canadiens had heart and desire but couldn't match the manpower."

Still, with a break here or there and the great Rocket Richard firing, Montreal still could win the game in overtime, the fifth consecutive heart-breaker.

"What the fans said out in the corridor during the ten-minute intermission sounded like gibberish," Dink Carroll remembered. "They mouthed words that made no sense, whacked each other on the back, and their hands shook when they lighted cigarettes."

When the teams trooped onto the ice for overtime, the big question was whether the Canadiens could withstand the psychological blow of losing the lead so late in regulation time. Primeau decided to use a line consisting of Howie Meeker, hero of past Cup triumphs, Cal Gardner, and Harry Watson, another playoff star. The coach had some qualms about sending Barilko out on defense.

"Bill had been committing himself too much, going on offense," Primeau later explained. "He would get caught out of position, which was dangerous with Rocket Richard on the ice. I finally told him I'd fine him if he didn't lay back and concentrate on defense."

Primeau finally decided to put Barilko onto the ice, and Selke once again fidgeted in his seat. Earlier in the series the Canadiens' managing director had said he hated Barilko so much he wanted him on the Montreal team!

Referee Chadwick dropped the puck that launched the sudden-death overtime. Without hesitation the Maple Leafs took command and forced their way past the Canadiens' defense. Meeker took the first shot, but McNeil punted it out of danger. Montreal's attack was feeble, and in no time at all the Leafs captured momentum. "The Canadiens were inconsequential and indecisive," said Baz O'Meara of the Montreal *Star*. "The tired defense was wobbling in front of McNeil."

All the Canadiens needed, however, was someone to shovel the puck to Richard. With a quick burst he could round the Toronto defense and test young Rollins. But the Montreal attack was deflated soon after it got going, and with more than two minutes elapsed Harry Watson's legs pumped mightily as he skated across center ice to no man's land. Richard made a futile attempt at intercepting him, but Watson skimmed the puck into the Canadiens zone with linemate Howie Meeker in speedy pursuit.

Meeker took control of the puck behind Montreal's net. His plan was simple; to swerve sharply in front of the goal and take McNeil by surprise. The play almost worked, but McNeil covered up in time, stopping the shot and the rebound drive by Watson. But McNeil couldn't control the second rebound, and he fell to the ice as the puck slid tantalizingly out to the blueline, where Bill Barilko should have been positioned.

Barilko had remembered coach Primeau's warning about not drifting too deep into the enemy zone and had deliberately placed himself "safely" on the wrong side of the blueline. Suddenly, he saw the puck coming at him. In that split-second he had to decide whether to chance getting caught out of position and rush in for the puck or to play it safe and allow it to drift over the blueline, where he could organize another rush. He decided to gamble.

Literally running on the tips of his skates, Barilko lurched over the blueline, and in one motion hurled his 5' 11", 185-pound body at the puck.

As he stroked the puck from his left, Barilko momentarily floated in the air, his legs spread out behind him, his hands clutching the stick, which was held horizontal across his body, and his head tilted slightly upward so that he could follow the trail of the flying puck.

Richard was to Barilko's left, Butch Bouchard to his right, but neither was close enough to block the hard drive. Cal Gardner was directly behind Barilko. In that brief second of flight Barilko's eyes changed from an expression of anxiety to expectant glee. He was still aloft when the puck cleared McNeil's raised right glove and barely eluded the neck of his stick. Two minutes and fifty-three seconds after the start of the sudden-death period it hit the twine, at a height of three feet. By the time Barilko landed, he was practically atop McNeil's right skate. For one breathless split-second the 14,577 witnesses to one of the greatest hockey games ever played held their collective breath. Then they realized it was over. "The walls of the rink vibrated with noise," said Carroll.

Toronto players left the bench and swarmed on the ice to join their teammates as they mobbed Barilko. The defeated Canadiens stood still, looking disconsolate, until they remembered their manners and skated over to congratulate the winners.

Primeau, who had coached two Memorial Cup champion teams and one Allan Cup champion, was one of the first on the ice. He dashed to Barilko, hugged him several times, and shouted, 'I won't fine you for charging on that one!'

Later, in the Leaf dressing room, captain Teeder Kennedy sipped champagne from the Stanley Cup once more and wrapped his arms around coach Primeau. "If anyone deserves credit more than any other," said Kennedy, "it's our coach."

A deathly silence pervaded the visitors' dressing room just a few yards away. McNeil and Richard sobbed openly. "Those two long overtime games against the Red Wings in the semifinals took a lot out of our guys," said coach Irvin. "And the Leafs had a fairly easy time with Boston. That may have been the difference."

Of course, it was more than that. Smythe had constructed a dynasty in 1946, and it still was evident in 1951. "Max Bentley," said Smythe, "is the greatest pivot man the game ever has seen." There were other aces, to be sure: Thomson, Mortson, Sloan, Meeker, Watson, and Gardner, to name only a few. But Bill Barilko was the guts of the Maple Leafs, and as long as he was around, there was a very good chance that Toronto would retain the Stanley Cup.

Bill Barilko had the world on a string during the spring of 1951. His electrifying Cup-winning goal had made him the toast of Toronto, if not of all Canada. He was a star who could relate to people, and everyone, from newsmen to fans in the cheapest seats, savored Barilko's glory. He was a hero in the finest tradition of Syl Apps and Teeder Kennedy. Apps and Kennedy were more the serious types, lacking Barilko's natural *joie de vivre*. By contrast, "Bashing" Bill could laugh it up with anyone — the guys at the neighborhood tavern or kids playing street hockey on the corner.

In August Barilko was invited to take an airplane ride over the northern Ontario lake and forest country with Dr. Henry Hudson, a pilot friend. A native of Timmins, Barilko was familiar with the vast virgin land with its bountiful fish and game, and he looked forward to the flight with his usual enthusiasm. He bade his pals goodbye and said that he would report to training camp in top shape.

It was the last time anyone heard from Bill Barilko.

The plane disappeared among the dense trees in the unmarked territory. Search parties probed the area continually until October, 1951, but failed to uncover any sign of the plane or passengers.

When the Maple Leafs skated out for the opening home game against the Chicago Black Hawks, on October 13, Barilko's sweater, number five, was hanging in the locker room. "Until the fate of Barilko is definitely known," said the *Globe and Mail*, "the Leafs refuse to acknowledge that he won't be back."

But Barilko never did return, and it soon became clear that the Leafs would never be the same without him. Conn Smythe said that Toronto would drop to fourth place without the defense ace. "The loss of Bill Barilko," said Rangers manager Frank Boucher, "will be felt a great deal more than anyone realizes."

The loss of Barilko was the major plank ripped out of the Maple Leafs' foundation, but there was another. Howie Meeker announced that he was going to retire in order to pursue a career in politics.

Although Broda was still on the Leafs' roster, Rollins was regarded as the number-one Toronto goalie. But even angular Al had lost the Vezina-Trophy touch. "Since the Fat Man stopped breathing down his neck," Smythe explained, "Rollins hasn't been going too well. Some of the shots that have been beating him shouldn't be beating him."

Even New York Rangers coach Bill Cook put the rap on Rollins. "He's first class when he's ahead and coasting," said Cook, "but he's likely to go to pieces when things are going against him."

Cook also predicted: "I can't see Toronto keeping the Cup. The Maple Leafs aren't championship caliber anymore. Smythe always brings the cream of the crop up from the minors, but the cream has curdled."

The extent of the curdle would be determined by the Stanley Cup playoffs. Toronto, without Barilko, had finished the regular season in third place, behind first-place Detroit and second-place Montreal. If there was any substance to the Leaf club, it would become evident in the playoffs against the Red Wings.

The series opened at Olympia Stadium with Detroit emphatically on top, 3–0. "Don't worry, fellows," said captain Kennedy, "only four more games against these guys and we'll have them." It was a hollow promise.

Smythe realized that his club was in trouble and decided to execute his ace in the hole. He benched Rollins and started ancient Broda in the second match, on March 27, 1952. Just shy of thirty-eight years old, fat Turk played brilliantly, giving up only one goal. But the Leafs were held scoreless and returned to Toronto down two games to none.

"Turk," said Smythe, "is the greatest champion of them all." Conn asked him to play again the third game, at Maple Leaf Gardens. Broda held fast for one period, giving up two goals while the Leafs scored one. But he couldn't stop Detroit's mighty machine after that, and when the final buzzer had sounded, the score was 6–2 for the Wings.

"In simple language," wrote Al Nickleson in the Toronto *Globe and Mail*, "the defending champions had a lesson in how to play hockey thrown at them by possibly the greatest Detroit team in a long line of standout clubs."

The Red Wings were awesome, to be sure, but the Maple Leafs could do nothing right anymore. "The puck rolls when it should slide," said Max Bentley. "It hops over your stick instead of onto it. We shoot and it hits a leg and deflects away. They shoot, and it hits a leg and goes in."

But the series wasn't over, and diehard Toronto fans recalled the gallant 1942 comeback in a effort to restore their faith in the Leafs. Surely the Leafs would not be beaten in four-straight games.

Harry Watson put Toronto ahead 1–0, beating Detroit goalie Terry Sawchuk at 2:56 of the first period, and the hopes of 13,574 fans in Maple Leafs Gardens soared. "The Leafs came out like the fighting, hard-hitting Toronto teams of old," said Al Nickleson. "They battled fiercest when the odds were greatest."

It was unfortunately too little and too late. Ted Lindsay tied the game for Detroit, and Tony Leswick put the Red Wings ahead to stay before the first period had ended. From that point on Toronto played a desperate and heart-breaking game of catch-up and never could haul down the sensational Red Wings. Sid Abel scored for Detroit in the second period, and the game ended with the Wings on top 3–1. The mighty Red Wings then went on to rout the Montreal Canadiens in four-straight to take the Stanley Cup.

Smythe was ready to concede what he had suspected when Bill Barilko disappeared: the Toronto monarchy, which had won the Stanley Cup four times in five years, had crumbled. Reverting to race horse parlance, "Smythe explained: "If a horse goes to the track too often, you don't get the best racing out of it. Our fellows have been whipped and whipped for a long time. I should think that a change of scenery would be part of the answer, so someone will be getting some good hockey players."

In seasons past Smythe could always count on the Toronto farm system to send Cup-winning players to the big team. This time they failed him. "I thought our young talent would improve more than they did," he explained. "Other clubs got wise that we had thinned out. They checked our big line and blanketed Bentley. We had a lack of scoring defensemen too."

A year earlier his scoring defenseman was Bill Barilko. Smythe could not replace him, and the Leafs continued to flutter downward.

Smythe had hoped that Hugh Bolton, a Toronto university student, could replace Barilko, but the awkward Bolton proved to be injury-prone and lacked Barilko's galvanic qualities. Smythe was persuaded that Rollins could not make it as Maple Leaf goalie, and traded him to Chicago for Harry Lumley. Once again Smythe's luck failed him, Rollins led Chicago into the playoffs for the first time in seven years; the following season he won the Hart Trophy as the NHL's most valuable player.

With Lumley in goal the Leafs finished out of the playoffs for the first time in seven years. They briefly rebounded into third in 1953–54 and 1954–55 but were wiped out of the Cup rounds by Detroit in five games and four games, respectively. Detroit put them out again in five games a year later, by which time it was obvious that Toronto was no longer a challenging factor in the NHL.

The old order changed. Smythe's interests had drifted more to racing than to hockey. At the age of sixty he resigned as manager of the Maple Leafs in favor of Day, but he retained the presidency of the team. Bereft of ability, the Toronto brass turned to slogans. With King Clancy coaching the team in 1955–56, Day promised a team with "guts, goals and glamour." They had only a smidgen of each, however, and dropped from fourth to fifth with Howie Meeker behind the bench. Amid all this confusion a power struggle developed for control of Maple Leaf Gardens and the hockey club. A group led by Smythe's son Stafford spearheaded the revolution, and soon Conn's "little boy" was running the show.

A coach and manager as an eleven-year-old while playing minor hockey, a coach and manager during student days at the University of Toronto, and a manager with the Marlboro Juniors, Stafford alternately lauded and feuded with his father.

"My dad gave me lots or rope and lots to do," said Stafford. "When I was thirty, I was ten years ahead of everybody, and at forty I was ten years behind everybody." He meant that after his father had allowed him to learn so much so soon, Conn continued to regard him as an employee and refused to permit him to make significant decisions. As a result, the younger Smythe decided he had to challenge his father, no matter what the reaction, public or private.

"The people my father respects," said Stafford, "are those who stand up to him and fight. After I learned to do this, he respected me, but we had plenty of scraps."

In 1957, during the Maple Leafs' depression, Conn Smythe decided to pump new blood into the organization. He appointed Stafford chairman of a new Maple Leafs hockey committee. He fired Howie Meeker, who had become general manager. "Meeker," Stafford said, "was too inexperienced."

Stafford Smythe gradually laid the groundwork for a revitalization of the Maple Leaf machine, in much the same way his father had done thirty years earlier. Stafford hired George "Punch" Imlach as assistant general manager to share responsibilities with coach Billy Reay. Then Conn announced in 1958 that he was preparing to relinquish his control of the Gardens and the Leafs' operation.

Meanwhile quite a battle was raging behind the scenes for control of the Leafs on the ice. At first it appeared that Billy Reay, who had succeeded Meeker as coach in 1957–58, would hold the reins for a few years, but the emergence of the ambitious Imlach changed things completely.

At the time few observers expected any significant change in the state of the Maple Leafs. There was certainly nothing about Imlach that suggested great days ahead. But he quietly began making moves that would have long-range value and would, at least for a time, restore to Toronto the dignity exemplified in the past by the likes of Clancy, Conacher, Primeau, Apps, Kennedy, Broda, and Bentley.

Imlach's first critical move was to board a jet for Saskatoon, Saskatchewan, where he signed thirty-three-year-old Johnny Bower to replace Ed Chadwick in goal for the 1958–59 season. It seemed insignificant at the time, but it would prove momentous in what developed into the greatest regular-season comeback ever accomplished by an NHL team.

Imlach's entrance to Maple Leaf Gardens had been something less than arresting. When he came to call on coach Reay in the autumn of 1958, Punch was shunted to the corner of the reception room and told to wait. As Imlach related in his autobiography, *Hockey is a Battle*, he felt as if he were being treated like a bug spray salesman. "And I realized right then," said Imlach, "that what went for that receptionist went for everybody else around Toronto, both in and out of the rink. They didn't know me. I was nothing to them until I made some sort of a reputation with them, some mark."

Just how long Billy Reay would have lasted under Imlach with a winning team is a moot question. Those who believed that they understood the Imlach psyche insisted that, sooner or later, whether the Maple Leafs finished first or last, Punch would take over the entire team, and Reay would get the boot.

Scott Young, one of the few genuinely brilliant hockey writers, was keeping a diary during the 1958–59 season. He later turned his diary into a book, *The Leafs I Knew*. On November 17, 1958, Young made the following entry: "Imlach is emerging as an interesting personality. . . . His shoved-back brown fedora, open gabardine coat, hand-in-pockets stance, and aggressive, quizzical look I think soon will be known in every rink in the land . . . . He is one of the most keep-punching types I've ever met . . . ."

Unfortunately for Reay the Leafs were not in first place by November, 1958; in fact, they were closer to the botom of the league. On November 15 they were beaten at home, 4–1, by Detroit, and even worse they were soundly booed by the Maple Leaf Gardens crowd. Imlach stepped in and warned the players that they would be fined $200 each if they lost their next two games. Ron Stewart's goal with forty seconds remaining enabled them to tie in Boston, but they lost 7–4 in New York.

Imlach was summoned before the Maple Leaf Gardens hockey committee. The question before the brass was simple — to fire or not to fire Billy Reay. In his autobiography Imlach explained his position:

I told them that the team obviously wasn't playing for Reay. I thought he wasn't tough enough on them, that he was trusting them to do things and they were letting him down. They asked me what I would do about it. I said I wasn't the general manager. In a way I put it up to them. That's when they decided to make me the general manager, to be fully responsible for making the rules for the hockey club and for seeing that the coach and players alike stuck to them . . . . I was just wishing that I was more confident that we'd get through the whole thing without anybody losing his job.

It was Grey Cup time in Canada. Even the most rabid hockey fans were turning their attention to the national football classic played that year in Vancouver on November 26. During the week the Leafs had lost two successive games to Detroit. Imlach was on edge. He finally made his move. First he visited Conn Smythe and told him that he was going to fire Reay. Smythe could have stopped the decision and fired Punch on the spot, but instead grudgingly approved. Imlach then proceeded to the office he had shared with Reay. "I'm relieving you of your duties as coach," he asserted.

Reay, who never was enamored of Imlach, leaped out of his chair in disbelief. He demanded to know whether Imlach had informed Smythe. He said he had. By late afternoon the news was on the streets. Reay had been given his walking papers; Imlach would coach and manage the team. Toronto's foremost columnists and sports editors were in Vancouver for the Grey Cup game at the time, and they resented the timing of Imlach's decision. Even Scott Young, who later collaborated with Imlach on his autobiography, was angry. "They wait until every Toronto sports columnist is 3,000 miles away," he wrote, "and sports pages are full of Grey Cup, then they fire Reay." But Young also insightfully observed: "Reay wasn't as easy-going as some people say, but he did think that usually the pride of professionals should be incentive enough. With the Leafs it wasn't."

Imlach's hyperactive ego was nurtured by Stafford Smythe, who gave Punch carte blanche. "Imlach," said Stafford, "has full authority to make whatever changes he sees fit. His main objective is the playoffs. I have dumped the whole building on his shoulders."

To which Punch replied: "If I'm going to be shot, I'd sooner be shot as a lion than as a lamb!"

Reay didn't walk out of Maple Leaf Gardens like a lamb either. He claimed that he had known as far back as training camp that the axe would fall and that Imlach would pull the lever.

"If I had thought about it at the time," said Reay, "I could have named the date. I've been coaching since I was twenty-four, all over the country, working my way up to this job — and then I get undermined."

But the hockey public was not really interested in Reay's post mortem. The fans wanted a winner in Toronto and they were quite willing to see what Imlach could do for them. Punch, in turn, predicted early in December that the last-place Leafs would, in fact, rise up and smite the Rangers, coached by volatile Phil Watson, and finish in a playoff berth.

"Imlach can crow all he wants," laughed Watson. "But it will be the same this year as last. The Rangers will make it; the Leafs won't."

Thus a feud between New York and Toronto that would grow more bitter with each passing month had begun. With a likely playoff team Watson was riding high while Imlach still was struggling, trying to make a winner out of the Maple Leafs. In an attempt to confuse the opposition, one night Imlach started a lineup of five defensemen — Carl Brewer at center, Noel Price at left wing, Bob Baun on the right, and Tim Horton and Al Stanley playing back. But the Leafs still were in last place in January, and Watson's needles became sharper.

"All the time," Watson snapped, "Imlach is saying 'I did this and I did that. I've won so many games since I took over.' Before that it was always 'we' or 'those guys.' Wasn't Imlach with the club at that time? Always he's predicting what the Leafs are going to do. The only crystal ball he's got is on his shoulders. What a beautiful head of skin!"

Although it was not evident to most casual observers, the Leafs were shaping up under Imlach. Carl Brewer had developed into a mature rookie defenseman, Bower was playing a solid goal, and youngsters such as Frank Mahovlich and Dick Duff were complementing such diligent and dependable veterans as Bert Olmstead and Allan Stanley.

Punch tried deals whenever possible, using his minor league experience as a guide. He remembered how Gerry Ehman had scored forty goals for him at Springfield, and he dealt Willie Marshall for Ehman. Placing Ehman on right wing with center Billy Harris and Frank Mahovlich gave Imlach two solid lines; the other was a unit centered by Bub Pulford with Ron Stewart on right wing and Bert Olmstead on the left. As February, 1959, came to a close, the Leafs appeared far from a playoff berth, and speculation about a new Leaf coach was rampant.

One thing was certain: if the Leafs were going to make the playoffs they would have to do so at the expense of one team, Phil Watson's Rangers. Torn by dissension and unnerved by Watson's temper tantrums, the Rangers started to wobble early in March but recovered to defeat Detroit, 4–2, on March 8 at Madison Square Garden. On March 11 the Leafs lost 6–2 to the Canadiens in Toronto. Imlach's team was nine points out of fourth.

The Leafs were dead. Phil Watson thought so; Madison Square Garden Corporation thought so; and the NHL schedule-makers thought so.

The Garden Corporation began printing playoff tickets. The NHL schedule-makers prepared playoff dates for Montreal, Boston, Chicago, and New York, omitting Toronto. While Watson awaited the playoff-clincher, Imlach kept telling himself and his players that there still was time for a miracle. Yet only two weeks remained, and the staggering Maple Leafs were still a big nine points away from fourth place.

Imperceptible as it was at the time, the turnabout began in Manhattan on Wednesday night, March 11, while the Leafs were losing, 6–2, to the Canadiens in Toronto. On that same night the Black Hawks invaded Madison Square Garden and delivered a 5–3 defeat to Watson's Rangers.

The stage was set for the New Yorkers to deliver their *coup de grace* to Imlach and his Leafs. On Saturday, March 14, Watson brought his Rangers to Maple Leaf Gardens for the first of a home-and-home series with Toronto. All New York required was a single victory on either night in order to finish Toronto. The New York victory on Saturday would give the Rangers a nine-point bulge over Toronto, and with four games remaining on their schedule the Leafs would never be able to make up the difference.

Only the most insightful critic would have given Toronto a chance — and then only by the slimmest margin. The Rangers were just short of open rebellion against Watson at the time. He had worked them to exhaustion in practices, and in the process had tired his lighter forwards such as Camille Henry and Red Sullivan. Once Watson put his team through a workout after a loss!

Imlach hoped against hope that he could capitalize on the negative Ranger factors. On the other hand, the New Yorkers had several top professionals, including high-scoring Andy Bathgate, Dean Prentice, Bill Gadsby, and Lorne Worsley. In spite of Watson they wanted the playoff money as much as the Leafs did.

Try as they might, the Rangers could never get untracked that Saturday night. George Armstrong scored for Toronto at 7:23 of the first period, and Frank Mahovlich got another one for Toronto at 16:26. Dick Duff scored twice in the second period, and Mahovlich collected his second goal in the last period. Final score: Toronto 5, New York 0.

The victory, balm that it was for Imlach, did not torpedo Watson or his Rangers. They never expected a win at Maple Leaf Gardens; even a tie would have been gravy. But on Sunday night, March 15, in New York, Watson did expect a victory, the final chop of his guillotine over Imlach and the Leafs.

New York defenseman Bill Gadsby delivered the first blow less than four minutes after the game began, putting the Rangers ahead 1–0. But Duff and Armstrong rallied Toronto with a pair of goals, and the game soon took on wild proportions. Bathgate tied the match, 2–2, early in the middle period, only to have Mahovlich and Armstrong put Toronto into a 4–2 lead. Then Jimmy Bartlett of the Rangers narrowed it to 4–3 a few minutes before the second period closed.

Imlach nearly crushed his fedora in his palm when big Hank Ciesla tied the contest for New York at 5:37 of the last period, and he almost leaped off the bench when Armstrong put him ahead again at 12:40. But Bower was having an unusually inept night in the Toronto goal, and at 15:21 Red Sullivan scored for the Rangers and the game was tied once again.

With only four minutes remaining, Watson beseeched his players to concentrate on defense, and they did just as he ordered. At last the Toronto attack seemed to be defused, and Worsley was expected to repulse what long shots were hurled at him from center ice. Watson fixed his eyes on the round time clock hanging from the mezzanine directly across from the Rangers bench. His calm was restored when he saw that defensemen Gadsby and Harry Howell were throwing a fortress across the New York blueline.

Punch Imlach hoped for a miracle. Then it happened. Allan Stanley moved the puck away from Bower and toward the Rangers zone. He passed it to Bert Olmstead on the left. Two more strides and Olmstead detected Bob Pulford in motion at center ice. The pass was true, but Pulford chose not to bisect the Rangers defense. Instead, he cracked his wrists and sent a rather ordinary long shot at Worsley. Imlach's hope was that the Rangers goaltender would deflect it to the corner, where a Toronto player could retrieve it for a close-in play on goal.

With the stunned silence that inevitably follows disaster, the packed crowd at Madison Square Garden sat thunderstruck as Pulford's shot breezed past Worsley's arm, glove, and leg pad. Toronto won the game 6–5 and pulled to within three points of the Rangers with three games remaining.

Panic descended on New York. Rangers manager Muzz Patrick

blasted Worsley; Watson singled out hard-rock defenseman Lou Fontinato for criticism. Earlier in the season Fontinato had been beaten up in a fight with Gordie Howe of Detroit and had played poorly ever since. "Fontinato was my policeman," Watson lamented. "But he became a changed man since the fight. He went into a shell; I don't know why."

Still, the odds favored the Rangers, who next would play the Bruins on Wednesday night, March 18, at Madison Square Garden. Boston put three goals past Worsley by the five-minute mark of the second period, and when the Rangers appeared to rally, low-scoring Larry Leach of the Bruins beat Worsley on a stoppable drive and the Rangers went on to lose 5–3. If any one player can be singled out for the collapse," said Muzz Patrick, 'it's Worsley. I can't understand why he's lost his touch."

Imlach moved on to Montreal with his team for a Thursday night game against the Canadiens at the Forum. The Bruins had also arrived there for a Saturday night match, and when Imlach saw Fleming Mackell of the Bruins, he asked about the win over New York. "Watson," said Mackell, "took it was if he was being hit in the head with a mallet. He sank slowly behind the boards, over on their bench. I could see less of him every time I looked."

Imlach's confidence had reached the bursting point. "I told the Boston guys," Imlach wrote in his autobiography, "then, in public, with some of the Leafs listening and grinning, that we were going to play them in the playoffs, because we were going to finish fourth, and they were going to finish second."

But the Leafs still were trailing, and they needed a win over league-leading Montreal. Imlach needed another stroke of luck, and he got it. Montreal's Vezina Trophy-winning goalie Jacques Plante was sidelined, and the Canadiens imported raw rookie Claude Pronovost as a replacement. The Rangers brass screamed "foul," but Pronovost took his spot in the Montreal net on March 19.

Phil Goyette lifted Montreal into the lead, beating Bower at 12:04 of the first period, but the aroused Leafs rebounded with four-straight goals, and swept the game 6–3. For the first time in the season Toronto had won three consecutive games and had pulled to within one point of the Rangers. Fourth place would not be settled until the final weekend of the season.

Just to make things more difficult for Imlach, Watson finally rallied his club on Saturday, March 21, when the Rangers defeated the Red Wings, 5–2, in Detroit. Toronto, three points away from fourth, was to play Chicago on Saturday night, and the Red Wings at Olympia in Detroit on Sunday. All the Leafs needed to expire was a loss to the third-place Black Hawks.

The Leafs reacted with the same vigor they had displayed against the Canadiens and virtually swept Chicago out of the rink. Pulford and Mahovlich scored to give the Leafs a 2–1 lead after two periods; then Stewart, Ehman, and Mahovlich sealed the victory with third-period goals.

On Sunday, the final night of the season the Rangers played host to the Montreal Canadiens, who had clinched first place and were trying to avoid injuries before the playoffs. Instead of using goalie Claude Pronovost, the Canadiens elected to play substitute goalie Charlie Hodge.

The Rangers opened the game as if they intended to demolish the Canadiens. Within six minutes defenseman Harry Howell had put a long shot past Hodge, and the Madison Square Garden crowd went wild with joy. If the Rangers were to win or if Toronto should lose, New York would have the playoff berth. But the Canadiens didn't turn over and die. Dickie Moore and Jean Beliveau got goals in the first period, and Henri Richard added another for Montreal at 6:17 of the third. Trailing 3–1, the Rangers desperately pushed their way into the Canadiens' ice, and Camille Henry scored at 14:38 to make it 3–2, Montreal. Beliveau coun-terattacked and scored again, and the Rangers lost 4–2.

The Toronto-Detroit game had started an hour later in Detroit, and the Leafs still needed a victory to beat New York. By the time the final score of the Rangers game was flashed, Toronto was behind 2–0. The score stayed that way until 2:41 of the second period, when Larry Regan beat Detroit's Terry Sawchuk. Then Bobby Baun tied the game for Toronto.

Norm Ullman gave Detroit a 3–2 lead, but Brewer and Regan scored for the Leafs. Then Marcel Pronovost scored for the Red Wings, and the second period ended with the teams tied 4–4.

In New York's Madison Square Garden, General John Reed Kilpatrick, president of the Rangers, sat in the press cage over-hanging the mezzanine. He was accompanied by his publicity assistant, Marvin Resnick, and a reporter. They watched the West-ern Union ticker report the third period of the Maple Leafs-Red Wings game from Detroit. "Let's hope the wire doesn't move until the end of the game," said Resnick. Kilpatrick remained silent. He was thinking of the $90,000 worth of playoff tickets the once-confident Rangers had sold in advance.

The minutes passed but not fast enough to outrace the Maple Leafs. Suddenly the wire machine next to Kilpatrick jerked, and all heads peered at the metal fingers pounding out the news.

It was a score — but for whom, Toronto or Detroit?

One minute earlier there had been a faceoff in the Toronto zone. Regan cocked his head next to Dick Duff and whispered loud enough for Duff to hear: "Dick, you're going to get the winner. I'm going to give it to you. Just be there."

Regan won the faceoff and dipsy-doodled so adroitly through the Red Wings' defense he reminded onlookers of Max Bentley at his best. But the curly-haired center had skated too far to the side to make a play. Instead, he kept control of the puck and wheeled behind the Detroit net; he saw Duff skating headlong to the goal. Regan's pass was true, and Duff walloped the puck past Sawchuk almost in the same motion. On the Madison Square Garden ticker it read: "DUFF, 2:51 — TORONTO 5, DETROIT 4."

Kilpatrick turned to Resnik. "It looks bad," he said, and his face was crimson with anger. Morbid silence reigned until twelve minutes had elapsed. Then there was more clicking, perhaps a Detroit goal.

Seconds before the ticker began, Billy Harris had skated into the Detroit zone and skimmed a pass to Bob Baun at the blueline. Baun shot the puck two feet off the ice toward the net. Harris saw it coming and arched his stick as a baseball batter might in attempting a bunt. The puck deflected off the wood and caromed past Sawchuk. The ticker clicked: "HARRIS, 14:40." The general said nothing. More minutes passed and then more clicking. "ONE MINUTE TO GO." 30 SECONDS. "GAME OVER."

One area of Detroit's Olympia Stadium was bedlam as the Maple Leafs and their small but vocal retinue of well-wishers celebrated the miracle. In its own way it matched the immortal Toronto comeback of 1942. Screaming at the tops of their lungs, the jubilant Leafs trooped into the dressing room and continued to whoop and holler.

Imlach, the man who would never give up, strutted from skater to skater, pumping each hand. "He had the dazed, glazed look of a man who has come through shell-shock," wrote Scott Young in *The Leafs I Knew*. "Bob Pulford broke down in one corner and could not compose himself for a minute or two."

Stafford Smythe, who had walked out of Olympia Stadium in the second period because of the tension, celebrated with his troops. Later Imlach added: "I feel sorry for Phil Watson. I won't gloat about the man who didn't make it."

At long last the glory that had been the Maple Leafs of bygone years was restored, and Punch Imlach, who only six months earlier had come to Toronto an obscure hockey professional, had become the hero of all Canada. In his autobiography Imlach offered this retrospective look at the amazing comeback:

> Even a week before the season ended, you could have got a-hundred-to-one against us even making the playoffs. I remember hearing later that Conn Smythe had said to somebody on Toronto's hockey committee, "What did you get, did you get a coach or did you get a madman?" This because I'm saying, "We're gonna make it, we're gonna make it." They got a madman, all right, but they didn't know it at the time.

Jim Proudfoot, sports editor of the Toronto *Star*, covered the Leafs during that unforgettable stretch. "The Leafs' effort," said Proudfoot, "rates as one of the most spectacular sports comebacks of all time."

Imlach's formula was nothing more than an updated version of Conn Smythe's 1946 plan ("Put the kids in with a few old pappy guys who still like to win and the combination is unbeatable"), with a minor modification here and there.

While Smythe had had old man Broda in goal, Imlach had old man Bower. Smythe had the "Gold Dust Twins," Thomson and Mortson, on defense; Imlach had Brewer and Baun. Both Smythe and Imlach had the same distillation of youth and experience up front, and the results were just short of stupendous. The Leafs followed the 1959 comeback with a seven-game triumph over Boston in the semifinals, but were subsequently defeated by Montreal.

Despite the loss, the Leafs had made it to the finals and, beyond a doubt, were serious contenders once again. The balance of power in the ancient Hab-Leaf rivalry was beginning to shift, perhaps imperceptibly at first, but unmistakably, as the dawning of the new decade would prove, in Toronto's favor.

1960
TO
1969

It takes a very special personality to end an era with his retirement. In baseball it happened when Babe Ruth hung up his uniform and in 1960 it happened in hockey when Rocket Richard hung up his skates after the Canadiens had taken their fifth-straight Stanley Cup.

Not only was Richard captain of the Canadiens he was the lion of hockey and his departure left a spiritual void which could not be filled. Although the Canadiens still had a lot of firepower they were short in the physical part of the game and were out-muscled by an up-and-coming Chicago team in the 1961 playoffs.

Physical hockey was to be an integral part of the game in the 1960's, a fact that never eluded Imlach. He not only recognized the usefulness of muscle but, more than anyone, valued experience and employed several discarded but valuable older players. The combination was as volatile and productive as Conn Smythe's 1940's formula and like an earlier Leaf team, Imlach's sextet wheeled off three-straight Stanley Cups while the Habs groped for a new identity.

The Canadiens' revival was predicated on the realization by new Montreal general manager Sam Pollock that the Habs would go nowhere without some strong-armed relief.

With that in mind Pollock made two franchise decisions, one involving defense and the other forward. To toughen up the backline he obtained career minor-leaguer Ted Harris, a tall, mean-spirited, stay-at-home type who had studied under the master, Hall of Famer Eddie Shore, at Springfield of the American League. Harris became a presence, not only for his solid bodywork but also for his fighting ability. His bouts with heavyweight champ Orland Kurtenbach were fistic classics.

To provide protection for the non-belligerent Beliveau, Pollock obtained a muscular forward from the AHL's Cleveland Barons — John Bowie Ferguson, a two-fisted slugger with a knack for scoring timely goals. Placed on a line with Beliveau, Ferguson immediately blossomed and was a rookie-of-the-year candidate in 1963–64.

Montreal's new additions did not produce a championship until after the Leafs' three-Cup run (1962–64). Whether Imlach could have squeezed a fourth-straight Stanley Cup out of his Maple Leafs had he been less of a martinet, is debatable. But Punch would not relent and drove several of his stars — most notably Frank Mahovlich — to distraction while diminishing their potential.

By 1965 the Leafs were in a state of disarray while the Canadiens under Blake began another renaissance, winning Cups in '65 and '66.

Somehow — like Captain Bligh making his last positive move before the mutiny — Imlach rallied his Leafs for one more run for the roses and in 1966–67, the NHL's last season as a six-team league before expansion, the Leafs regained the Stanley Cup, employing much of the nucleus that had helped them orchestrate the 1962 triumph.

Imlach lost his touch and his grip on his players and the Leafs finally succumbed to abject disintegration as the sixties wound down. Conversely the Canadiens, though hardly a juggernaut, combined two key ingredients — teamwork and talent — to win Stanley Cups in 1968 and 1969. In each case, the Habs were beneficiaries of the NHL's expansion which doubled the league's size from six to twelve teams. Instead of having to face a strong foe in the finals, the Canadiens were challenged by the St. Louis Blues, an expansion club composed of over-the-hill big leaguers and minor leaguers who had been drafted to fill out expansion rosters. The Habs won both series in four-straight games in what critics considered a mockery of Stanley Cup competition.

Nevertheless, the Canadiens had won fair and square and had enough talent to remain a challenger into the new decade, which was more than could be said for Toronto's representatives.

MONTREAL:
RETOOLING THE POST-RICHARD CANADIENS

From time to time the Canadiens would elevate a brilliant little netminder named Charlie Hodge from their minor-league affiliate and Hodge would play like a champion. Plante still had all the ability in the world but he had been hit in the face by an Andy Bathgate slapshot during a game in New York and donned a protective face mask, the first goaltender in modern hockey to do so. Once again Plante offered a portent of things to come, but Blake was not the least enamored of the mask idea, although he publicly asserted that as long as it helped Plante keep pucks out of his net it would be all right. For 1959–60 the mask proved effective enough to enable Plante to win the Vezina Trophy.

The Rocket signed his eighteenth NHL contract with the Canadiens that season, but in November a puck smacked into his face, smashing a cheekbone, and deactivated him for a month. Montreal managed without him, and when Richard returned, the Habitants staged another successful assault on first place. Ab McDonald had not been an adequate replacement for Bert Olmstead, so Selke tried the French-Canadian Marcel Bonin whose claims to fame included wrestling with bears and eating glass. Another interesting newcomer was Bill Hicke, a right wing with an extraordinary burst of speed and a wide repertoire of stickhandling maneuvers. Unfortunately, a reporter tabbed him "the next Rocket Richard" and Hicke had to bear that onus for the rest of his playing career in Montreal.

Hicke and Bonin were among the young Canadiens to lead the team to a four-game sweep of Chicago in the semifinals. They then proceeded to do the same thing to Toronto, only the second time an NHL club has swept to the Stanley Cup in eight consecutive games.

Never one to stand pat, Selke was acutely aware of one problem — the Rocket was fast approaching the end of the line. If he decided to retire, a new captain would have to be selected and some way had to be found to replace Richard's extraordinary effect on his teammates and fans alike. This would prove to be an impossible chore. There would never be another quite like Maurice Richard; not Jean Beliveau, not Bernie Geoffrion, not Henri Richard. And nobody knew that better than Selke.

The Rocket dropped his bomb on September 15, 1960, and announced he was through as a hockey player. Selke promptly revealed that Maurice would become a "vice president" of the team and its goodwill ambassador. Richard had participated in 978 regular-season games and 133 playoff matches. He was selected to one of the NHL's two All-Star Teams for sixteen-straight seasons. Both the Lady Byng Trophy and the league scoring championship eluded him; the latter would remain the tragedy of his career.

Now the Canadiens turned to the delicate task of picking a new captain to succeed the Rocket. The logical choices were Doug Harvey, Jean Beliveau, and Boom Boom Geoffrion. Harvey, who had seniority over the others, got the nod and led Montreal to still another first-place finish. They went into the playoffs favored to win their sixth-straight Stanley Cup and found themselves confronted by a tough Chicago sextet that finally had found a formula for routing the Habs.

Montreal won the first match, 6–3, but the big, tough Hawks battered the smaller Canadiens at every turn. One by one, Hicke, Marshall, and Beliveau were sent to the hospital with injuries. Blake denounced the Hawks for their back-alley tactics but it was too late. Former Montrealer Ed Litzenberger came up with the winning goal for Chicago in the second game at the Forum, putting the Habs behind the eight ball.

By Chicago's standards, the third game of the series in cavernous Chicago Stadium was a classic. Three overtime sessions were required before Murray Balfour, once Montreal property, scored for the Hawks. Blake, who had been seething over the officiating since the second game, raged when the red light signaled Balfour's goal. The traumatized coach headed for referee Dalton McArthur and swung at the official. Blake was fined two thousand dollars for his behavior and McArthur became a marked man as a result of the incident. The Canadiens recovered briefly in the fourth game, but Chicago goalie Glenn Hall blanked them in the fifth and sixth contests and Montreal found itself in the unusual position of not hosting a Stanley Cup final for the first time in eleven years!

Now that the unthinkable had actually taken place, it was time for housecleaning. The Canadiens' lack of a policeman to protect the smaller forwards was an albatross that hovered over Selke for years. A deal was in order, and Selke obtained the oft-hated Lou Fontinato from the Rangers in return for Doug Harvey. To say the least it was a very controversial deal. Big and strong, Fontinato was nevertheless a clumsy defenseman, the antithesis of the smooth-skating, sharp-passing Harvey. Even Fontinato's fighting ability was debatable ever since Gordie Howe had plastered him with a broken nose during a notorious battle in New York. But Louie still liked to hit and that was what mattered most to Selke; besides, he was considerably younger than the thirty-six-year-old

Harvey who was mistakenly believed to be in the twilight of his career.

In a related deal, Selke peddled young defenseman Al "Junior" Langlois to New York for John Hanna, another stocky and rough defenseman. Thus, Montreal sacrificed ability for brawn and hoped for the best. Harvey was named player-coach of the Rangers and immediately went about the business of embarrassing his former employers. He scored six goals and twenty-two assists and won the Norris Trophy as the league's best defenseman. While he was at it, Harvey led the Rangers to a playoff berth.

Finding an heir to Harvey's throne as team captain was an even more difficult task for Selke than replacing the Rocket. For now the choice narrowed down to a pair of worthies — Boom Boom Geoffrion and Jean Beliveau. The electrifying Boomer had seniority over Beliveau and appeared a slight favorite in the balloting. On the other hand, Beliveau was admired as a virtuoso and a gentleman. He won the captaincy on the second ballot and that might have been a bigger mistake than the Canadiens imagined.

Geoffrion was crushed by the decision. When Beliveau learned of his teammate's depression, he went directly to management and offered, unsuccessfully, to step aside. Several observers doubted whether the diffident, mild mannered Beliveau was psychologically equipped to be the new Montreal leader. They suggested that he could never galvanize the team to action like the volcanic Rocket or the lighthearted but determined Harvey. In a sense, they were to be proved wrong. Montreal finished first, by thirteen points, and Plante won the Vezina Trophy again. In addition, fleet Bobby Rousseau won the Calder Trophy as rookie of the year. "Rousseau," said Peter Gzowski, "makes up in zest and recklessness (he always seems to be shooting from his knees, or lying down, or leaping high in the air) what he lacks in size." But Rousseau had that characteristic fragility that so many of the Canadiens' youngsters had, and although Rousseau developed into a superb artist, he always had difficulty when the checking became overly rough. The Canadiens finally unloaded him to Minnesota in 1970.

The easy conquest of the 1961–62 regular-season schedule proved to be a deception. Chicago lost the opening pair of games of the semifinal in Montreal, then breezed to victory in the remaining four contests. It was a fate both Montreal rooters and captain Beliveau found difficult to accept.

"We began to feel the pressure of losing," said Beliveau. "We had been winning for so long we did not know what it was like to lose. The people started to talk."

They continued talking when Montreal finished third the following season and Beliveau scored only eighteen goals for the second year in a row. "By that time" said Le Gros Bill, "I was ready to quit. If Senator Molson had told me to leave, I would have gone."

A patient man, Molson realized that Beliveau had been tormented by injuries and personal problems that affected his play on ice. "Jean," Molson comforted him, "you've given us so many good years you could have some bad ones and we'd still owe you a lot. We need you now more than ever."

Molson persuaded Beliveau to stay on, which was a good move all around. Beliveau went on to play superb hockey for the Habs and became vice-president with Molson's Brewery. Nevertheless, his lyrical style never captured the imagination of Montrealers the way Morenz, Richard, and Geoffrion did and nobody was more keenly aware of this than Beliveau himself.

Meanwhile, Plante was assailed by more frequent asthma attacks and became more and more estranged in his relationship with Blake. In addition, Plante's defense literally crumbled in front of him. A fractured cheekbone sent Tom Johnson to the hospital and a freak accident to Fontinato shocked Forum onlookers almost as much as the Morenz mishap.

In a game against the Rangers, Vic Hadfield of New York pursued Fontinato, who was skating close to the end boards, behind the net. The Montreal defenseman detected the onrushing Ranger and used one of his favorite checking devices. Fontinato crouched low in the expectation that Hadfield, upon hitting him, would sail over his body and into the boards. But the impact was such that Hadfield's body caught Fontinato in the shoulders and neck. As the Montreal strongboy hit the wooden boards, his neck broke. The combined dislocation and fracture of the neck permanently injured Fontinato; he never played for the Canadiens again, although he was later able to regain some mobility in his neck.

Fortunately for Selke, the vast farm system was still dispatching players to the big team. Eager but clumsy, Terry Harper, almost a replica of Fontinato was called to Montreal along with tall, stylish Jacques Laperriere. The Canadiens, symbolically, gave Laperriere Harvey's number-two sweater, and for a while he appeared to be almost as accomplished as his predecessor.

Left wing Gilles Tremblay was another with great potential. He scored thirty-goals in 1961–62, but was soon afflicted with an asthmatic condition, even worse than Plante's, and had to retire permanently in the 1969–70 campaign at the age of thirty.

In the 1963 Stanley Cup semifinal Toronto ousted the Habs in five games. That was as much humiliation as Selke could absorb. "Too many chiefs and not enough braves," was Ken Reardon's explanation. Plante's behavior, for one thing, had grated both Blake and the front office. He had to go, and he did. A major trade was concluded with New York in which Plante, Don Marshall, and Phil Goyette were transplanted to the Rangers for goalie Gump Worsley and forwards Dave Balon, Leon Rochefort, and Len Ronson.

"I really believe it was all for the best," said an enthused Blake who finally had Plante off his back. "I think the players involved as well as the clubs are going to benefit. I also feel we're going to benefit more in the long run because we gained a big edge in youth as well as getting an extra player.

"There simply has to be changes made. You can't stand pat after being eliminated from the playoffs like we were. As for Plante, I always said, when he played for our club, that he was the best goalie in the league. But last season I found a big change in Jacques. He was nervous — very nervous. I don't know who made him nervous, whether it was the club, or the people in the stands, or what, but something was bothering him. He wasn't sure whether he'd be able to play or not play. I think he needed a change, and I think the trade will help him."

Blake commended Marshall but noted that in the "last couple of years I thought Donnie hadn't been extending himself — with us he just didn't seem to be going all out anymore." He also lauded Goyette but pointed out that Montreal was strong at center and Phil, therefore, was expendable.

Just which benefited most from the trade can be debated to this day. Only Worsley was good enough to stick with Montreal for a substantial length of time. Plante failed, despite occasional histrionics, in New York, but Goyette and Marshall became rejuvenated as Rangers and Marshall remained with the team through the 1969–70 season.

When Dickie Moore announced his retirement after twelve years with the club, *Les Canadiens* redoubled their efforts to find a hard-checking forward. A tip from former Montreal ace Floyd Curry resulted in the signing of John Ferguson, a muscleman with the Cleveland Barons, of the American League. "Fergie" was an awkward skater with limited ability, but his addition to the squad would turn out to be of utmost importance in years to come. In some ways it was the most important decision made by the Canadiens in the 1960's.

No player since Rocket Richard had exuded so much raw fire as Ferguson. As a matter of personal policy he never talked to the opposition either on or off the ice, and he would resort to any means available to score a goal or stop an enemy. He was complemented by another, although smaller, hitter named Bryan Watson whose career in Montreal was considerably less extensive than Ferguson's.

Worsley, the great new and corpulent goaltending hope, was lauded by Blake as a notable replacement for Plante. "With the Rangers," said Blake, "he was getting nowhere. Maybe, just maybe, he got to feel that it didn't matter too much whether the team won or lost. There was no future. But it'll be different now. It's bound to be. He's got an opportunity for his talents now that he never had before in his career."

The blimpish Gump responded by getting injured early in the season. Little Charlie Hodge stepped in and played brilliantly for sixty-two games, winning the Vezina Trophy. Thanks to Hodge, Montreal went on to fool the experts and finished in first place, but Toronto came on strong and beat them, four games to three, in the semifinal playoff round.

Ever since he had become owner of the Canadiens, Senator Molson had remained unobtrusively behind the scenes as Selke diligently put together the pieces of the Montreal hockey empire. That Selke was succeeding was evident by the first-place finish in March, 1964, but the Canadiens' elimination in the playoffs underscored the fact that there still was work to be done. Selke acknowledged this just as he had realized there was a formidable task ahead of him in the late forties when he first arrived in Montreal.

Selke had reached the age of seventy-one by the spring of 1964 but he had the attitude and energy of men thirty years his junior. He loved hockey as passionately as he had as a kid in Berlin, Ontario, and saw no reason for not continuing in his position. Flanked by the dynamic Reardon and clever Sam Pollock, Selke could see the Stanley Cup only about a season away.

However, behind the scenes a big-business power play was under way that would ultimately reshape the entire structure and character of the Canadiens. Hints of a shakeup were heard during the 1964 Stanley Cup finals after Montreal was eliminated. Word was out that instead of the traditional player shakeup that follows defeat it would be the high command that would face the inquisition. Early in May, the first signs of trouble bubbled to the surface. Ken Reardon, who had served so loyally under Selke and who was expected to succeed him as managing director, resigned as vice-president. Since Reardon had been closely aligned with Selke, the move startled the hockey world and set off even more speculation as to the Habitants' palace revolution.

On Friday, May 15, the cat was out of the bag, and all hell broke loose in the front office. Senator Molson announced that sweeping changes were being made in the Canadiens' organization from Selke to Rocket Richard to Sam Pollock!

Big business had finally extended its tentacles and completely engulfed Le Club de Hockey Canadien. What had once been a rather homey operation run by Leo Dandurand and later by Senator Raymond and Selke had now become a high-pressure outfit with a new president and a new managing director.

To begin with, Selke "resigned," although the circumstances and remarks he made to newsmen suggest that the veteran hockey man had been ceremoniously pushed out of his job. "I'm disappointed," he said soon after he stepped out. "I'd have liked at least one more year to finish reconstructing the team. We're almost there, but not quite."

The sop proffered to Selke was an obscure title, "vice-chairman of the board of the Canadian Arena Company." "I'll help with the selection of new players," Selke said with an overdose of wishful thinking. "If they don't . . . if they don't, it's so long . . . those who ask your advice really want your support of their opinion and will be content with nothing less . . . I feel lost."

And well he might have. His successor was thirty-eight-year-old Sam Pollock, who had been director of the Canadiens' farm system since 1958 and was now the youngest club manager in the NHL. Pollock's appointment immediately clarified the meaning behind Reardon's departure a week earlier. Sam had outfought Kenny, somehow, in the behind-the-scenes infighting for Selke's job.

Pollock's credentials were quite sound. He had devoted nineteen of his years to hockey management, seventeen of them as a full-time employee of the Forum. He was instrumental in developing the Junior Canadiens and led them to the Memorial Cup, emblematic of national supremacy, in 1950. In more recent years

Pollock had taken a more active role in the actual manipulating of players on the NHL Canadiens and helped negotiate the famed Worsley-Plante deal.

Pollock knew what he wanted, and he was going to run the Canadiens his way. Thus, having Selke around would soon prove to be an embarrassment and an irrelevancy until the elder states-man finally moved gracefully to the background. But there were others crowding Pollock for the limelight.

In another interesting move Rocket Richard was appointed "assistant to the president of the Canadiens" with emphasis on public relations. The front-office communique also said he would aid in the development of hockey personnel. At first, Richard was overjoyed to be back with the club on a full-time basis. It appeared, at least superficially, that the New Order would rely on Richard's hockey wisdom instead of merely trading on his good name. This, however, would prove to be untrue and Richard eventually detected the deception and left the organization.

Frank Selke, Jr., son of the former managing director, was named vice-president for sales and publicity of the Canadian Arena Company. This was expected because of a desire to keep the Selke name affiliated with the team and also because the thirty-four-year-old had been master of ceremonies of the between-periods shows of the hockey telecasts.

Zeroing in on the target with the same flair he had displayed as a player with the Montreal Junior Royals was dashing, blond, thirty-five-year-old David Molson, who succeeded his cousin, the Sen-aotr, as president of the Canadiens' hockey business.

Just about the only key member of the organization to survive the upheaval was coach Blake. In Toronto's *Globe and Mail*, sportswriter Dick Beddoes chastised the Hab organization for discarding the venerable Selke, charging the Molson family with "what James Russell Lowell called 'the elbowing self-conceit of youth.'" Bernie Geoffrion's on-ice performance had slipped in recent years. When a coaching job opened at Quebec City, the Boomer announced his retirement from the NHL and became coach of the Quebec Aces of the American League. Geoffrion hoped that with a couple of good years under his belt in Quebec he might — just might — get Blake's job when Toe decided to quit the Habs.

The Rocket was provided with a small office in the Forum and awaited his assignment with the enthusiasm of a rookie. Unfortunately, the work never came. One afternoon, early in the 1964–65 season, Peter Gzowski paid a visit to the Rocket. He came away with this report:

> However executive Maurice Richard's manner has become, a visitor to his vice-presidential office at the Forum can still see the fire in his eyes has only been banked; through an interview he twists and fiddles restlessly, as if wishing he could start just one more explosive rush down the boards, and hear "vas-y Maurice" once more.

Nobody had come along to fill the Rocket's role on the ice. Bill Hicke was a failure and now the Canadiens turned to another small, chunky forward, Yvan Cournoyer, who had been promoted from the junior ranks. The handsome slick-haired skater betrayed flashes of speed and an enormously dynamic shot for his size. Cournoyer would prove to be an asset as a sniper but owned nothing like the tough fiber the Rocket displayed. He would become, at best, a very efficient but not a great hockey player.

Another significant addition was tall, gangly Ted Harris, a raw-boned defenseman who would, in time, aid John Ferguson as the team tough guy. Goaltending was shared by Charlie Hodge and Gump Worsley, and the scoring, surprisingly, was paced by hard-checking Claude Provost, who skated with an abnormally wide stance.

The Canadiens finished second to a surprisingly strong Detroit sextet in March, 1965. This placed Montreal against Toronto in the first round of the playoffs and they disposed of the Leafs in six games with Provost and young Bobby Rousseau leading the attack. They had even less trouble with Chicago in the final, winning the Cup in five games. A new award, the Conn Smythe Trophy, for the most valuable player in the playoffs was won by captain Beliveau.

The success formula devised by Blake was interpreted in various ways by different analysts of the game. One theory had it that Toe was the ultimate tyrant who frightened his players by slamming doors, shouting at them on the bench, and doing sardonic dances in the dressing room. Selke, who was admittedly closer to Irvin than Blake, insisted that Toe was not a martinet. He contended that Blake emphathized with his skaters more than most coaches and was a master psychologist.

For Henri Richard, maturity came fast. He fought on even terms with his tormentors. He would not be run out of the league and would become a very accomplished hockey player although never the electrifying personality the Rocket was.

By contrast, the Pocket Rocket was determined but not explosive, strong but not overpowering. If the Rocket was the home-run hitter, Henri was more the base-stealer and opposite-field hitter. He also had the Rocket's touch of the brooder in him.

The younger Richard was an essential cog in Selke's rebuilding plan, and was an asset to Pollock, too, in Sam's first years in Montreal. The Canadiens finished first in 1965–66, breezed past Toronto in the first round of the playoffs with four straight wins, and appeared capable of disposing of the Detroit Red Wings at will in the Cup finals, especially since the series opened with two games at the Forum. But Detroit's hot hand, goalie Roger Crozier, was sizzling, and the Red Wings upset the Habs in the first two games. They became favorites as the series shifted to Olympia Stadium. But Blake rallied his crew and Montreal didn't lose again. The Cup-winning goal was scored by the Pocket Rocket in sudden-death overtime.

In Quebec City, Boom Boom Geoffrion was leading the Aces to first place in the American League and casting an eye on Montreal where it was assumed that, sooner or later, Toe Blake would retire. Naturally, Geoffrion was hopeful that it would be sooner, but when Toe announced he would return to the Montreal bench for the 1966–67 season, Geoffrion figured that Blake's retirement would never come. That, as well as disenchantment with the Quebec situation, inspired Geoffrion to try a comeback, but not with the Canadiens. He was acquired by the New York Rangers and went on to prove there was still life in his old legs and plenty of radar in his stick.

Pollock surprised the NHL when he imported a green goaltender named Rogatien Vachon from the minors to replace Worsley. Toronto's vocal Punch Imlach said Vachon was nothing but "a junior B goalie," but little Rogie managed to play capably, if not frequently with a spectacular flair.

Despite the injuries, the Canadiens finished second in 1966–67 and defeated the Rangers in the opening round of the playoffs.

When the Canadiens entered the 1967 Cup final against Toronto, of the Montreal team that had won the Stanley Cup in 1960 only Henri Richard and Beliveau remained. The total power of the fifties' dynasty was missing, and the goaltending of Worsley and

Vachon could not match the perfection of vintage Jacques Plante. As a result, Toronto bumped Montreal out of the finals in six games.

The defeat marked the end of an era for Montreal as it did for the other five NHL clubs. Expansion had finally come to hockey, and in June, 1967, representatives from Pittsburgh, Los Angeles, Oakland-San Francisco, Minneapolis-St. Paul, Philadelphia, and St. Louis participated in the draft to stock the six new teams of the West Division. The Canadiens were on the spot because they owned the most abundant stockpile of young talent in the NHL and figured to be riddled by the hungry new clubs. But the genius of Sam Pollock intervened to protect the glittering herd. Wheeling and dealing with expansion teams, Pollock peddled off enough fringe talent to enable *Les Canadiens* to retain the nucleus of a future winner and they entered the 1967–68 season as strong as possible under the circumstances.

This time it required more than the usual time for the Canadiens to get going. They were in last place in December, 1967, but soon achieved a relentless climb to the top that placed them first in the newly created East Division of the NHL. They then wiped out the Bruins and Black Hawks in short order and proceeded to the East-West final against the St. Louis Blues to take the Stanley Cup.

The former managing director, Selke, was forgotten as Pollock accepted the compliments as big-league hockey's presiding genius. "Sam," wrote Dick Beddoes in the *Globe and Mail*, "is the smartest man now connected with hockey in any front-office job."

Toe Blake finally gave in to his better judgment and his nerves and retired after the 1968 championship sweep. In his thirteen years as coach, Blake had finished first nine times and won eight Stanley Cups. Few would argue that he was the finest all-around coach the NHL has known.

"Under Toe's stabling influence," wrote Jim Proudfoot of the Toronto *Star*, "the Rocket earned the stature he surely would have missed otherwise. This might have been Blake's finest achievement as a coach. Another would be the rehabilitation of the Montreal club after it came apart in 1961 and 1962. In two years, the Canadiens were back in first place and, a year after that, they won the Stanley Cup again."

Blake's replacement was neither Rocket Richard nor Floyd Curry, as had been speculated by many, but Claude Ruel, who had been one of the best junior defensemen in Canada before losing an eye. He later coached the Junior Canadiens, and in time became the director of player personnel for the Habs.

Blake was a tough act to follow, but Ruel proved his mettle as the Canadiens took it all in 1969, defeating Bobby Orr & Co., the powerful Boston Bruins.

The glow of victory in Montreal completely obscured some ominous storm clouds which were relentlessly gathering over their horizon. They were, however, visible to many hockey men in Boston and other parts of the NHL. It was pointed out that the mainstay of the Canadiens, captain Beliveau, was aging rapidly and would be less and less effective. It was also noted that goalie Worsley was getting older and Henri Richard was no longer young. The Bruins, by contrast, would ice a strong, young team, led by the irrepressible Bobby Orr, and the Montreal dynasty would surely end in 1969–70.

Perhaps Ruel had that in the back of his mind as he returned home to relax through the summer of 1969. "Just wait until next year," he warned. "They will write that I had nothing to do with this. They will write this, I know."

TORONTO: THE IMLACH ERA — STANLEY CUPS AND CHAOS

Imlach lifted the Leafs to second place in each of the seasons following the 1959 comeback, and won his first Stanley Cup in 1962, defeating Chicago four games to two. It was that season that Stafford Smythe completed his annexation of the Maple Leaf Gardens hierarchy.

Ever since Imlach had outwitted Phil Watson in 1959, Stafford had argued with his father for interfering too much in the club's management. He objected to his father's emphatic endorsement of Imlach as coach as well as manager. Friction between the two continued to produce sparks until early November, 1961, when Stafford resigned as chairman of the hockey committee.

He told his father that he planned to move on to other interests and would remain in the Maple Leaf Gardens organization only if he could be in complete command. Within three weeks Stafford had gotten his way. On November 23, 1961, Stafford — along with Harold Ballard and John Bassett — bought Conn Smythe's stock at $40 a share with a $21-million bank loan that was repaid in four years.

"Stafford," said Toronto *Star* sports columnist Milt Dunnell, "was determined to be his own man — not the son of Canada's most famous sports figure." Every so often Stafford would underline his point by telling acquaintances: "I waited until my dad joined the army — then I joined the navy."

Dunnell added: "Stafford got more nettles than he deserved — but he didn't seem to mind that either." He didn't seem to mind Imlach either, especially after the 1962–63 season, when Punch's club duplicated the 1947–48 team's twin championships: first place and the Stanley Cup. It was the second of three-straight Cup wins (same as Hap Day) for Toronto, and Punch Imlach's name had become a household word in hockey.

More than any of his colleagues, Imlach was an existentialist, always thinking of the present more than the future or the past. During the 1963–64 season he realized he needed a scoring boost to win the Stanley Cup. In February, 1964, he completed a staggering trade with New York, sending Dick Duff and Bob Nevin — members of previous Cup-winners — as well as young stars Arnie Brown, Rod Seiling, and Bill Collins to the Rangers for forwards Andy Bathgate and Don McKenney.

Bathgate was the most significant factor in the 1964 Cup victory. He also was among the most important factors in alerting the hockey world to the change in Imlach's personality and the disastrous effect it was beginning to have on the Maple Leaf hockey club.

The metamorphosis was due partly to Imlach's enormous success, his popularity, and the fact that he enjoyed more autonomy than anyone in the Maple Leaf organization since Conn Smythe ran the club. Where once he had been sensitive and close to his players, he now drifted away from them a little more with each Cup victory. As a result, the more sensitive — and also the best — players began to rebel against his rule.

Defenseman Carl Brewer, one of the best ever to skate for Toronto, was among the first to challenge Punch. Brewer had become friendly with Toronto attorney R. Alan Eagleson, who later was named executive director of the NHL Players Associations. Punch was openly opposed to Eagleson and was not at all pleased that Brewer, Pulford, and other Leafs were friendly with the attorney.

Imlach's admiration for Bathgate disappeared after the gifted right wing helped Punch win the Stanley Cup. A free-wheeling type of the Max Bentley school of hockey, Bathgate could not adapt his style to Imlach's restrictive, overly defensive blueprints, and Imlach's personality conflicted with his. The animosity finally bubbled forth at the end of the 1964–65 season, when Bathgate told a newsman what he thought was wrong with the Maple Leafs.

"Imlach never spoke to Frank Mahovlich or myself for most of the season," said Bathgate, "and when he did, it was to criticize. Frank usually got the worst. We are athletes, not machines, and Frank is the type that needs some encouragement, a pat on the shoulder every so often."

Bathgate was echoing the sentiments of other players not brave enough to speak out. In time Toronto players such as Brewer, Baun, Ron Stewart, Jim Pappin, Mike Walton, and Brian Conacher trained their verbal fire on Punch, and Toronto's civil war was brought into the open.

Brewer chose to quit hockey in 1965–66 rather than play for Imlach, but the Leafs managed to win the Stanley Cup without him in 1966–67. It was to be Imlach's last moment of true hockey glory and, in a very real sense, the culmination of the Toronto-Montreal rivalry.

The Leafs had finished the regular season in third place. While much of the nucleus of the 1964 Cup-winning Leafs was still in place — Mahovlich, Keon, Armstrong, Kelly, Baun, Horton, Stanley, and Bower — for instance, the team was aging. Stanley was forty-one, Bower, forty-two. Sharing the nets with Bower was thirty-seven-year-old Terry Sawchuk, acquired from the Red Wings after they left him unprotected in the 1964 draft. In the Stanley Cup finals of 1967, Canada's centennial year, the Leafs met the Canadiens.

Sawchuk injured his ankle in the opener, a 6–2 loss. Bower played the next two, winning 3–0 and 3–2. When Bower pulled a groin muscle in the pregame warmup before the fourth match Sawchuk started in a 6–2 loss. When Bower was unable to start the fifth, many believed that the psychological advantage had swung, perhaps insurmountably, to the Canadiens. After all, Sawchuk had been as dismal in his two games as Bower had been stellar. But the veteran netminder confounded the armchair experts and, as if an apparition of himself from one of the Detroit powerhouses of the late forties or early fifties, played spectacularly, frustrating the Canadiens' best efforts. The Habs were relentless, using every weapon in their arsenal, urged on by a packed Forum. When it was over, Toronto was victorious, 4–1, and a game away from the Stanley Cup.

Back at the Gardens the Leafs checked the Habs fiercely. Sawchuk was again brilliant. In the final minute of regulation time, down 2–1 and facing elimination, the Canadiens opted for six attackers — and an empty net.

What turned out to be the pivotal faceoff in the series saw Allan Stanley against big Jean Beliveau, deep in Toronto territory. Stanley won the draw and fed the puck to Kelly. Then it was Kelly to Pulford to Armstrong. The Leaf captain fired from ninety feet away. The series was over.

As the Leafs swarmed over the boards one of them in particular seemed almost on the fringes of the celebration, at least emotionally. Frank Mahovlich, despite his performance in the series, was desperately unhappy and underproductive under the iron rule of Punch Imlach. His arrival in Toronto as rookie of the year in 1957–58 can be seen as the beginning of the Leafs' return from the wilderness of the 1950's. When he was traded to Detroit in 1968 the Leafs were entering a period of failure absolutely unparalleled in the team's history. The rise and fall of Mahovlich's career with the club symbolizes the making and breaking of rapport between Imlach and his Leafs. Mahovlich's case history, better than any other, describes the decline and fall of the 1960's Leafs hockey fortunes and the ultimate ousting of Imlach himself from the organization.

To Frank Mahovlich Toronto represented a big haunted city. He was recognized and hounded wherever he went by fans who were not satisfied with his play. He clashed with teammates over his temporary refusal to join the Players Association. And he was tormented by the specter of Punch Imlach, who bothered him more than everything else combined.

Punch felt that he commanded with the authority of Napoleon, the wisdom of Socrates, and the insight of Einstein. The Leaf boss believed that all players, though constructed differently, would be treated equally. "Yeah," added one ex-Leaf, "equally bad!"

When it came to Mahovlich, Imlach lost points immediately. Either he couldn't or wouldn't pronounce the ace left wing's name correctly, calling him "Ma-hal-a-vich" instead of "Ma-hov-lich."

"Imlach refused to understand him," said Paul Rimstead, former sports editor of *The Canadian* magazine. "The relationship deteriorated to the point where Mahovlich no longer could play his best hockey for the Leafs."

It wasn't always that way. Punch and Frank had been almost chummy from the time Mahovlich joined the team until 1960–61, when he scored forty-eight goals and was regarded as the Maple Leafs' superstar.

Many observers say that the crack in their relationship first developed at a banquet late one evening in London, Ontario. A day later Frank and his teammates were on a plane heading for a road game when the Big M picked up the morning paper. He fidgeted nervously as he read the headline and then proceeded down to the story.

The account asserted that Mahovlich had told the banquet audience that teammate Red Kelly was not contributing that much to Frank's success. The Big M pulled himself together, walked over to Kelly, and insisted he had been misquoted. Kelly was sympathetic and told Frank to forget the whole bloody thing.

Mahovlich then approached Imlach and pointed out that the story was all wrong, but Imlach wasn't impressed. That was the beginning of the end of the Mahovlich-Imlach friendship, although it took several seasons before their rift became irreparable.

"I actually liked the guy for about five years," Mahovlich said. "Then things weren't the same after that. He just wasn't the guy I once knew. He started to do a lot of funny things; I later told some of the guys on the Red Wings what he did, and they refused to believe me. They gave me the double look."

One of the favorite tortures in the Imlach concentration camp was inflicted after a losing weekend of hockey for the Leafs. They would often play at home on Saturday night and travel as far as Chicago or Boston for a Sunday night game. Mahovlich explained:

> We'd catch a plane back to Toronto on Monday morning, and then he would take us directly from the airport to the rink for a practice. If that were the case, why didn't he practice us on the ice right after the game? After a while I began to wonder how long I could take this kind of thing. A day off from hockey does a man a lot of good, but we never seemed to get a day off with Imlach.

Then there were the demands from the supposedly sophisticated Toronto fans. If Frank had scored forty-eight goals when he was twenty-three years old, they reasoned, he should score at least fifty goals a year later. On top of that Chicago owner Jim Norris allegedly had offered $1 million for Mahovlich, but the Leafs had turned him down. When Frank slipped to thirty-three goals in 1961–62, a few vocal purists in Maple Leaf Gardens began what was to be a chronic chorus of boos whenever the Big M played a mediocre game. Soon the hoots began grating on his nerves, not to mention those of the other stars around the league.

"If Toronto fans would appreciate his great talent and give him the cheers he deserves instead of booing him, maybe the pressure wouldn't cook the guy," said Gordie Howe.

But the warning came too late. Mahovlich couldn't conceal his anxiety. He became introverted and distant. On November 12, 1964, Mahovlich succumbed to his first breakdown. He was suffering from what doctors later described as "deep depression and tension," but the exact diagnosis wasn't made public at the time. "We did not have Frank's permission," said Dr. Hugh Smythe, the team's physician.

Mahovlich remained in seclusion for a couple of weeks before returning to the Leaf lineup. He remained secretive about his ailment, and he became exceptionally confidential about his interviews with reporters.

Once, a season later, Paul Rimstead asked to talk to him. "Okay," said Frank, "but not on the team bus. "I'll see you later sometime."

They eventually held their rendezvous at a Montreal hotel, where Mahovlich allowed that his relationship with Imlach was worsening. The Big M pointed out that his doctor advised him to ignore Punch whenever possible. "He told me to pull an imaginary curtain around myself whenever Punch was around," Frank said. "I've been doing it, and I feel a lot better."

But there were other problems and annoyances. Some people close to the Leafs' scene believe that the team's policy toward endorsements helped to turn Mahovlich off even more.

"Each Toronto player collected a flat $1,500 from Maple Leafs Sport Productions, the Leafs' company," said Al Eagleson, adviser to the Players Association. "That hurt Mahovlich. There were years when he could have picked up $25,000 from endorsements. I had an offer of $5,000 from one firm for one season. He had to decline because of the Leafs' commitment."

The boos from the crowds became more frequent and more annoying. In the middle of the 1967–68 season Mahovlich played superbly, and the Leafs routed the Montreal Canadiens, 5–0, at Maple Leaf Gardens. Frank scored a goal and two important assists. Even his arch-critic, Imlach, described Frank's game as "outstanding."

Mahovlich was named the second of three stars picked after every home game by broadcaster Foster Hewitt. Normally a "star" is greeted with cheers or, at worst, mild applause when he skates out onto the ice to acknowledge the selection. When Frank planted his blades on the ice, he heard some applause, but there was no mistaking the boos that were uttered by some spectators.

Mahovlich completed the home-game ritual and returned to the dressing room. He showered and changed into street clothes and later headed for the team's sleeping car, which would carry the Leafs to Detroit for their next game. He boarded the sleeper and prepared to go to bed, but somehow he couldn't shake the memory of the catcalls, and he couldn't get to sleep.

Torn by his anxiety, Mahovlich finally walked off the sleeper at about 4 A.M. He contacted a club doctor and was escorted to a hospital. This time his ailment was no secret. Dr. Hugh Smythe disclosed that Mahovlich was suffering from "deep depression and tension" and was in the care of Dr. Allen Walters, a psychiatrist.

"The barbs hurt him," said Toronto *Star* sports writer Milt Dunnell. "Many players could shake it off, but Mahovlich never was able to do it. He retreated within himself. The club officials have to ask themselves whether a person of the Big M's temperament ever can attune himself to the animosity of their sport — the animosity which he hears — not the violence which he feels on the ice."

The Maple Leaf brass had begun thinking about dealing Frank to another team, but they couldn't make a move until he returned to the lineup and proved to the satisfaction of prospective buyers that he was capable of playing big-league hockey again.

The sabbatical proved beneficial to both Mahovlich and the Leafs, and he rejoined the club after a few weeks' rest. Recalling his mood at the time, Frank commented: "It was getting pretty bad. By this time I hadn't talked to him (Imlach) for five years. I would have liked to talk to somebody about it, but the way the Leafs setup worked, Imlach was boss of everything, so I couldn't talk to anybody."

Early in March, 1968, Imlach finally concluded a deal with Detroit. The Leafs would receive Norm Ullman, Floyd Smith, and

Paul Henderson in return for Mahovlich, Pete Stemkowski, and Garry Unger, all forwards.

In addition the Leafs would receive the right to obtain ace defenseman Carl Brewer, who had quit pro hockey but who might be induced to return.

The deal was one of the most spectacular trades ever negotiated in the NHL. Ullman, an efficient center, was the ninth-highest goal-scorer in league history. Henderson was a very promising young scorer, and Smith was a journeyman with a knack for scoring goals. In addition to Mahovlich the Leafs lost Stemkowski, a hard-checking center, and Unger, a rookie with great potential.

Mahovlich, of course, was delighted to be free of Imlach's, shackles. For years the Red Wings were renowned as a relaxed team with an obvious *joie de vivre*. During playoff time manager Abel would take his men to the racetrack rather than seclude them in some distant hideaway. Frank was aware of this, but he wasn't quite sure about how the Detroit players would react to him.

"There was pressure at first," he recalled. "Some of them heard the Frank Mahovlich stories, and they were wondering if they were true. And I was never the kind of guy who tried to sell myself."

Players and newsmen gradually began to notice the metamorphosis. The Big M began to laugh and joke with his cronies, and soon he became one of the boys. "I really feel bad that I didn't take the time or make the effort to get to know him in Toronto," said Baun, by this time also with Detroit.

The escape from Imlach was obviously the prescription Mahovlich required. He sparkled on a line with Howe and Delvecchio and scored forty-nine goals one season. But what of the other Toronto players? The Mahovlich supporters were for the most part players who believed in the Players Association and Eagleson. Conacher, Walton, Pulford, and Jim Pappin had become vehemently anti-Imlach, and Punch knew it. The day after Mahovlich walked out on the team for a second time, Imlach called a meeting but specifically omitted Conacher, Walton, Pulford, and Pappin. After conferring with his "loyal" players Imlach ordered a scrimmage.

"That day," said Conacher, "we had an Association-Nonassociation practice. Punch had managed to split the team right down the middle."

His early successes seemed to have persuaded Imlach that he could do no wrong and that his increasingly vigorous practices were the one and only way to hone his team to sharpness — no matter how tired the players were from previous games. In his *Hockey in Canada: The Way It Is*, Brian Conacher asserted that Imlach's practices were designed more as punitive devices than as a forum for working out new plays and other techniques.

"On one occasion," wrote Conacher, "he kept the team on the ice for two hours of straight skating.

> There was no purpose to the practice. As I skated around the rink beside Tim Horton, we looked at each other and asked what we were doing there, it all seemed so pointless . . . the practice had been the most useless I had ever experienced as a hockey player. If Punch was trying to get the team in shape, he was doing it the wrong way as far as I could see. What our team needed was a day off, not two hours of solid skating.

One by one the Leafs defected from Imlach's rule, and Toronto plummeted in the standings. The Leafs finished out of the playoffs, in fifth place, during the 1967–68 season, thus setting the stage for Imlach's last major uprising — "L'affaire Mike Walton" — which was the catalyst for the firing of Punch Imlach.

A creative and speedy center, Mike Walton had two strikes against him in Imlach's estimation. For one thing, Walton tended to accent his offensive play and ignore his defensive chores (as far as Punch was concerned), and for another he was related by marriage to Stafford Smythe, who had become Imlach's arch-enemy.

Like Mahovlich and Brewer, Walton was high-strung, and he objected to the tactics, psychological and otherwise, used by his coach. He was once benched during a game with Montreal, and brooded about it for days afterward. "I don't think my defensive playing merits my being benched," said Walton, "but there's no point griping directly to Punch. That's a waste of time." Two nights later he was back in the lineup, starting against the St. Louis Blues. Within minutes, Walton had two goals, and the Leafs were on their way to a win.

But Walton was benched again almost as quickly, and the pattern continued. The player's friendship with attorney Eagleson helped to widen the gap between him and Imlach, as it had in Mahovlich's case and those of other Leafs. The big break occurred during the home stretch of the 1968–69 season, when the Leafs were striving for a playoff berth.

On Thursday, February 20, 1969, Walton walked out on the

Leafs because of his problems with Imlach. After several days of public declarations on both sides — Imlach said he would welcome Walton back if he came with "the right attitude" — the two finally huddled, and a brief reconciliation was effected. "The reason I came back," said Walton, "was that the pressure was on me from the rest of the fellows. Several talked to me individually, and indirectly the whole team was in on it."

Maple Leaf center Norm Ullman, who then was president of the NHL Players Association, agreed: "We discussed it, and everybody felt that Mike should be back with the team."

The rift finally ended on February 26, 1969. Late that afternoon Walton phoned Imlach, and the boss invited him to his office, suggesting that he "come up the back way." As a result of the conference Walton dressed that night for the game against St. Louis. His return was greeted with more enthusiasm than criticism by the discreet Leafs fans.

Back-to-back victories over St. Louis and Philadelphia gave Toronto the thrust they needed for a playoff berth. The Leafs finished fourth, but the bitterness between Imlach and Walton lingered on. It was obvious that one of the two would have to go after the 1968–69 season ended. Much would depend on Imlach's handling of the team in the opening playoff round, against the Boston Bruins.

The end for Imlach and the Maple Leafs came with the suddenness and violence of a bolt of lightning. Although Toronto had finished fourth, the Leafs compiled a commendable record — thirty-five wins, twenty-six losses, fifteen ties — and were given a better-than-fair chance of taking a game or two, if not the series, from second-place Boston. But Punch had run out of the kind of miracles he had produced in 1959, and the Leaf hockey club was destroyed as no Toronto hockey club had ever been annihilated in Stanley Cup competition. They were beaten 10–0 and 7–0 at Boston Garden and returned to Maple Leaf Gardens, where they sealed the humiliation with 4–3 and 3–2 losses to the Bruins.

"You might have suspected," said Rex MacLeod of the Toronto *Globe and Mail*, "that the Bruins had a copy of the Leafs' plan, but it was apparent that the Leafs didn't have a plan."

As the triumphant Bostonians trooped off the ice, Imlach positioned himself in the aisle near the visitors' exit so that he could shake their hands. One of the surprised Bruins was center Derek Sanderson. Moments later Sanderson told reporters: "When Imlach said good luck to me just now, it was the first time he's ever talked to me. But I'll tell you this. He's an egomaniac, and I'm glad we knocked him out."

At the time neither Sanderson nor anyone else realized how potent the knockout blow had been. Even before all of the Boston players had passed Imlach, Stafford Smythe invited Punch to speak privately with him. Minutes later Imlach was informed that he had been fired, and word quickly spread throughout the arena and into the dressing rooms.

The announcement was greeted with a curious distillation of surprise and expectancy. "I'm amazed," said Bruins manager Milt Schmidt. "It's hard to understand. Punch got the Leafs into the playoffs ten out of eleven years. I missed eight years in a row, and they didn't fire me. It's hard to understand. Punch is a good hockey man and a good friend."

By contrast, *Globe and Mail* reporter Louis Cauz observed: "Imlach's dismissal was not a surprise — he has repeatedly been under fire from the hockey committee during the past season — but the timing caught everyone off guard."

Punch agreed. In his memoirs he commented: "I didn't expect it to happen at that particular time. I mean I wouldn't have done it like that. I would have shaken hands with the guy and said, 'Well, you got in the playoffs. I didn't expect you'd get in. You did a pretty good job.' The next day, maybe, you take the guy and tell him he's through."

Considering that he went out a loser, Imlach went out in style. The city of Toronto tendered an official banquet in Punch's honor. Besides, he had the luxury of having Smythe pay him one season's salary, or approximately $35,000. "Imlach is no donkey," wrote Milt Dunnell in the Toronto *Star*. "He undoubtedly knew the axe was poised. It scarcely is likely he expected it to fall before he had a chance to wash off the blood of defeat."

AFTER 1967

MAPLE LEAF BLUES, THE FLOWER AND THE GLORY

In the seventies, the contrast between the Leafs and the Canadiens was, quite simply, the difference between winning and losing. Although in 1970, the Habs missed the playoffs for the first time in twenty-two years, they quickly recovered. Spearheaded on the offense by Frank Mahovlich, who had been acquired from the Red Wings for Mickey Redmond, and backstopped by a sensational Ken Dryden, the Habs upset the Cup-defending Boston Bruins in the spring of 1971 and then came back with a Cup win two years later. The real capper would come in the last four years of the decade when the Habs reeled off four consecutive Stanley Cups and recorded one of the best won-lost records in league history (229-46-45).

In the spring of '71, Dryden was almost unbeatable as he turned back the best efforts of a stellar Bruins cast, including the Orr-Esposito offensive dynamite, defensive center Derek Sanderson, and crack penalty killer Ed Westfall. Not even the retirement of the majestic Jean Beliveau and belligerent John Ferguson could limit Montreal. New stars moved into the firmament, including Yvan Cournoyer, and then Guy "the Flower" Lafleur, each of whom, in succession, became the new Francophone hockey hero of the province of Quebec.

On the strength of his junior career, expectations for Lafleur had been enormous. *Maclean's* magazine ran a cover story featuring a photograph of the Rocket, Beliveau, and Lafleur in their Hab jerseys, the implication clearly being that the torch had been passed. Lafleur took a few years to develop into the superstar his junior career had indicated. Perhaps coincidentally, his discarding his helmet seemed to result in his blossoming as a legendary Canadiens ace. His greatest years were played on a line with centerman Jacques Lemaire and right wing Steve Shutt.

Montreal's return to the pinnacle was assisted greatly by an extraordinary collection of superior defensemen headed by Larry Robinson, Serge Savard, Guy Lapointe, and Carol Vadnais who fronted for Dryden.

In the mid-1970's, to become dominant, the Canadiens had to dethrone the intimidating Philadelphia Flyers. Unaffectionately known as the Broad Street Bullies, the Flyers were led by the hyper-competitive Bobby Clarke and policed by the likes of Dave "the Hammer" Schultz and "Mad Dog" Kelly. Bernie Parent, a former Leaf, guarded the Philly nets. In the view of many, the classy Habs were engaged in a good-vs-evil crusade in which the seamier (vicious) side of hockey would lose out to the classical (artistic) element as represented by the Canadiens. The supreme test would finally come in the 1976 playoffs when both Montreal and Philadelphia reached the finals. In a series that would alter the course of hockey history, the Habs tamed the Flyers in four-straight games. In a pivotal episode, Montreal's Larry Robinson battered Flyer strongman Dave Schultz. After the final buzzer had sounded, the NHL image-makers breathed a huge sigh of relief as the Canadiens carried away the Cup.

Not only did the victory cause rejoicing throughout the hockey world, it gave the Canadiens the confidence they needed to play their skating game without fear of intimidation. The results were arresting to say the least. The Habs proceeded to take over the league, winning Cups as easily as their illustrious predecessors in the mid-to-late fifties. Scotty Bowman was acclaimed as a genius coach not unlike Toe Blake, as the Habs took three more Cups in succession in 1977, '78 and '79.

Meanwhile, the Leafs were increasingly dominated by their turbulent, often erratic, and never silent owner, the bellicose Harold Ballard who, choosing to ignore the upstart WHA, lost much of his talent roster, including captain Dave Keon and goalie Bernie Parent, who had been a very worthy successor to the aged Bower. (In the late '60s, when Ballard, Stafford Smythe, and John Bassett shared control, the Leafs shortsightedly sold the farm teams and, therefore, much of the team's future.) There were bright spots to be sure — offense stars Darryl Sittler and Lanny McDonald; defensive forward Ron Ellis, a member of the 1967 Cup-winning Leafs; Team Canada '72 hero Paul Henderson; Borje Salming on defense; super-tough forward and crowd pleaser Dave "Tiger" Williams; and Jacques Plante in the Toronto nets — but there were too few of them to carry the team. At times the Leafs were an embarrassment to the club's rich heritage while on other occasions, the 1978 playoffs in particular, with Red Kelly behind the bench, they actually posed as contenders. But they never won a championship and as a result Ballard changed coaches almost as often as the Habs won Stanley Cups. As new avenues of futility were explored, Punch Imlach briefly reappeared as Leaf general manager.

By the late 1970's, Ballard was still regarded more with amusement than revulsion by his critics. Only the most confirmed cynic would have ventured that, for the Leafs, the worst was yet to come.

As for the Canadiens, the era of the eighties would be complicated by the resignation of Bowman, the retirement of Ken Dryden, and the wilting of the Flower, the superlative Guy Lafleur. Montreal's halcyon hockey years were over, but to the Canadiens' credit, they would never slip to the subterranean depths inhabited by the Leafs.

The 1980's appeared promising, at least on paper, for both the Leafs and the Canadiens. Montreal not only had won four-straight Stanley Cups, but seemed to have enough of a nucleus to remain a threat if not a champion. Toronto had sufficient solid personnel, particularly sharp little goaltender Mike Palmateer, to challenge the best clubs for the Stanley Cup. Sniper Rick Vaive and aggressive left wing Wendel Clark emerged as other Leaf stars of the decade.

Ironically, the decline of the Canadiens in the eighties was attributable to wholly unexpected causes. After all, Scotty Bowman had proved himself one of the winningest coaches of all time. Who could have expected him not to try for a fifth-straight Stanley Cup? But, as one-time Canadiens coach Dick Irvin would have commented, the unseen hand intervened.

Motivated by ambition to advance to the Hab general manager's spot, Bowman found it absolutely intolerable that the Canadiens' high command had rejected him in favor of a less experienced hockey man named Irving Grundman. The furious Bowman walked out on the Canadiens and accepted a job as GM and coach of the Buffalo Sabres. His departure would have reverberations — mostly negative — for years to come.

Compounding the Habs' woes was goaltender Dryden's decision to retire after the 1979 Stanley Cup win. It was a demoralizing blow. The scholarly netminder not only was in the prime of his career (he had had a superb 2.30 goals-against average in 1978–79), but had only played seven full NHL seasons. Considering his astute deportment between the pipes, and his age and physical condition, he could have had at least two more good seasons ahead of him. But he was interested in pursuits in the realm of law and writing and could not be persuaded to return.

Thus the Habs were now crippled in two vital positions. No less debilitating was Guy Lafleur's slow, yet perceptible decline in productivity, a descent that would be dramatized as the new decade progressed. The Bowman-Dryden-Lafleur factor resulted in a precipitatory if not calamitous drop in the Habs' fortunes. Montreal was able to reverse the losing trend and, in 1986, engineer a surprise Stanley Cup win over the Calgary Flames. Unfortunately, the organization suffered irrevocable public relations damage in its handling of the underproductive Lafleur's forced retirement. Canadiens management, particularly former Lafleur-teammate-turned-GM, Serge Savard, and former linemate Jacques Lemaire, earned harsh criticism from the player who had been the soul of the late-'70's Hab championships. Somewhat like the Rocket, the Flower did not go happily into the sunset.

After the 1986 win, the Canadiens remained contenders but were unsuccessful in gaining any more Cups in the decade as Wayne Gretzky's Edmonton Oilers and the Calgary Flames controlled Stanley Cup play. Nevertheless, they remained contenders. Goaltender Patrick Roy and sniper Stephane Richer became new Canadiens heroes.

If the Canadiens suffered in any department, it was in the area of coaching. Jean Perron, who led the club to the 1986 championship, proved too much of a disciplinarian for some of his players and was eventually replaced by Pat Burns. Burns was a superb choice and kept the Canadiens at or near the top of the Adams division.

In Toronto, under Ballard's "direction," the Leafs' tragedy of errors intensified. In the late 1970's, he had deposed a brilliant coach in Roger Neilson, then went on to do the fanciful and foolish at the expense of logic and prudence. In the early 1980's, he opted for cronieism over craft in hiring the mediocre Mike Nykoluk, a Ballard favorite, as his coach.

At a time when most teams were developing sophisticated coaching techniques and using more and more advanced scouts and supplementary specialty coaches, the primitive-thinking Ballard refused to catch up and the Leafs suffered accordingly in the technology department.

For a time, Ballard's machinations amused much of the Toronto media but by the middle of the decade even his most loyal cronies began to tire of him. In 1984–85, for example, when the Canadiens had climbed atop the Adams division (41–27–12), the Leafs were ensconced at the bottom of the Norris division (20–52–8).

Once the most desirable city in which to play, Toronto, because of Ballard, became the hell-hole of the NHL. But the more his critics urged reform, the more stubbornly "Pal Hal" dug in his heels and defied his "enemies," as did his general manager, Gerry McNamara, who had replaced Imlach. Leaf coaches became a source of embarrassment to the team and the city, particularly John Brophy, a former minor league supergoon, who brought all his pugilistic know-how to the job of coaching the Leafs. In a final insult to the team, Brophy and then-new Leaf GM Gord Stellick traded speedy Russ Courtnall to the Habs in exchange for the very limited John Kordic. Kordic quickly proved incapable of making the grade as a Toronto goon; Courtnall starred with the Habs. George Armstrong, Doug Carpenter, and Tom Watt followed Brophy as coach; Floyd Smith replaced Stellick.

All in all, the 1980's were an extended nightmare of folly and despair for the Leafs. While the Canadiens organization invoked and maximized Hab tradition at every turn, Toronto's rich heritage became comatose, suppressed by Johnny-Come-Lately Ballard, who, on one occasion went so far as to incinerate Foster Hewitt's gondola.

The death of Harold Ballard in March of 1990 opened a new struggle for ownership and managerial control of the Leafs. In 1991, Cliff Fletcher, who had led the Calgary Flames to the Stanley Cup in 1989, but who also traded away Brett Hull to the St. Louis Blues, was named Leaf president, CEO, and general manager.

Conn Smythe, founder of the Maple Leaf dynasty, once observed of Harold Ballard: "I wouldn't give him a job around here at ten cents a week." In Toronto, the hope is that the Leafs can recover from the disastrous Ballard decades and one day regain hockey supremacy.

Perhaps at that time the historic Hab-Leaf rivalry will be legitimately reinstated, and the successors of Morenz, Joliat, the Rocket, Plante, Harvey, Geoffrion, Beliveau, and the Flower — and the heirs to Conacher, Clancy, Apps, Broda, Barilko, Mahovlich, Keon and Armstrong will again carry the banners of *le bleu, blanc et rouge*, and the blue and white, proudly, into the Stanley Cup finals.

CANADIENS vs LEAFS: THE RIVALRY AT A GLANCE

	1927–28 to 1928–29	1929–30 to 1938–39	1939–40 to 1948–49	1949–50 to 1958–59
Biggest team surprise:	Toronto makes the playoffs in 1928-29.	Toronto wins the 1932 Stanley Cup.	Toronto wins the 1947 Stanley Cup.	Toronto makes the playoffs in 1958–59 after being nine points behind the fourth-place New York Rangers with only two weeks left in the regular season.
Biggest individual surprise:	George Hainsworth, Montreal, finishes the 1928–29 season with an 0.98 goals-against average after playing in all 44 games.	Turk Broda, Toronto, becomes an instant star (1936–37).	Frank (Ulcers) McCool, Toronto, records three-straight shutouts in the 1945 Stanley Cup finals.	Goalie Johnny Bower makes the Toronto club at the age of 34.
Biggest team disappointment:	Conn Smythe's failure to land a superstar for Toronto in 1927–28.	Demise of Montreal in the late 1930's.	Montreal fails to win the Stanley Cup in 1947.	In the 1951–52 finals Montreal is swept by the Red Wings.

CANADIENS vs LEAFS: THE RIVALRY AT A GLANCE (continued)

	1959–60 to 1968–69	1969–70 to 1978–79	1979–80 to 1988–89	1989–90 to Present
Biggest team surprise:	Toronto wins three-straight Stanley Cups (1962, 1963, 1964) despite having a relatively old team.	In 1971, Montreal upsets the Boston Bruins in the first round of the playoffs en route to capturing the Stanley Cup.	Montreal wins the 1986 Stanley Cup.	Toronto declines abruptly from 1989–90 to 1990–91.
Biggest individual surprise:	Toronto goalie, Johnny Bower, excels in the Toronto nets to the age of 46.	Ken Dryden, Montreal.	Patrick Roy, Montreal.	Russ Courtnall, Montreal.
Biggest team disappointment:	In the late 1960's team-wide dissent runs rampant under the eccentric iron rule of Toronto GM and coach George (Punch) Imlach.	In 1969–70 Toronto misses the playoffs.	The Toronto Maple Leafs.	The 1990–91 Toronto Maple Leafs.

CANADIENS vs LEAFS: THE RIVALRY AT A GLANCE (continued)

	1927–28 to 1928–29	1929–30 to 1938–39	1939–40 to 1948–49	1949–50 to 1958–59
Biggest individual disappointment:	None.	None.	Toronto's Bucko McDonald and Gordie Drillon are benched in the 1942 finals after two-straight losses.	Hailed as the Leafs' answer to Jean Beliveau, Eric Nesterenko fails to live up to advance billing.
Best goalie:	George Hainsworth, Montreal.	George Hainsworth, Montreal.	Turk Broda, Toronto.	Jacques Plante, Montreal.
Best defenseman:	Clarence (Hap) Day, Toronto.	Michael Francis (King) Clancy, Toronto.	Butch Bouchard, Montreal.	Doug Harvey, Montreal.
Best defensive team:	Sylvio Mantha and Albert (Battleship) Leduc, Montreal.	King Clancy and Hap Day, Toronto.	Jim Thomson and Gus Mortson, Toronto.	Doug Harvey and Tom Johnson, Montreal.
Best forward:	Howie Morenz, Montreal.	Charlie Conacher, Toronto.	Maurice (Rocket) Richard, Montreal.	Jean Beliveau, Montreal.
Best stickhandler:	Aurel Joliat, Montreal.	Joe Primeau, Toronto.	Max Bentley, Toronto.	Jean Beliveau, Montreal.
Cleanest player:	Aurel Joliat, Montreal.	Joe Primeau, Toronto.	Syl Apps, Toronto.	Don Marshall, Montreal.
Toughest defenseman:	Red Horner, Toronto.	Red Horner, Toronto.	Bill Barilko, Toronto.	Bob Baun, Toronto.

CANADIENS vs LEAFS: THE RIVALRY AT A GLANCE (continued)

	1959–60 to 1968–69	1969–70 to 1978–79	1979–80 to 1988–89	1989–90 to Present
Biggest individual disappointment:	Toronto's Brit Selby, 1965–66 rookie of the year, a total bust after first season.	Montreal fires head coach Al McNeil after winning the 1971 Stanley Cup because Henri (Pocket Rocket) Richard didn't like him.	Because of injuries, Wendel Clark, Toronto.	In 1990–91 Toronto's Gary Leeman has an injury-riddled season after scoring 50 goals the previous year.
Best goalie:	Gump Worsley, Montreal.	Ken Dryden, Montreal.	Patrick Roy, Montreal.	Patrick Roy, Montreal.
Best defenseman:	Tim Horton, Toronto.	Serge Savard, Montreal.	Larry Robinson, Montreal.	Dave Ellett, Toronto.
Best defensive team:	Carl Brewer and Bob Baun, Toronto.	Larry Robinson and Guy Lapointe, Montreal.	Larry Robinson and Rick Green, Montreal.	Chris Chelios and Petr Svoboda, Montreal.
Best forward:	Frank Mahovlich, Toronto.	Guy Lafleur, Montreal.	Bobby Smith, Montreal.	Stephane Richer, Montreal.
Best stickhandler:	Jean Beliveau, Montreal.	Guy Lafleur, Montreal.	Bobby Smith, Montreal.	Denis Savard, Montreal.
Cleanest player:	Dave Keon, Toronto.	Guy Lafleur, Montreal.	Mats Naslund, Montreal.	Russ Courtnall, Montreal.
Toughest defenseman:	Ted Harris, Montreal.	Terry Harper, Montreal.	Chris Chelios, Montreal.	Luke Richardson, Toronto.

CANADIENS vs LEAFS: THE RIVALRY AT A GLANCE (continued)

	1927–28 to 1928–29	1929–30 to 1938–39	1939–40 to 1948–49	1949–50 to 1958–59
Toughest forward:	Howie Morenz, Montreal.	Harvey (Busher) Jackson, Toronto.	"Wild" Bill Ezinicki, Toronto.	Bert Olmstead, Montreal.
Most valuable player:	Howie Morenz, Montreal.	King Clancy, Toronto.	Ted (Teeder) Kennedy, Toronto.	Maurice Richard, Montreal.
Best rookie:	Joe Primeau, Toronto.	Syl Apps, Toronto.	Howie Meeker, Toronto.	Bernard (Boom Boom) Geoffrion, Montreal.
Best coach:	Cecil Hart, Montreal.	Dick Irvin, Toronto.	Hap Day, Toronto.	Hector (Toe) Blake, Montreal.
Best general manager:	Conn Smythe, Toronto.	Conn Smythe, Toronto.	Conn Smythe, Toronto.	Frank Selke, Montreal.
Best leader:	Howie Morenz, Montreal.	King Clancy, Toronto.	Syl Apps, Toronto.	Maurice Richard, Montreal.
Montreal turning point:	The emergence of George Hainsworth as a super-goalie in the tradition of Georges Vezina.	Howie Morenz is traded to the Chicago Black Hawks in 1934.	Montreal management refuses to give up on Maurice Richard despite his being injury-prone early in his NHL career.	Toe Blake becomes head coach, 1955.
Toronto turning point:	Conn Smythe gains control of the Toronto St. Patricks and renames them the Toronto Maple Leafs.	Conacher, Primeau, and Jackson are united to form the "Kid Line."	Max Bentley is acquired from the Chicago Black Hawks in a five-for-two deal.	1951 playoff hero, Bill Barilko, dies in a plane crash, August 1951.

CANADIENS vs LEAFS: THE RIVALRY AT A GLANCE (continued)

	1959–60 to 1968–69	1969–70 to 1978–79	1979–80 to 1988–89	1989–90 to Present
Toughest forward:	John Ferguson, Montreal.	Dave (Tiger) Williams, Toronto.	Chris Nilan, Montreal.	Wendel Clark, Toronto.
Most valuable player:	Jean Beliveau, Montreal.	Ken Dryden, Montreal.	Patrick Roy, Montreal.	Patrick Roy, Montreal.
Best rookie:	Jacques Laperriere, Montreal.	Ken Dryden, Montreal.	Patrick Roy, Montreal.	Stephan Lebeau, Montreal.
Best coach:	Punch Imlach, Toronto.	Scotty Bowman, Montreal.	Pat Burns, Montreal.	Pat Burns, Montreal.
Best general manager:	Punch Imlach, Toronto.	Sam Pollock, Montreal.	Serge Savard, Montreal.	Serge Savard, Montreal.
Best leader:	Leonard (Red) Kelly, Toronto.	Serge Savard, Montreal.	Larry Robinson, Montreal.	Mike McPhee, Montreal.
Montreal turning point:	Tough-guy defenseman John Ferguson is signed.	Scotty Bowman becomes head coach.	Patrick Roy is made number-one goalie.	The youth movement.
Toronto turning point:	In November of 1961 control of the team passes from Conn Smythe to his son, Stafford.	Swedish defense ace Borje Salming is signed.	The new decade. The franchise declines further.	Team owner, Harold Ballard, dies, 1990.

CANADIENS vs LEAFS: THE RIVALRY AT A GLANCE (continued)

	1927–28 to 1928–29	1929–30 to 1938–39	1939–40 to 1948–49	1949–50 to 1958–59
Best game:	March 19, 1929. Toronto defeats the Detroit Red Wings, 3–1, in the team's first playoff game as the Maple Leafs.	April 3, 1933. In game five of the semifinals Toronto's Ken Doraty scores the game-winning goal in the sixth overtime as the Leafs defeat the Boston Bruins, 1–0.	April 18, 1942. In game seven of the finals Toronto defeats the Detroit Red Wings for the Stanley Cup.	April 8, 1952. Maurice Richard is knocked out in a game against the Bruins then comes back, later in the match, to score the winner.
Biggest impact:	The Montreal Canadiens finish first in the NHL's Canadian division but are eliminated in the second round of the playoffs by the Montreal Maroons, 1927–28.	Toronto wins the 1932 Stanley Cup, defeating the New York Rangers, three gaes to none.	Toronto wins the 1949 Stanley Cup after finishing the regular season under .500 and in fourth place.	Toronto overcomes the Rangers to reach the playoffs in 1959.

CANADIENS vs LEAFS: THE RIVALRY AT A GLANCE (continued)

	1959–60 to 1968–69	1969–70 to 1978–79	1979–80 to 1988–89	1989–90 to Present
Best game:	Game six of the 1962 Stanley Cup finals. Toronto vs Chicago. Hawks lose momentum after jubilant hometown fans, celebrating a Bobby Hull goal, litter the ice. When play resumes Leafs score two quick goals to win the Cup.	Game seven, opening round, 1971 Stanley Cup playoffs. Montreal defeats the Bruins, 4–2 to win series.	May 24, 1986. Montreal defeats the Calgary Flames, 4–3, to win its first Stanley Cup since 1979.	None
Biggest impact:	In the 1965 semifinals Montreal defeats Toronto en route to capturing the Stanley Cup.	In the 1978 quarter-finals Toronto defeats the heavily favored New York Islanders in seven games.	In the 1989 Stanley Cup finals the Flames recover from a two-games-to-one deficit to defeat Montreal and win the first Cup in franchise history.	Montreal finishes second in the Adams division (behind the Bruins) with an all-kid defense.

CANADIENS vs LEAFS: THE RIVALRY AT A GLANCE (continued)

	1927–28 to 1928–29	1929–30 to 1938–39	1939–40 to 1948–49	1949–50 to 1958–59
Best series:	Toronto defeats the Detroit Red Wings in the first playoff round, 1928–29.	Montreal defeats the Chicago Black Hawks, three games to two, to win the 1931 Stanley Cup.	In the 1942 Stanley Cup finals, against the Red Wings, Toronto rallies from a three-games-to-none deficit to take the Cup.	In the 1951 Stanley Cup finals Toronto and Montreal battle as every game goes into overtime. Leafs win series, four games to one.
Biggest comeback:	Toronto reaches the playoffs in 1928–29 after falling short the previous year.	Montreal rallies from a two games-to-one deficit, against the Black Hawks, to win the 1931 Stanley Cup.	Toronto defeats the Red Wings in the 1942 Stanley Cup finals.	Toronto loses first game of the 1951 Stanley Cup semifinals, against Boston, then loses only one more game, against Montreal in the finals, en route to the Cup.
Biggest choke:	None.	In the 1938 Stanley Cup finals a weaker Black Hawk team defeats Toronto, three-games-to-one.	Montreal loses to Toronto in the first round of the 1945 playoffs.	None.

CANADIENS vs LEAFS: THE RIVALRY AT A GLANCE (continued)

	1959–60 to 1968–69	1969–70 to 1978–79	1979–80 to 1988–89	1989–90 to Present
Best series:	None	In the 1976 Stanley Cup finals Montreal ends two-year reign of terror of "Broad Street Bullies," the Philadelphia Flyers. Four-game sweep captures first of four-straight Cups for Habs.	1989 Stanley Cup finals between Montreal and Calgary.	None
Biggest comeback:	Montreal loses first two games (at home) to the Detroit Red Wings then wins four in a row in the 1966 Stanley Cup finals.	Down two games to none, Toronto rallies to upset the Islanders in seven games, 1978 Stanley Cup quarter-finals.	Montreal loses first game of the finals, against the Flames, then comes back to win four-straight and the Cup in 1986.	None
Biggest choke:	None.	In 1969–70 Montreal misses the playoffs after winning Stanley Cup the previous year.	None.	In 1990–91 Leafs fail to catch the Minnesota North Stars and, therefore, miss the playoffs.

BIBLIOGRAPHY

Batten, Jack. *The Leafs in Autumn: Meeting the Maple Leaf Heroes of the Forties*. Toronto: Macmillan, 1975.

Coleman, Charles L. *The Trail of the Stanley Cup*. Montreal: National Hockey League, Vol. 1 (1966); Vol. 2 (1969); Vol. 3 (1976).

Conacher, Brian. *Hockey in Canada: The Way It Is*. Toronto: Gateway Press, 1970.

Diamond, Dan, and Stubbs, Lewis. *Hockey — Twenty Years: The NHL Since 1967*. Toronto: Doubleday, 1987.

Duplacey, James, and Romain, Joseph. *Toronto Maple Leafs: Images of Glory*. Toronto: McGraw-Hill Ryerson, 1990.

Fitkin, Ed. *Broda of the Leafs*. Toronto: Baxter Publishing, 1950.

Germain, Georges-Hébert. *Overtime: The Legend of Guy Lafleur*. Toronto: Viking, 1990.

Goyens, Chrys, and Turowetz, Allan. *Lions in Winter*. Toronto: Prentice-Hall, 1986.

Harris, Billy. *The Glory Years: Memories of a Decade, 1955–1965*. Toronto: Prentice-Hall, 1989.

Hewitt, Foster. *Foster Hewitt: His Own Story*. Toronto: The Ryerson Press, 1967.

Hewitt, Foster. *Hockey Night in Canada*. Toronto: The Ryerson Press, 1961.

Houston, William. *Ballard: A Portrait of Canada's Most Controversial Sports Figure*. Toronto: Summerhill Press, 1984.

Houston, William. *Inside Maple Leaf Gardens: The Rise and Fall of the Toronto Maple Leafs*. Toronto: McGraw-Hill Ryerson, 1989.

Imlach, Punch, and Young, Scott. *Hockey is a Battle*. Toronto: Macmillan, 1969.

Kariher, Harry C. *Who's Who in Hockey*. New York: Arlington Press, 1973.

Liss, Howard. *Hockey's Greatest All-Stars*. New York: Hawthorn Books, 1972.

McAllister, Ron. *Hockey Heroes*. Toronto: McClelland and Stewart, 1949.

McAllister, Ron. *Hockey Stars . . . Today and Yesterday*. Toronto: McClelland and Stewart, 1950.

McAllister, Ron. *More Hockey Stories*. Toronto: McClelland and Stewart, 1952.

McFarlane, Brian. *50 Years of Hockey: A History of the National Hockey League*. Toronto: Pagurian Press, 1967.

Melady, John. *Overtime, Overdue: The Bill Barilko Story*. Toronto: City Print, 1988.

O'Brien, Andy. *Headline Hockey*. Toronto: The Ryerson Press, 1963.

O'Brien, Andy. *Rocket Richard*. Toronto: The Ryerson Press, 1961.

Orr, Frank. *The Story of Hockey*. New York: Random House, 1971.

Roxborough, Henry. *The Stanley Cup Story*. Toronto: The Ryerson Press, 1964.

Selke, Frank J., Sr., with Green, Gordon. *Behind the Cheering*. Toronto: McClelland and Stewart, 1962.

Young, Scott. *100 Years of Dropping the Puck: A History of the OHA*. Toronto: McClelland and Stewart, 1989.

Young, Scott. *The Leafs I Knew*. Toronto: The Ryerson Press, 1966.